GROWING POPULATIONS, CHANGING LANDSCAPES

Studies from India, China, and the United States

Indian National Science Academy

Chinese Academy of Sciences

U.S. National Academy of Sciences

NATIONAL ACADEMY PRESS
Washington, D.C.

NATIONAL ACADEMY PRESS • 2101 Constitution Avenue, NW • Washington, D.C. 20418

NOTICE: The project that is the subject of this report was approved by the Governing Board of the National Research Council and by competent members of the Chinese Academy of Sciences and the Indian National Science Academy. The members of the committee responsible for the report were chosen for their special competences and with regard for appropriate balance.

This study was supported by Grant No. 95-31825A-POP/PCE and 96-41812A-WER between the National Academy of Sciences and John D. and Catherine T. MacArthur Foundation and Task Order #34, NO1-OD-4139 of the Department of Health and Human Services. Any opinions, findings, conclusions, or recommendations expressed in this publication are those of the authors and do not necessarily reflect the views of the organizations or agencies that provided support for the project.

International Standard Book Number 0-309-07554-8
Library of Congress Catalog Card Number 2001117395

Additional copies of this report are available from National Academy Press, 2101 Constitution Avenue, N.W., Lockbox 285, Washington, D.C. 20055; (800) 624-6242 or (202) 334-3313 (in the Washington metropolitan area); Internet, http://www.nap.edu

Cover Art: Photograph by Anamaria Viveros
JR

Indian National Science Academy

The Indian National Science Academy, formerly known as the National Institute of Sciences, is a nonprofit society of distinguished scientists. Established in 1935, it received the recognition of the Government of India in 1945 as the premier scientific society representing all branches of science in India. The Academy is dedicated to the promotion and coordination of scientific research in the country and its practical applications to problems of national welfare.

Chinese Academy of Sciences

The Chinese Academy of Sciences was founded on November 1, 1949, on the basis of the institutions of the former Academia Sinica and Beiping Academy of Sciences. It is the country's highest academic institution and comprehensive research and development center in the natural sciences and high technology. The Academy has five academic divisions, 121 institutes, more than 200 scientific and technological enterprises, and more than 20 supporting units, including three universities, five documentation and information centers, two printing houses, and five research and development centers for scientific instruments. They are distributed over various parts of the country. Thirteen branches of the Academy have been established. They are in Shanghai, Nanjing, Hefei, Changchun, Shenyang, Wuhan, Guangzhou, Chengdu, Kunming, Xi'an, Lanzhou, Xinjiang, and Hainan.

U.S. National Academy of Sciences

The National Academy of Sciences is a private, nonprofit, self-perpetuating society of distinguished scholars engaged in scientific and engineering research, dedicated to the furtherance of science and technology and to their use for the general welfare. Upon the authority of the charter granted to it by the Congress in 1863, the Academy has a mandate that requires it to advise the federal government on scientific and technical matters. Dr. Bruce M. Alberts is president of the National Academy of Sciences.

The National Academy of Engineering was established in 1964, under the charter of the National Academy of Sciences, as a parallel organization of outstanding engineers. It is autonomous in its administration and in the selection of its members, sharing with the National Academy of Sciences the responsibility for advising the federal government. The National Academy of Engineering also sponsors engineering programs aimed at meeting national needs, encourages education and research, and recognizes the superior achievements of engineers. Dr. William A. Wulf is president of the National Academy of Engineering.

The Institute of Medicine was established in 1970 by the National Academy of Sciences to secure the services of eminent members of appropriate professions in the examination of policy matters pertaining to the health of the public. The Institute acts under the responsibility given to the National Academy of Sciences by its congressional charter to be an adviser to the federal government and, upon its own initiative, to identify issues of medical care, research, and education. Dr. Kenneth I. Shine is president of the Institute of Medicine.

The National Research Council was organized by the National Academy of Sciences in 1916 to associate the broad community of science and technology with the Academy's purposes of furthering knowledge and advising the federal government. Functioning in accordance with general policies determined by the Academy, the Council has become the principal operating agency of both the National Academy of Sciences and the National Academy of Engineering in providing services to the government, the public, and the scientific and engineering communities. The Council is administered jointly by both Academies and the Institute of Medicine. Dr. Bruce M. Alberts and Dr. William A. Wulf are chairman and vice chairman, respectively, of the National Research Council.

Preface

This collaborative study of population and land use change grew out of conversations among representatives of the academies of science of India, China, and the United States. They were attending the "Science Summit" on World Population, a gathering of the world's scientific academies held in New Delhi in October 1993. The three academies expressed their desire to engage in studies of important issues of mutual interest. Once they agreed on a study of population and land use, they explored issues of comparability of data and approaches to studying the issue in their respective countries. In the end, they decided to identify two sites in each country that would serve as the basis for comparison. A panel made up of representatives of each of the three academies was established to guide the effort.

The panel suggested criteria for selection of the study sites, but each country chose its own. Site selection depended on the existence of data, the availability of research personnel, and the specific interests of each country, balanced by the desire to provide comparable rural and urban settings.

Despite a variety of simplistic arguments about the relationship between population and land use change, many studies have demonstrated that the relationship is complex, influenced by a multitude of physical, social, economic, and political factors. Investigators also have recognized that correlations alone do not translate directly into explanations of cause and effect. Although the study design emphasized issues of transnational collection and comparison of data on population and land use change, the interests of the research scholars at each site inevitably moved toward focus on the nature of the processes leading to change. Thus the studies of the individual sites reflect the richness and complexities of reality rather than the bland results of generalization.

To the general public, a study based on statistical research and comparisons of data across different jurisdictions in different countries conjures up one word: dry. To a professional in the social sciences, it suggests another word: risky. "Dry" is easy to understand. Statistics alone do not explain how people and land interact. They do, however, capture some facets of the dynamism of human societies, their differences as well as their commonalties, and in this report they are often wrapped in a narrative that sheds light on the rich histories, evolution, and day-to-day life of the study regions. For example, although the numbers describe the spectacular growth of Shenzhen City in southern China, from a town of 45,000 to a city of 2.5 million in 15 years, they do not convey the dynamism of the site as experienced by an observer on the ground. In the surrounding Pearl River Delta, 7 kilometers of furniture manufacturing establishments are abruptly truncated by fish ponds a few kilometers from a major toll highway flanked by raw quarry faces supplying rock for highways and high-rises. A retired farmer in a new concrete three-story house with an electric fan and a TV describes the sale of the communal lands to industry, with each farmer claiming a share. His only complaint: he has three married children but only one grandchild, a common occurrence under China's population policy.

In China's Jitai Basin, three sisters and a younger brother live in a farmhouse, next door to a family with a son home for a holiday from his job in Guangdong Province, which includes the Pearl River Delta. His father complains that the son sends home too little money; the son replies that his father does not understand the high cost of living in the Delta. There, a new hotel with a marble lobby and dining room that seats hundreds suggests he is right. Elsewhere in the province, three families are living side by side in a new compound for workers. In the yard outside the compound stand three separate, identical wells, one for each family, instead of a single shared one.

In Kerala in southwest India, where roads are clogged with decoratively painted trucks, the international beachcombers and opulent retirement homes of overseas workers in a small village contrast with the small paddy fields and bullocks in the countryside. In northern India, at the western desert edge of Haryana State, a new sprinkler irrigation system provides the hope of new crops even as salinization of soil and groundwater threaten the system. In the words of a village elder, hushed by the younger generation, people have replaced wildlife on the landscape. At a half-day's drive away in eastern Haryana, poultry barns have replaced chicken yards, and a huge automated rice mill is shipping its products to the world, a sign of the Green Revolution. On a major highway on the outskirts of New Delhi, whose streets teem with people, a Mercedes is slowed by cows in the roadway.

And then there is South Florida, a plumber's paradise on an immense scale, a landscape engineered to control floods and protect the land devoted to sugarcane and cattle. Immigrants continue to come, settling in urban areas of the Atlantic Coast, where they are hemmed in by the Everglades wetland. The Everglades itself, once subject to massive drainage, is now the site of a major "restoration" project aimed at, among other things, returning the Kissimmee River from a straight canal to its meandering former self.

In the U.S. Midwest, Chicago, site of one of the world's highest office towers built by a company that has since moved its headquarters 40 miles to the west, has a thriving downtown and waterfront playland. The city continues to expand across land that was once prairie, then farmland, and now exurbia laced with interstate highways.

Much of the riskiness perceived by professional colleagues relates to the definition of variables and the compatibility of data used. Early in the study, "common variables" became a rallying cry, lamentation, or denunciation as the Tri-Academy panel and associated research scientists traveled to the study sites in India, China, and the United States. Everyone knows that true comparative analyses are impossible without identically defined, relevant variables expressed in comparable units. Save for some demographers, geographers, economists, and sociologists who have tried to compare spatial data in the international context, few researchers are aware of how each country respects its own land classification scheme and special definitions. Still fewer are aware, for example, that "urban" may refer to neither city nor metropolitan area, and that "rural" may not imply agricultural. Each category may contain some of the other, and definitions may change between censuses, unbeknownst to the unwary researcher. In the absence of comparable and unchanging spatial units and definitions, the numerical size of a population within political boundaries of varying scales produces uncertain measures of migration or population density. Does a sudden increase in rural population and decrease in urban population stem from people moving or definitions changing? Researchers also encountered the problem of verifying data sources and the differences in languages (only two of the six jurisdictions speak the same language). It is a measure of the goodwill and cooperative spirit of all of the participants from the three countries that we remain on speaking terms.

That said, a word on compromises is warranted. This study was based on the premise that international comparisons of recorded social transformations may yield insight into principles that could lead to broader generalizations, or at least to recognition of common experience, generalizable or not. A perfect design would call for the selection of study sites carefully matched across a spectrum of attributes such as population, land cover, occupations, and geography. Although the panel encouraged such design criteria, each country was responsible for selecting its own sites, under the significant constraint that the studies rely on ongoing work or existing material and not on the collection of new data. One result is that all sites have large populations and high population densities. A base period, roughly the last half-century, was adopted for the comparison of trends, but, where available, much earlier data were used in the analyses. Even though the case studies described here do include some anecdotal narrative, the panel has emphasized, to the extent possible, quantitative measures of trends. As the findings demonstrate, however, some explanations of changes in land use and population draw on qualitative as well as quantitative observations.

The three academies intend to continue their discussions of this important topic, including lessons learned from this initial experiment in collaboration. At the same time, new opportunities for discussion and the exchange of ideas should continue to be pursued. After all, researchers, policymakers, and others are paying greater attention to the ways in which diverse societies throughout the world are evolving socially, culturally, and economically. Cross-disciplinary and cross-national studies can, despite the obstacles they face, contribute to our understanding of a rapidly changing world. As chairman of such a study, my special thanks go to the staff and to my colleagues on the panel from India, China, and the United States. The process from beginning to end has been a long one, complete with much debate, drafting, and redrafting. But most of us, new to each other initially, have become friends, drawn together by mutual interest, harrowing field excursions, and humor.

M. Gordon Wolman, Chairman
Tri-Academy Panel

Acknowledgments

The first four chapters of this report are the work of the Tri-Academy panel and represent a synthesis of the material presented in the six case study reports and the gender analysis. The country studies were carried out by Tri-Academy panel members and their colleagues. The Kerala study (Chapter 5) was conducted by the Centre for Development Studies, Thiruvananthapuram, Kerala, under the direction of P. S. George. The Haryana study (Chapter 6) was undertaken by the Agricultural Economics Research Centre of the University of Delhi under the leadership of Prem S. Vashishtha. In a complementary study (Chapter 7), Sumati Kulkarni of the International Institute for Population Sciences in Mumbai analyzed the gender dimensions of the relationship between population and land use in the two Indian study sites. P. S. Ramakrishnan of Jawaharlal Nehru University provided coordination on behalf of the Indian National Science Academy. A. K. Jain of the Indian National Science Academy provided indispensible administrative and logistic support.

The Chinese studies of the Jitai Basin (Chapter 8) and the Pearl River Delta (Chapter 9) were accomplished through the collaboration of the Institute of Geographic Science and Natural Resources, the Nanjing Institute of Soil Sciences of the Chinese Academy of Sciences, and the Institute of Population Research at Peking University. Zhao Shidong served as the Chinese study director.

In the United States, the South Florida case study (Chapter 10) was carried out by a group at Florida State University, led by William D. Solecki and Robert T. Walker. The Chicago study (Chapter 11) was conducted by Edwin S. Mills of Northwestern University and Cynthia S. Simmons, a consultant to the U.S. National Research Council (NRC) presently at Michigan State University. The U.S. studies were coordinated by M. Gordon Wolman of Johns Hopkins University, chairman of the NRC's Committee on Population and Land Use.

Leaders of the science academies of India, China, and the United States encouraged the work of this project, and the John D. and Catherine T. MacArthur Foundation, the U.S. National Institutes of Health, and the U.S. National Research Council provided financial support. Billie Lee Turner of Clark University and Edwin Mills of Northwestern University aided in the design of the effort and in its execution. T. R. Lakshmanan of Boston University contributed an early review of a portion of the text, and Barbara Torrey, executive director of the NRC's Division on Behavioral and Social Sciences and Education, not only helped to initiate the study but also reviewed a major portion of the panel's text.

This study of population and land use would not have gotten off the ground had it not been for the energy and indefatigable work of the original study director, Judith Bale, staff member of the U.S. National Research Council, and it would never have been completed without the commitment, eye for standards, and good sense of her colleague and successor as study director, Michael Greene. Project consultant Sabra Bissette Ledent edited the report.

This report was reviewed in draft form by individuals chosen for their diverse perspectives and technical expertise, in accordance with procedures approved by the NRC's Report Review Committee. The purpose of this independent review is to provide candid and critical comments that will assist the institution in making its published report as sound as possible and to ensure that the report meets institutional standards for objectivity, evidence, and responsiveness to the study charge. The review comments and draft manuscript remain confidential to protect the integrity of the deliberative process. We wish to thank the following individuals for their review of this report:

John S. Adams, University of Minnesota
D. Gale Johnson, University of Chicago
Ronald Lee, University of California, Berkeley
Clifton Pannell, University of Georgia
G. William Skinner, University of California, Davis
T. N. Srinivasan, Yale University
David Sui, Texas A&M University
James Wescoat, University of Colorado
Thomas Wilbanks, Oak Ridge National Laboratory
Yue-man Yeung, The Chinese University of Hong Kong

Although these reviewers provided many constructive comments and suggestions, they were not asked to endorse the conclusions or recommendations, nor did they see the final draft of the report before its release. The review of this report was overseen by Brian J. L. Berry of the University of Texas, Dallas, and F. Sherwood Rowland of the University of California, Irvine. Appointed by the National Research Council, they were responsible for making certain that an independent examination of this report was carried out in accordance with institutional procedures and that all review comments were carefully considered. Responsibility for the final content of this report rests entirely with the authoring committee and the institution.

Contents

PART IV   United States

LIST OF TABLES AND FIGURES

Tables

Figures

Executive Summary

In 1999 the world's population reached 6 billion, after doubling in only 40 years. Much of this recent population growth took place in the poorer regions of the world. Fertility and mortality rates began to decline in the Western industrialized regions in the nineteenth century (a process called the demographic transition), but only in the last decades of the twentieth century did some of the developing regions begin to realize significant declines in fertility. Given the population momentum provided by a youthful age structure, populations in many parts of the world will continue to grow for many years to come.

These unprecedented rates of growth, which could have alarming effects on the environment and the life support system of the planet, have renewed the debate about the future prospects for human societies. The high rates of economic and industrial development that accompanied population growth in the twentieth century fed fears about depletion of resources and fouling of the land, air, biota, and water in nearly all parts of the globe. Today's intense debate over the relationship between numbers of people and use of available land has resurrected both Malthus's hypothesis and its critics. The original publication of Thomas Malthus, an eighteenth-century English economist, and those who followed him predicted that the needs of a growing population eventually would exceed the capacity of a finite earth to support it. More optimistic scholars have suggested that limitless human ingenuity will overcome mere physical constraints. Indeed, thus far scientific and technological advances in agriculture have enabled food production to more than keep up with a burgeoning population—on a global level. At the regional and local levels, and at particular times in history, however, hundreds of millions of people have lacked sufficient food or food of adequate quality.

Because the conversion of land from its natural state to human use is the most permanent and often irreversible effect that humans can have on the natural landscape, a critical aspect of these debates is the relation of growing population numbers to changes in land use. In general, to meet demands for food farmers must either expand the area of land under cultivation or intensify agricultural practices, which often requires applying large quantities of fertilizer, herbicides, insecticides, and irrigation water and risking their potentially damaging impacts on the environment. Beyond agriculture, other aspects of human consumption, itself a product of increasing population coupled with economic development, may further degrade natural resources and the environment. There is, however, no simple and universal relationship between population growth and land use change. Many other factors, such as geography and climate, come into play, and governments are not without influence on land use conversions. An understanding of the forces at work in regions where land use change has been particularly notable may clarify the issues.

In October 1993, representatives of 58 of the world's science academies gathered in New Delhi for a "Science Summit" on World Population. During the meeting, the representatives of the science academies of India, China, and the United States agreed to undertake a unique, multinational collaboration (called here the Tri-Academy Project) that would utilize a case study approach to explore the interactions between population growth and changes in land use in the world's three most populous countries. The study reflects a desire to experiment with inter-academy collaboration as well as intrinsic interest in the topic of the study itself. Bringing together natural and social scientists from the three countries, the project would seek to cast light on the transformations in demographics, land use, and consumption. The John D. and Catherine T. MacArthur Foundation, the U.S. National Institutes of Health, and the U.S. National Research Council agreed to support the undertaking.

This study was based on the premise that international comparisons of recorded social transformations may yield insight into principles that could lead to broader generalizations, or at least to recognition of common experience. A perfect design would call for the selection of study sites carefully matched across a spectrum of attributes such as population, land cover, occupations, and geography. Although the panel encouraged such design criteria, each country was responsible for selecting its own sites, under the significant constraint that the studies rely on ongoing work or existing material and not on the collection of new data. One result is that all sites have large populations and high population densities. A base period, roughly the last half-century, was adopted for the comparison of trends, but, where available, much earlier data were used in the analyses. Even though the case studies described here do include some anecdotal narrative, the panel has emphasized, to the extent possible, quantitative measures of trends. As the findings demonstrate, however, some explanations of changes in land use and population draw on qualitative as well as quantitative observations.

Because data on population and land use are collected within different geographical boundaries by different agencies in the three countries, establishing a comparable primary database for the six studies was a difficult undertaking. Early in the study an attempt was made to establish a common database, relying on official, published records in each country, and, generally, the study teams were expected to draw on existing published sources rather than undertake new surveys and measurements. It was recognized from the beginning that there would be problems related to the definition of variables and the compatibility of data used. True comparative analyses are impossible without identically defined, relevant variables expressed in comparable units, but each country has its own land classification scheme and holds to special definitions. Researchers also encountered the problem of verifying data sources. In each case study, team members used both the common database and additional data from more specialized and local studies. Inevitably, there were some inconsistencies between the common database and the case studies, and in the comparative analyses these were resolved in favor of the case studies.

STUDY REGIONS

The objective of the Tri-Academy Project is to examine the structure of population and land use interactions in six regions. The sites were selected by the respective academies, based on the prior existence of data, availability of research personnel, and the specific interests of each country. They are: in India, Kerala, a subtropical state in southwest India, and Haryana, a state north of New Delhi; in China, the Jitai Basin in Jiangxi Province in southern China and the Pearl River Delta just to the south on the coast; and in the United States, South Florida in the southeastern United States and Chicago and the surrounding region in the American Midwest. Study teams in each region analyzed basic trends in population growth and land use change since World War II and sought to identify drivers of the observed changes. Each case study chapter is authored by members of the local study team. The project team then as a whole compared the trends and drivers across sites and identified general relationships.

Kerala has a high life expectancy, a high education rate, and one of the lowest population growth rates in India. The major industry in Kerala is agriculture, and the state's average per capita income is low. The state economy benefits, however, from remittances from expatriate workers.

Land use in Kerala is currently influenced by state government policies that encourage cash crop production and by migration from the cities to the highland areas within the state.

Haryana and its neighbor state Punjab to the north are the wheat-growing "breadbasket" of India. Haryana's population growth rate is among the highest in India, but it has benefited from the introduction of Green Revolution technologies, and agricultural productivity has been able to keep pace with population. The agricultural land area has remained fairly constant during the state's high-growth period, even though Haryana continues to be an important supplier of food for the country.

The inclusion of a chapter on gender issues in development in Kerala and Haryana represents the realization of a fortuitous opportunity. The panel was unable to pursue comparable studies in China and the United States.

The Jitai Basin, a center of revolutionary activity in the forties and fifties, was considered a less-developed region of China for most of the twentieth century. Beginning in the 1950s, this agricultural region was heavily affected by radical government policies, including the Great Leap Forward, the "grain production first" system, the Cultural Revolution, and the "household responsibility" system, all of which had detrimental effects on the physical environment. The region is now a focus of Chinese environmental policies. Meanwhile, population has grown slowly, some natural areas (such as wetland, forestland, and grassland) are being restored, and the region remains a source of "floating" workers for the Pearl River Delta to the south.

The Pearl River Delta, long a commercial region open to the West, was at one time a center of food production for the South China region. It also was a major source of Chinese immigrants to the West and to Southeast Asia. In 1978 the Chinese government designated several special economic zones in the Delta, areas where foreigners are permitted to invest and local companies are free to export. Since then, the region has experienced rapid urbanization and industrialization and has become a magnet for migrant and "floating" workers from many parts of China.

In the United States, South Florida developed rapidly after 1900; throughout the twentieth century decadal growth rates exceeded 100 percent. The primary industry is agriculture, but since World War II tourism and, more recently, financial and trading activities have become key industries. The interaction between population and land use in South Florida is dominated by the influx of migrants from northern U.S. states and immigrants from the Caribbean and Central and South America. Government policies to protect the Everglades and to provide water control structures for agriculture have created a highly inhomogeneous population pattern.

Chicago, a small city of 5,000 in 1840, grew at a rate of 10.4 percent per year from 1840 to 1900, when it became known as the world's greatest rail center. Grassland, timber, and livestock provided successive bases for commercial development. The city's population peaked in 1950, and the metropolitan region continues to grow as suburbanization encroaches on agricultural land. People initially migrated to the region to exploit the natural resource base, but with the growth of transportation, communication, and financial institutions, employment in the modern era has shifted from the secondary to the tertiary sector, which provides services to both the regional agricultural sector and the global economy.

PROJECT DESIGN AND FINDINGS

The research objectives of the Tri-Academy Project are to explore the relations among population growth, consumption patterns, and land use change in the six study regions and to identify issues that will illuminate the principal forces driving the observed changes. The study protocols focused on three broad questions:

1. What is the nature of the significant population and land use transformations in the study regions?
2. To what extent have local population growth and consumption directly influenced the changes in land use?
3. From a comparison of the case studies, what can be learned about the general nature of the forces driving the transformations and about the influence of government policies on population growth and mobility, land use, and economic development?

Three general findings emerged from the case studies:

1. *The Intertwined Effects of Population, Consumption, and Technology.* As noted, the population of each study region is increasing. Migration, as opposed to natural population growth, is the dominant source of these increases in the Pearl River Delta and South Florida, two of the three fastest-growing regions. The effect of local consumption on land use patterns often is less important than that of external consumption. In all regions, the area devoted to subsistence crops has decreased over time and the area sown to market crops has increased. In some regions, local consumption has changed in response—for example, meat, milk, and fish consumption has risen in the Jitai Basin and grain consumption has fallen in Haryana. In the study regions, the impact of technology on the environment was found to be positive or negative, depending on the time and the situation. In Haryana and the Jitai Basin, technological change led to environmental degradation, but more recently in Florida and the Jitai

Basin it permitted restoration of natural areas. Green Revolution technology has played a major role in transforming the nature of agricultural land use.

2. *Stability and Change on the Land.* Contrary to common perceptions, forest areas seem to be stable or even increasing in the study regions of high population density. Grassland and wetland areas, by contrast, are declining and may be more at risk of land use transformation. From 1970 to 1995, total agricultural land in most study regions did not undergo major changes, even though the populations of the regions did grow significantly. Thus, population increases are not uniformly associated with decreases in agricultural land areas. Recovery and restoration of land are possible with appropriate and effective land use policies; however, the ecological and political settings in which they occur may be complex. Finally, land use change has affected the social groups within regions differently. The case studies document differences in effects on upland and lowland groups, on landless people, on women, and on the rural poor.

3. *The Importance of Government Policy.* Of the various factors mentioned in this report, government policy generally appears to have the greatest single effect on land use change. In the study regions, the effects of government policies are amplified by the fact that no region is a closed system; people, capital, and goods flow across all boundaries. As a result, external forces sometimes have the dominant effect on land use changes. The case studies also reveal that policies often are not motivated by the pressure of population growth and that some policies result in land use changes that provoke increased migration or movement of people. Policies in the study regions that have had a major effect on land use change include: price controls on agricultural inputs and outputs, infrastructure support, taxation, privatization, and reforestation programs. Economic policies have been especially important in the Chinese regions and in Kerala; infrastructure support was important in Haryana and South Florida.

CONCLUSION

In an increasingly globalized world, places are linked more strongly over greater distances. Understanding the role of government action is critical to understanding how global forces reshape regions and countries. Government policies can offset or mitigate the effects of natural population growth on land use, or they can force or encourage land use changes first, which in turn causes movement of people. At best, policy becomes an important mechanism through which jurisdictions can channel global forces and define opportunities for growth. At worst, global flows of people and capital cause unintended consequences that subvert the intention of government action. Any understanding of the interaction between land use and population in any place will depend on taking into account external and global forces.

This observation has important implications for local sustainability initiatives. The true drivers of local environmental change must be identified, and policies intended to foster more sustainable development must be carried out in recognition of the larger context. For example, the success of water restoration projects currently proposed for Haryana depends strongly on a shift in Indian national food supply policies. Similarly, in South Florida transformations in land use are influenced as much by commodity prices, tax incentives, and government infrastructure projects as they are by the pressures of increasing population density. Recognition of the importance of these types of spatial linkages can be a significant step toward more effective environmental management.

The case studies in this investigation do not support a view of the world in which land use change and environmental degradation stem purely from the numerical population and its consumption pattern. The most obvious deficiency in most formulas relating population change to development is that the role of social organization—be it economic, political, or cultural—is ignored. In the regions studied here, it is precisely these social actions—from government policy to attitudes toward women—that affect population, consumption, land use, and the environment in profound ways.

PART I

Population and Land Use in India, China, and the
United States: Context, Observations, and Findings

1

Introduction to the Tri-Academy Project

Human population growth changed in character and form in the twentieth century. In the roughly 40 years after 1950, the world's population grew at an unprecedented rate. Not until 1830 did the population reach 1 billion, but only 100 years more were required for it to reach 2 billion. From 1960, when the world population stood at 3 billion, just 40 years, to 1999, were required for the total world population to reach 6 billion. Much of this recent population growth took place in the poorer regions of the world. Fertility and mortality rates began to decline in the Western industrialized regions in the nineteenth century (a process called the demographic transition), but only in the last decades of the twentieth century did some of the developing regions begin to realize significant declines in fertility. The population momentum resulting from a youthful age structure, however, ensures that the populations of the developing world will continue to grow for many years.

These unprecedented rates of population growth have sparked alarm about their impact on the global environment and future prospects for human societies. All human activities since antiquity have disturbed a "pristine" nature. Thus it is not surprising that the high rates of economic and industrial development that accompanied population growth in the twentieth century resulted in the depletion of natural resources and fouling of the land, air, biota, and water in many regions of the globe. The intense modern debate over the relationship between numbers of people and use of available land has resurrected both Malthus's hypothesis and its critics. Although he later revised his views, Thomas Malthus predicted, late in the eighteenth century, that the needs of a growing population would eventually exceed the capacity of a finite earth to support it. Others have suggested that limitless human ingenuity will overcome mere physical constraints. Thus far, scientific and technological advances in agriculture have enabled food production to more than keep pace with a burgeoning population—on a global level. However, at the regional and local levels, and at particular times in history, hundreds of millions of people have lacked sufficient food or food of adequate quality.

A critical aspect of these debates is the relation of increasing population to changes in land use. Humans need land first and foremost to produce food. In general, a rising demand for food leads to expansion of land under cultivation, intensification of agricultural practices, or both. The latter, in turn, often requires application of large quantities of fertilizer, herbicides, insecticides, and irrigation water, which can have damaging impacts on the environment. Beyond agriculture, other drivers of land use change include industrialization and urbanization, which may further degrade natural resources and the environment.

The objective of this Tri-Academy Project is to examine the interactions between population, land use, and consumption by studying six regions in the world's three largest countries (Figure 1-1). The regions are: in India, Kerala, a state in southwest India, and Haryana, a state north of New Delhi; in China, the Pearl River Delta in the south and the Jitai Basin in Jiangxi Province just to the north; and in the United States, South Florida in the southeastern part of the country and the Chicago region in the American Midwest. Study teams in each region analyzed basic trends in population growth and land use change since World War II and sought to identify drivers of the observed changes. Afterward, members of the local study team prepared each case study chapter. The project team then as a

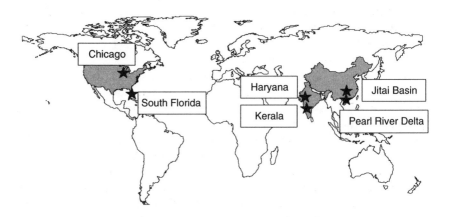

FIGURE 1-1 Tri-Academy study regions.

whole compared the trends and drivers across sites. Although initially it was assumed that population growth alone might be a significant driver of land use change in many of the regions, the results indicate that many other factors also played important roles in the transformations. These factors include government policies, changes in consumption patterns, and the effects of economic integration and globalization.

ORIGIN OF THE STUDY

In October 1993, representatives of 58 of the world's science academies gathered in New Delhi for a "Science Summit" on World Population. Over the course of four days of discussion, scientists from all continents prepared a joint statement intended for use at the United Nations Population Conference scheduled for Cairo in June 1994.[1] The statement read in part:

> Throughout history, and especially during the twentieth century, environmental degradation has primarily been a product of our efforts to secure improved standards of food, clothing, shelter, comfort, and recreation for growing numbers of people. The magnitude of the threat to the ecosystem is linked to human population size and resource use per person. Resource use, waste production, and environmental degradation are accelerated by population growth. They are further exacerbated by consumption habits, certain technological developments, and particular patterns of social organization and resource management.

The statement went on to say:

> The relationships between human population, economic development, and the natural environment are complex. Examination of local and regional case studies reveals the influence and interaction of many variables. For example, environmental and economic impacts vary with population composition and distribution, and with rural–urban and international migrations. Furthermore, poverty and lack of economic opportunities stimulate faster population growth and increase incentives for environmental degradation by encouraging exploitation of marginal resources.

During the meeting, representatives of the science academies of India, China, and the United States agreed to participate in a unique, multinational collaboration (called here the Tri-Academy Project) that would utilize a case study approach to explore the interactions between population growth and changes in land use. Bringing together natural and social scientists from the three countries, the project would seek to cast light on

---

[1]See Population Summit of the World's Scientific Academies. 1999. Washington, D.C.: National Academy Press.

the transformations in demographics, land use, and consumption. The John D. and Catherine T. MacArthur Foundation, the U.S. National Institutes of Health, and the U.S. National Research Council provided support for the undertaking.

RESEARCH OBJECTIVES

As noted, the research objectives of the Tri-Academy Project are to explore the relations among population growth, consumption patterns, and land use change in the six study regions and to compare the findings in a way that will illuminate the principal driving forces of the observed changes. A Tri-Academy panel made up of representatives of the academies of science of the three countries was appointed to design the project and oversee its progress. Each academy selected its own study sites, seeking to identify areas undergoing significant changes in population yet embracing a variety of land uses, including agricultural, urban, and natural.

This study was based on the premise that international comparisons of recorded social transformations may yield insight into principles that could lead to broader generalizations, or at least to recognition of common experience, generalizable or not. A perfect design would call for the selection of study sites carefully matched across a spectrum of attributes such as population, land cover, occupations, and geography. While the panel encouraged such design criteria, each country was responsible for selecting its own sites, under the significant constraint that the studies rely on ongoing work or existing material and not on the collection of new data. One result is that all sites have large populations and high population densities. A base period, roughly the last half-century, was adopted for the comparison of trends, but, where available, much earlier data were used in the analyses. Even though the case studies described here do include some anecdotal narrative, the panel has emphasized, to the extent possible, quantitative measures of trends. As the findings demonstrate, however, some explanations of changes in land use and population draw on qualitative as well as quantitative observations.

The inclusion of a chapter on gender issues in development in Kerala and Haryana represents the realization of a fortuitous opportunity. The panel was unable to pursue comparable studies in China and the United States.

The project participants entrusted with the task of creating a common study design for the six study regions faced several constraints. For example, the study had to be based on existing data sets, whose variables did not generally coincide for all sites over the period of study, and on the availability of skilled research teams within the country specializing in the study sites. The common variables selected for the project were sometimes a compromise that took into account the specific data available for each site and the different data forms, units, time intervals, and standards of each country. Nevertheless, the six studies provide an opportunity for comprehensive cross-site comparisons.

The objectives of the study are embodied in three questions that embrace the many specific issues addressed at each site and in the chapters of this report:

1. What is the nature of the significant population and land use transformations in the study regions?

2. To what extent has local population growth and consumption directly influenced the changes in land use?

3. From a comparison of the case studies, what can be learned about the general nature of the forces driving the transformations and about the influence of government policies on population growth and mobility, land use, and economic development?

The first of these questions requires analysis of land use and population data, especially those indices that best describe the changes over time. For population, the project team analyzes the record of population and population growth, migration, urbanization, worker demographics, age and gender distribution, and other social indices. To describe land use change, it looks at the distribution of land cover, soil classification and condition, water tables and quality, and cropping patterns.

To answer the second question, the project team compares the time relationships of all these variables, looking for patterns in the recorded changes in the distribution of land among the natural, agricultural, and urban (called "built-up" in this report) categories vis-à-vis changing population densities and distributions and consumption patterns.

In exploring the third question and examining other forces causing change, researchers take into account the roles of government policies and economic integration and globalization. This question, often explicitly excluded from demographic and land use studies, can be answered only by analyzing how population and land use changes have been influenced by government policies and heightened economic integration either directly or through unintended consequences. The answer may suggest directions for future research.

THE STUDY REGIONS

The populations, resources, land use, and economies of the study regions encompass a broad range. These characteristics are described in Table 1-1 and in this section.

Kerala, a subtropical state in southwest India, has a high life expectancy, a high level of education, and one of the lowest population growth rates in India (see Chapter 5). The major industry in Kerala is

TABLE 1-1 Characteristics, Tri-Academy Study Regions, 1990

Study Region	Population Size (annual growth rate)	Geographical Context	Area (km^2)	Agriculture	Environmental Issues
Kerala	29.1 million (1.3%)	Primarily rural area with midsize cities and villages	39,000	Commercial, truck, and subsistence farming	Deforestation, agricultural land loss, water use
Haryana	16.5 million (2.4%)	Productive agrarian area with high density of farming villages and midsize market centers	42,000	Market-based farming using Green Revolution techniques	Falling water table, possible soil exhaustion, heavy chemical uses to maintain productivity, shrinking agricultural plots
Jitai Basin	2.5 million (0.4%)	Primarily rural area with midsize cities and villages	12,500	Subsistence and commercial farming	Agricultural land loss, deforestation
Pearl River Delta	17 million (3.4%)	Major metropolitan area with surrounding villages and rural areas	17,400	Truck farming	Major urban pollution issues, agricultural land loss, and water use
South Florida	5.4 million (2.6%)	Mixed area with major urban concentrations, nature reserves, and commercial agriculture	27,100	Commercial	Threatened unique biosphere reserve, water resources
Chicago CMSA	7.9 million (0.2%)	Major metropolitan area with surrounding suburbs and adjacent rural areas	13,100	Commercial and truck farming	Moderate urban pollution issues, farmland loss

NOTE: CMSA = Consolidated Metropolitan Statistical Area.

agriculture, and its average per capita income is low. The state economy benefits, however, from remittances from expatriate workers.[2] Land use in Kerala is currently influenced by state government policies that encourage cash crop production and by migration from the cities to the highland areas within the state.

Haryana and its neighbor state Punjab to the north are the wheat-growing "breadbasket" of India (see Chapter 6). Haryana's population growth rate is among the highest in India, but thanks to the introduction of Green Revolution technologies, agricultural productivity has been able to keep pace. The agricultural land area has remained fairly constant during the state's high-growth period, even though Haryana continues to be a major supplier of food for the country. The state is made up of two quite different regions, an arid one in the west and a semiarid one to the east.

The Jitai Basin, a center of revolutionary political activity in the 1940s and 1950s, has been considered a less-developed region of China for most of this century (see Chapter 8). Beginning in the 1950s, this agricultural region was heavily affected by radical government policies, including the Great Leap Forward, which called for cutting down forests to provide fuel for local small-scale smelters; the "grain production first" system, which dedicated more farmland to grain production; the Cultural Revolution, a political movement designed to completely remold society and change the thinking of the Chinese people; and the "household responsibility" system, which temporarily shifted the responsibility for management of farmland and forests from public to individual households. The region is now a focus of Chinese environmental policies. Meanwhile, population has grown slowly, some natural areas are being restored, and the region remains a source of "floating" workers for the Pearl River Delta to the south.

The Pearl River Delta, long a commercial region open to the West, was at one time a center of food production for the South China region (see Chapter 9). It also was a major source of Chinese immigrants to the West and to Southeast Asia. In 1978 the Chinese government designated several special economic zones in the Delta, areas where foreigners are permitted to invest and local companies are free to export. The government also allowed agricultural land to be converted to urban uses, under a regime of government incentives. Since then, the region has experienced rapid urbanization and industrialization and has become a magnet for migrant and "floating" workers from many parts of China.

---

[2]Remittances are funds sent back to the home country, usually to family, by overseas workers. They are often a large fraction of the workers' salaries and can be an important source of income for the families and the region.

In the United States, South Florida developed rapidly after 1900; throughout the twentieth century decadal growth rates exceeded 100 percent (see Chapter 10). The primary industry is agriculture, but since World War II tourism and, more recently, financial and trading activities have become key industries. The interaction between population and land use in South Florida is dominated by the influx of migrants from northern U.S. states and immigrants from the Caribbean and Central and South America. Government policies to protect the Everglades and to provide water control structures for agriculture have created a highly inhomogeneous population pattern.

Chicago, a small U.S. city of 5,000 in 1840, grew at a rate of 10.4 percent a year from 1840 to 1900, when it became known as the world's greatest rail center (see Chapter 11). Grassland, timber, and livestock provided successive bases for commercial development. The city's population peaked in 1950, but the metropolitan region continues to grow as the suburbs encroach on agricultural land. People initially migrated to the region to exploit the natural resource base, but with the growth of transportation, communication, and financial institutions, employment in the modern era has shifted from manufacturing to providing services to both the regional agricultural sector and the global economy.

All study sites are subdivisions of larger national political entities and are themselves divided into smaller subunits. In India, the study regions, the states of Haryana and Kerala, are composed of political districts. In China, the Jitai Basin in Jiangxi Province and portions of the Pearl River Delta in Guangdong Province are defined as geographical entities that followed land use development histories different from those of the rest of their respective provinces. Data for the larger provinces and the smaller counties and metropolitan districts are presented for comparison with those of the study regions. In the United States, the South Florida region is an aggregate of seven Florida counties, and the Chicago study region comprises six counties of the state of Illinois. The city of Chicago falls within Cook County and is not a subdivision in itself.

For the most part in this project, the study regions were treated as single entities, although data were compiled at the level of each administrative subdistrict within the regions. In some cases, analysis at the subregional level revealed interesting forces at work. In Kerala, for example, it was possible to study internal migration from one district to another, propelled by differences in government pricing policies for land and crops. In the Pearl River Delta, project team members learned how the local environmental laws influence relative population growth among districts. And in Haryana, they found that the arid and semiarid regions of the state were subject to different government policies. The forces at play at the district level help to illuminate the causes of the broader changes at the study region level.

PROJECT STRUCTURE

Each case study was carried out by a local or national research team following protocols devised and accepted by all. The research teams met four times. The first meeting, held in Washington, D.C., in 1995, featured a preliminary discussion on criteria for the selection of study sites and suggestions of possible sites. At the second meeting, which took place at the University of Kerala in 1996, project participants established the study protocols and a list of common variables. A third meeting at Florida State University in Tallahassee in October 1997 was devoted to formulating guidelines for the use of geographic information systems (GIS) in the studies. The Tallahassee meeting was combined with a training course, offered by Florida State University, on applications of the GIS methodologies. At the fourth and last meeting, held in Beijing in June 1998, the outline of this study report took form.

The structure of the project reflects some of the comparative international studies related to global environmental change carried out in the 1990s (for example, Turner et al., 1990; Kasperson et al., 1995; Strzepek and Smith, 1995). In these investigations, a diverse group of researchers developed a common research process and produced a set of case studies that yielded interesting analogies rather than formal comparisons. The Tri-Academy study used a similar modus operandi. Because data on population and land use were collected within different geographical boundaries by different agencies in the three countries, establishing a comparable primary database for the six studies was a difficult undertaking. Generally, the study teams were expected to draw on existing published sources rather than undertake new surveys and measurements. Once a set of common variables was selected, data from all research groups were sent to the research group at Florida State University. There, these data were compiled in four categories—demographic, land use, environmental, and consumption—on both regional and subregional scales for the Tri-Academy common variable data set. In each case study, team members used both the common database and additional data from more specialized and local studies.

It was recognized from the beginning that there would be problems related to the definition of variables and the compatibility of data used. True comparative analyses are impossible without identically defined, relevant variables expressed in comparable units. But each country respects its own land classification scheme and holds to special definitions. In the absence of comparable and unchanging spatial units and definitions, the numerical size of a population within political boundaries of varying scales produces uncertain measures of migration or population density. Researchers also encountered the problem of verifying data sources. Inevitably, there were some inconsistencies between the common data set and the case studies, and in the comparative analyses these were resolved in favor of the case studies.

Temporal scales of analysis differ among the study regions. The Tri-Academy Project was searching for patterns in the trajectories of land use dynamics. Thus the time periods of the six studies differ because the starting points needed to capture the major land use transformations differ by location. The Chicago study period is the longest, from 1840 to 1990. Other study periods are: Kerala, 1960–1990; Haryana, 1970–1990; the Jitai Basin, 1965–1994; the Pearl River Delta, 1950–1995; and South Florida, 1900–1990. For purposes of direct comparison, data primarily for the period 1970–1990, the period of greatest overlap in the Tri-Academy data set, are used.

Because the emphasis of the study is on transformations and the factors that influence them, comparisons from the different eras proved useful. In the chapters that follow, readers will find for several of the study regions graphs of similar shapes but with different time scales describing transformations with common elements. The driving forces revealed were not simple; they involved complex interactions of several factors. Moreover, it was not always possible to distinguish the dependent variable defining the transformation and the independent variable presumably driving it. This complexity is elucidated in the chapters that follow.

DESCRIPTIVE FRAMEWORK

Although a variety of models describe the interaction of population, land use, and development (see Chapters 2 and 3), participants in this study found no single one adequate to characterize the transformations occurring in the study regions. Because differentiation between the internal and external forces driving change within each region appears to be significant, a purely descriptive figure was formulated to capture the relationships among the several important variables in the study. The triangle depicted in Figure 1-2 with apices labeled government, population, and land distinguishes between factors "internal" and "external" to a region. Activities emanating from within and from outside a region affect the relationships between population and land use. For example, population is changed by births and deaths within the region and by migration to and from outside the region. The products of the land serve the population within the region and export markets elsewhere. Capital and technology can come from either side.

The arrows along the base of the triangle point in both directions. Family planning and migration choices are influenced by consumption and income, for which the land is an important resource. In turn, population growth affects land use through people's needs for housing and space, the conversion of land to agriculture to produce foodstuffs and other goods, and the deterioration of environmental quality from industry and agriculture. The land also affects population growth: eroded and degraded lands do not support large populations, whereas sites with productive soils or pleasant environments attract migrants, as do sites where worker housing has been constructed in anticipation of new growth.

In Figure 1-2, government actions are shown primarily as applied forces with little direct feedback. Government policies—local, regional, and national—were found to be important in all study regions, but the national government dominates in nearly all the cases, presently and historically. In the United States, land regulation is primarily determined at the state and local levels. The various levels of government control population growth through education and health services and through direct regulation of births and migration, as in China, or incentives and infrastructure that promote or discourage migration, in all sites. Government has profound effects on land use and the environment through direct regulation, in China and South Florida, and through infrastructure, incentives, and pricing policies, in all sites. These factors are discussed extensively in the case studies.

Perhaps most interesting are the forces originating outside the triangle—that is, those external to the study regions. On the left is the reservoir of people. In-migrants increase a region's population—with major

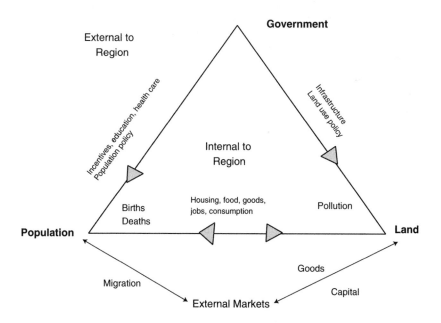

FIGURE 1-2 Relations among government, population, and land, and influences on population and land use emanating from within a region and from outside a region. Arrows show both the direction of influences and the loci of impacts.

impacts in Haryana, Guangdong Province, and Florida—and out-migrants send home remittances, and in some cases investment capital and know-how, to bolster income and support investments in the land—a big factor in Kerala and the Jitai Basin. External markets in goods, workers, technologies, and capital have great impacts on land use in all the study regions and provide an external link between consumption and land status that is, in many cases, stronger than the internal one. Each study region is linked to external markets that serve as a supplier of food and other imported products, purchase exported products of the region, and act as a source of the capital and human resources.

Chapters 2–4 offer a comparative analysis of the six case studies. Chapter 2 on population compares the characteristics of population growth in the study areas with worldwide trends and relates them to current theoretical models. Chapter 3 describes the land use patterns in the study regions and relates the patterns to population change in the regions by land use type. The conjoined findings are presented in Chapter 4.

REFERENCES

Kasperson, J. X., R. E. Kasperson, and B. L. Turner II, eds. 1995. Regions at Risk. Tokyo: United Nations Press.
Strzepek, K. M., and J. B. Smith. 1995. As Climate Changes: International Impacts and Implications. Cambridge: Cambridge University Press.
Turner, B. L., II, W. C. Clark, R. W. Kates, J. F. Richards, J. R. Mathews, and W. B. Meyer, eds. 1990. The Earth as Transformed by Human Action. Cambridge: Cambridge University Press.

2

Elements of Population Growth

India, China, and the United States are all undergoing major demographic and spatial transformations. The form of these transformations varies widely—not only among the three nations, but also within various regions of the three countries. Some major patterns are apparent, however, when the three countries and the six study regions in them (Kerala, India; Haryana, India; the Jitai Basin, China; the Pearl River Delta, China; South Florida, USA; and Chicago, USA) are compared on several dimensions: changes in the rates and components of population increase, geographic redistribution of the population, and the influences of external economic and demographic events.

This exploration of the findings from these six study regions runs head on into many of the major controversies in demography. Are the net effects of population growth positive (Simon, 1981) or negative (Ehrlich, 1968)? Does population growth cause innovation (Boserup, 1965)? Is population growth the major factor in environmental degradation, or does it play only a secondary role after factors such as economic development, consumption, and public policy (Jolly and Torrey, 1993; Meyer and Turner, 1992)?

Simple answers do not stand up to scrutiny given the interaction of population variables with other social and economic variables and with the physical environment. In some of these interactions population can best be viewed as the independent variable; in other contexts it must be viewed as the dependent variable. It is this complexity that makes analysis in the field both frustrating and exciting.

This Tri-Academy Project does not resolve that complexity. On the contrary, the results of the individual case studies indicate many areas where simple explanations do not hold and where the complexity of interactions among population, consumption, land use, the environment, and other social and economic variables must be addressed to understand the underlying processes. The role of this chapter is to place the case studies in context, to look for some common threads among them, to tie them to some of the relevant demographic theory, and to raise questions that remain unresolved.

POPULATION AND LAND AREA

The countries in this study—India, China, and the United States—are the world's most populous (see Figure 2-1). In 2000 the population of China was estimated at 1.262 billion, India at 1.014 billion, and the United States at 276 million (U.S. Census Bureau, 2000). Although the combined population of these three countries—2.5 billion—makes up 42 percent of the world's population, the countries only occupy 16 percent of the world's land area. How these countries handle their land and population relationships will have a major role on how the earth as a whole copes with population pressure on the land.

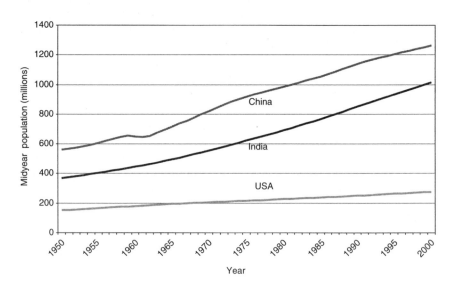

FIGURE 2-1 Population of India, China, and United States, 1950–2000. SOURCE: U.S. Census Bureau. 2000. International Data Base, May 10, online at *http://www. census.gov/ipc/www/idbnew/html*

The crudest measure of the relationship between population and land is simple population density, a gauge in which the three countries differ substantially. In 2000 the world's population density was almost 46.4 persons per square kilometer (U.S. Census Bureau, 2000). The population density of the United States, however, was only 30 persons per square kilometer, or substantially below the world average. With its 135 persons per square kilometer, China has a population density more than three times the world average, even though vast arid areas in western China are sparsely populated. India is one of the world's more densely populated countries. Its density of 341 persons per square kilometer is almost eight times the world average.

More important than the density of each country as a whole is the spatial variation within the country. The Tri-Academy Project studied six regions that are at or above the average population density of the nation in which they are located. The primarily agricultural regions, the Jitai Basin and Haryana, are close to the national averages for China and India, respectively. The two urban regions, the Pearl River Basin and the Chicago metropolitan area, show high densities as would be expected. The other two regions, Kerala and South Florida, have particular circumstances that lead to unexpected results. Although South Florida is 96 percent urban and is densely settled along the coasts, much of the inland area is reserved for national parks and conservation areas. As a result, the average density is as low as that of the Jitai Basin. At the other extreme, Kerala, which is only 26 percent urban, has a dense system of village settlements that results in a population density almost as high as those of the Chicago and Pearl River Delta regions.

CHANGES IN DENSITY AND POPULATION

As the world moves into the twenty-first century, one major reason for concern is not just the current population density level but also the rate at which it has been increasing over time. From 1950 to 2000 the world's population density more than doubled, from 20 persons to 46 persons per square kilometer. The population density of the United States increased somewhat more slowly, from 17 persons per square kilometer in 1950 to 30 by 2000—an increase of roughly 75 percent. During that period the population density of China increased 125 percent, from 60 to 135 persons per square kilometer, and India's population density increased over 175 percent during the last half-century, rising from 124 persons per square kilometer in 1950 to more than 341 in 2000 (U.S. Census Bureau, 2000).

Because land area varies very little with time, the changes in density have been directly associated with changes in population size. During the last half of the twentieth century, the combined population of India, China,

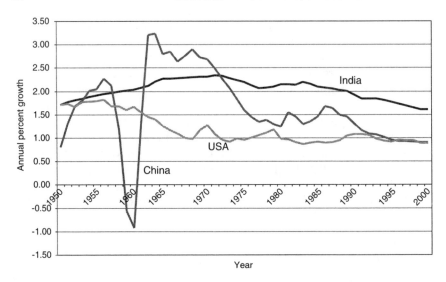

FIGURE 2-2 Population change in India, China, and United States, 1950–2000. Note the significant drop in the late 1950s and early 1960s due to the famine and deferred births associated with the Great Leap Forward in China. SOURCE: U.S. Census Bureau. 2000. International Data Base. May 10, online at *http://www. census.gov/ipc/www/idbnew.html*

and the United States increased 135 percent—roughly the same as that of the world as a whole. Yet the average annual rates of population growth varied markedly (see Figure 2-2). China's average growth rate rose from less than 1.0 percent in 1950 to over 3 percent in the 1963, interrupted by declines during the "Great Leap Forward" of the late 1950s and the early 1960s. The high birth rate was the response of the population to the huge losses of life during the Great Famine and was a catch-up in births to replace the children who died or who were not born in those years. The birth rate has since declined steadily, to 2.7 percent in 1970, 1.25 in 1980, and an estimated 0.9 percent in 2000. By contrast, India's rates of population growth have remained high, rising from an average annual growth rate of 1.7 percent in 1950 to 2.3 percent in 1970 (U.S. Census Bureau, 2000). A decline in recent decades brought the rate down to 1.9 percent in 1990 and an estimated 1.6 percent in 2000. In the United States, the average annual growth rate of 1.7 percent in 1950 and 1960 declined to 1.3 percent in 1970 and 1.0 percent in the 1980 and 1990. By 2000, the rate of population growth of 0.9 percent in the United States was the same as that of China but much lower than the 1.6 percent for India. But even India's growth rate had come down below the level that the U.S. rate was in 1950.

THE DEMOGRAPHIC TRANSITION AND COMPONENTS OF POPULATION CHANGE

As countries undergo the "demographic transition" (Davis, 1945), the traditional pattern of high fertility and high mortality is transformed by the technological, social, and market changes that reduce mortality while fertility remains high. The result of high fertility and low mortality is a major increase in population size. Later, fertility also begins to fall, eventually reducing the rate of population growth. The speed of the transition and the level to which fertility declines (above or below replacement level) varies widely from one society to another. Each of the three countries in this study has had its own pattern and timing for this transition.

The United States was one of the first countries to go through the demographic transition; crude death rates fell from 17 to 9 deaths per thousand persons between 1900 and 1950. Since 1950 the crude death rate has fluctuated slightly with improvements in life expectancy, sometimes outweighed by increases in the proportion of the population over age 65, so that by 1998 the crude death rate was eight deaths per thousand persons (Figure 2-3). The demographic transition in fertility in the United States was not as smooth as that in other countries with developed economies. Although the crude birth rate fell from 32 births per thousand persons in 1900 to 19 per thousand by 1940, the extended baby boom after World War II led to crude birth rates of 24 per thousand in the 1950s and 1960s (Figure 2-3). Fertility has dropped markedly since that time, but the crude birth rate of 14 per thousand total population at the end the twenti-

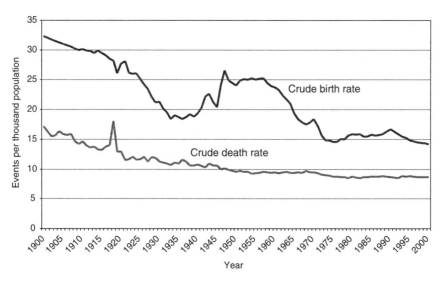

FIGURE 2-3 Demographic Transition of the United States, 1900–2000.

eth century was substantially higher than fertility levels in most other developed countries. The difference between the population growth rate of 0.9 percent a year and the rate of natural increase of 0.6 percent in 2000 stems from the large net flow of immigrants into the United States— roughly a million a year over the last decade.

China, with its population of more than 1.2 billion, has seen one of the world's most impressive transitions in population growth (Banister, 1985). In the last half of the twentieth century, death rates declined dramatically in China (Figure 2-4): from 30 deaths per thousand persons in 1950 and 35 per thousand in 1960, down to about 7 per thousand in 2000 (U.S. Census Bureau, 2000). In recent decades, the second part of the demographic transition has taken hold at a very fast pace, with dramatic declines in fertility coincident with the adoption of the one-child population policy (Feeney and Jianhua, 1994). Although the adherence to this one-child policy varies widely throughout the country, it has been particularly effective in urban areas (Cooney and Li, 1994; Zeng Yi, 1996). From 1950 to 1970 the crude birth rate dropped gradually, from 43 to 37 births per thousand persons. During the 1970s, the decline was much more dramatic, to 19 births per thousand persons by 1980. After a slight rise to 21 per thousand in 1990, the rate was down to 16 per thousand by 2000 (Figure 2-4). Today, China appears to have passed through all the stages of the demographic transition. As a result of falling death rates and even faster falling birth rates, China's rate of natural increase (and its rate of population growth) in 2000 was only 0.9 percent a year—well below the world average of 1.3 percent a year (U.S. Census Bureau, 2000).

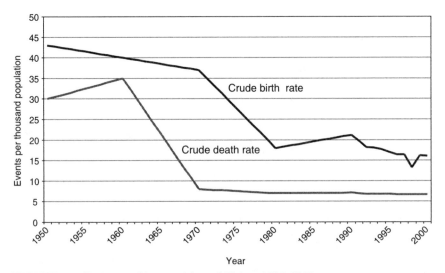

FIGURE 2-4 Demographic transition of China, 1900–1998.

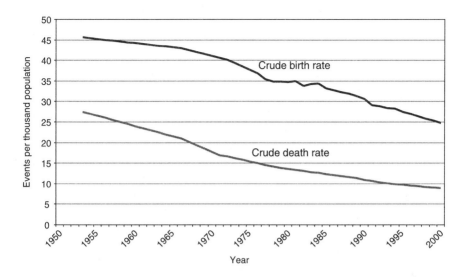

FIGURE 2-5 Demographic transition of India, 1950–1998.

During the second half of the twentieth century, India too showed gradual but steady reductions in its crude death rates—from 27 per thousand persons in 1950 to 9 per thousand in 2000—signaling the beginning of its demographic transition (Figure 2-5). Although the crude birth rate remained quite high at 45 per thousand in the 1950s, recent years have seen moderate declines in this rate, down to 26 per thousand in 2000. India's current rate of population growth at 1.6 percent a year in 2000 is still substantially higher than the world average.

Tables 2-1 and 2-2 provide a demographic comparison of the six sites for 1990–1991, the last years for which common data are available for all sites. For reference, national-level data for 1990–1991 are shown as well. These data were provided principally by the national statistical agencies responsible for the national censuses, the Office of the Registrar General of India, the Chinese Central Bureau of Statistics, and the U.S. Census Bureau. The data have been supplemented by that from municipal statistics and sample surveys.

The comparability of data across sites is limited by differences in concepts and measurement. The urban concept is particularly tied to administrative definitions that change between countries and over time within a given country. Similarly, differences in residence definition affect the counting of the "floating" population in China and illegal immigrants in the United States. Underenumeration of women in India, younger children in China, and illegal immigrants and minorities in the United States have had major effects. Such is the nature of comparative

TABLE 2-1 Population Size and Components of Population Change by Nation and Study Region, 1990

	China Study Regions			India Study Regions			U.S. Study Regions			
	Total China[a]	Pearl River[b]	Jitai Basin	Total India[c]	Kerala	Haryana	Total U.S.[d]	South Florida	Chicago	World
Total population (millions)	1,139	15.4	2.0	851	29.1	16.5	250	4.6	7.4	5,278
Annual population growth (percent)	1.4	4.0	1.3	2.1	1.3	2.0	1.0	2.6	0.2	1.7
Rate of natural increase (per thousand persons)	14	12	8	20	16	25	8	4	9	17
Residual rate of net migration (per thousand persons)[e]	.5	29	5		-3	-5	2	22	-7	—
Crude birth rate (per thousand persons)	21	17	13	31	23	35	16.6	14	17	27
Total fertility rate (births per woman)	2.2	2.3	2.6	3.8	1.8	4.0	2.1	2.1	2.1	3.4
Crude death rate (deaths per thousand persons)	7	5	6	11	6	10	8.6	10	8	10
Life expectancy at birth	68.4	77.6	68.7	57.2	69.6	62.7	75.5			61
Infant mortality rate (deaths per thousand births)	42.6	NA	45	79.9	17	75	8.6	7	8	58

[a]Average annual rates for calendar year 1990. Data from U.S. Census Bureau, 2000.

[b]Includes estimates for the "floating" population using known increment for Shenzhen to augment the value proportionally for each municipality in the Pearl River Delta. Data from the 1990 Census of China and the Guangdong and Shenzhen Statistical Yearbooks.

[c]Rates for total India from U.S. Census Bureau, 2000. Values for Kerala and Haryana are for 1991.

[d]Rates for total United States from U.S. Census Bureau, 2000.

[e]Calculated value of annual rate of population growth minus annual rate of natural increase.

SOURCES: U. S. Census Bureau. 2000. International Data Base. May 10, online at www.census.gov/ipc/www/idbnew.html; Statistical Yearbooks for Guangdong, Shenzhen, and Jiangxi, China; 1981 and 1991 Censuses of India.

TABLE 2-2 Selected Demographic Characteristics by Nation and Study Region, 1990

	China Study Regions			India Study Regions[a]			U.S. Study Regions			
	Total China	Pearl River	Jitai Basin	Total India	Kerala	Haryana	Total U.S.	South Florida	Chicago	World
Total population (millions)	1,139	15.4	2.4	851	29.1	16.5	250	4.6	7.4	5,278
Population density (persons/km²)	120	975	176	266	749	372	26	171	601	35
Sex ratio (men per hundred women)	106.5	101	105	107.9	96.5	116.0	95.1	93.6[a]	95.1	101.5
Percent under age 15	27.7			37.2	29.7	37.8	21.5	19.3	22.5	30.7
Percent age 65 and over	5.6			4.6	5.4	3.8	12.6	19.1	11.3	6.8
Percent urban population	26.4	70	17.8	27.0	26.4	24.6	75.2	95.8	96.4	46.7

[a] Values for Indian states are for 1991.

SOURCES: U.S. Census Bureau. 2000. International Data Base. May 10, online at www.census.gov/ipc/www/idbnew.html; Statistical Yearbooks for Guangdong, Shenzhen, and Jiangxi, China; 1991 Census of India.

research that the comparisons among these studies have led to several individual research projects aimed at exploring conceptual and measurement issues in more detail. Nevertheless, several general comparisons can be made across sites.

Age Structure and Age-Specific Vital Rates

Rates of population growth and natural increase and crude birth and death rates help paint a rough picture of population change, but a fuller understanding of the underlying population dynamics lies in a more detailed look at the population age structure and age-specific birth and death rates. For example, a young population with a pattern of relatively high age-specific mortality rates could produce a lower crude death rate than an older population with relatively low age-specific mortality rates. Thus, although the United States and India have roughly the same crude death rate, life expectancy at birth in the United States in 2000 was 77.1 compared with 62.5 in India (Figure 2-6). Because the Indian population in 2000 was younger—only 5 percent were over age 65 compared with 12 percent in the United States—the ratio of the number of deaths to the total population size is roughly equivalent. China, with 7 percent of its population over age 65 in 2000 and a life expectancy at birth of 71.4, has a crude death rate lower than those of either the United States or India. In infant mortality rates, the United States, with only 7 deaths per thousand births in 2000, is far below China's 29 deaths per thousand and India's 65 deaths per thousand.

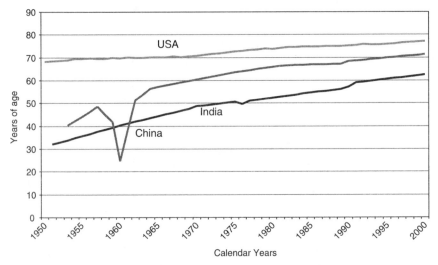

FIGURE 2-6 Life expectancy at birth, India, China, and United States, 1950–2000.

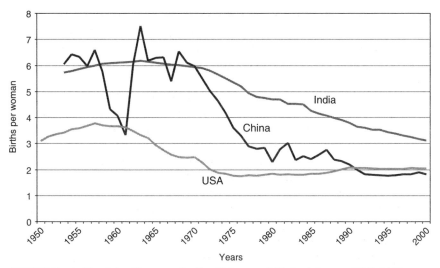

FIGURE 2-7 Total fertility rate, India, China, and United States, 1950–2000.

The percentage of China's population under age 15 in 2000 was 25 percent compared with 21 percent in the United States and 34 percent in India. The Chinese total fertility rate in 2000 at 1.8 children per woman was also lower than the U.S. rate of 2.1, but the larger percentage of the population that is of child-bearing age led to a larger crude birth rate in China in 2000 (16 per thousand persons) than in the United States (14 per thousand persons). India's total fertility rate of 3.1 births per woman and its crude birth rate of 25 per thousand persons in 2000 were far higher than those of the United States and China (Figure 2-7).

Spatial Redistribution

Another major aspect of population trends in all three countries is the change in the spatial distribution of the population. As economic development proceeds, the percentage of the labor force engaged in agriculture decreases and the percentage located in urban areas increases. In the United States the percentage of the labor force in agriculture declined from 51 percent in 1880 to 8 percent by 1960. During the same period the urban percentage increased from 28 percent to 70 percent. In recent decades Americans have remained highly mobile, with roughly one out of six persons changing residence each year. Much of the growth has been in the suburbs—often distant suburbs—of metropolitan areas, with the result that a larger and larger portion of the nation's territory has become urban. The two U.S. study regions grew dramatically for most of the last hundred years. Chicago's period of highest growth was from the mid-

1800s to the middle of the twentieth century. In recent years that growth has slowed (as has the growth of many older northern U.S. cities) to the point that the region as a whole shows net out-migration. South Florida began its growth later, at the beginning of the twentieth century, and still has significant in-migration.

For China, this migratory flux is a relatively new phenomenon (Goldstein, 1990)—and one that has spawned a new category of migration known as the "floating population" (a population with official residence in the countryside and temporary residence in urban areas). Increased migration, such as the heavy flow into the rapidly urbanizing Pearl River Delta—has accompanied economic development and the recent rapid growth of major cities as well as smaller towns (Ma and Lin, 1993).

India still has a large proportion of its labor force in agriculture and a relatively low rate of urbanization, but at the same time many of its cities are now so large that they count among the world's major metropolises. Migration—particularly rural to urban—has shown signs of expansion in recent years, consistent with the small net out-migration from largely rural Haryana, which attracts workers to its highly productive farms and agroindustry but loses more to the cities in other states. Kerala also is registering a small net out-migration, the result of continuing out-migration to urban centers in India and to overseas locations such as the Persian Gulf. This out-migration is partially balanced, however, by return migration from those areas.

THEORETICAL BACKGROUND AND STUDY FINDINGS

The theoretical literature related to population, consumption, environment, and technology is complex. However, it is possible to broadly classify theories by their positive or negative view of population growth. Those with a positive view tend to emphasize the productive side of population. Those with a negative view concentrate on consumption by the population. Each approach has a long intellectual tradition, each views consumption, environment, and technology differently, and each leads to strikingly different conclusions (Bongaarts, 1996; Keyfitz, 1996). Moreover, the earlier theoretical formulations often refer to closed societies, an untenable assumption with today's high levels of immigration and economic globalization.

People as Consumers and Producers

The view of people as consumers can be traced back to Thomas Malthus's "An Essay on the Principle of Population" published in 1798. In that essay, Malthus contends that agricultural production, limited by finite resources, cannot keep pace with population growth, but that "negative checks" such as famine and disease help to keep such growth in check. His theory holds that any increase in production is quickly consumed by the higher demands of a growing population. Thus society remains near the subsistence level. In this formulation, technology and social/economic organization are assumed to remain constant. Although Malthus relaxed this constraint in a later essay, yielding a more benign view of population growth, it was the first, more dramatic view that many writers later called "Malthusian."

In the centuries that followed, scholars made several attempts to translate Malthus's ideas into a sustainable population size. In one such formulation (Lipton, 1989), consumption per capita could remain high and population size would be held down by "checks" that would reduce fertility (or immigration). Recent formulations have developed the idea further into the notion of "carrying capacity."

More recently, the debate has switched emphasis again, to the effects of population and consumption on the natural environment; protection of the environment, unique ecosystems, and individual species (and their genome content) have become paramount. In this context, sustainability is as likely to refer to the sustainability of the natural system as to societal sustainability.

Within this literature, perhaps the I = PAT formulation is the most well known—that is, negative impacts on the environment are a direct function of population size, affluence, and technology (Holdren and Ehrlich, 1974). Thus the population of a highly developed country with high consumption levels would have a much more negative effect on the environment than a similar population in a country with lower levels of economic development and consumption.

The other major approach—viewing people as producers—also has a long intellectual tradition, stretching back to Adam Smith and Karl Marx. In both the classical and Marxist traditions, population is highly related to labor, one of the principal factors of production. A larger labor force will increase total production, capital and technology being held constant.

Neoclassical economics has followed this tradition of the importance of labor. Although neoclassical economists recognize that population growth could disrupt the savings necessary for capital investment and further development, they are likely to view other factors, such as technological and organizational change, as more important in assuring development. In fact, Boserup (1965) has proposed that population growth sometimes foments technological change by providing the need ("more mouths to feed") and the resources ("more available labor"). In recent years, Simon's advocacy of population as the "ultimate resource" has emphasized the producer aspect even more (Simon, 1981).[1]

---

[1]It is not only population that is viewed differently by the two theoretical traditions. Economic development could be either the source of destructive consumption or the means of providing the resources for coping with society's pollution. Technology has a similar duality.

Recognition that population has both consuming and producing functions leads to a broader scope of demographic/environmental inquiries. Any given person may produce items for another's consumption rather than directly producing for himself. Through markets and trade, food and other goods produced in one area can be consumed in another area some distance away. Combine this with the increases in agricultural productivity that have released workers from the land and the issue of population size broadens into one of population distribution.

As people leave an area with excess agricultural labor for nonagricultural pursuits in urban areas, a trade relationship develops in which the consumption of products in one area can have environmental consequences in a different area. Urbanization has led to a wide variety of environmental effects—local effects such as urban pollution and conversion of close-in agricultural land to urbanized areas and distant effects such as a reduction (or slower increase) in the rural population and a shift from producing food for local consumption to producing cash crops for distant markets.

Today, linkage with the global economy inevitably accompanies economic development. All three countries are now strongly influenced by the rest of the world economy, and trends in one area or country cannot be analyzed without taking into account other international factors and flows of money, goods, and people across national boundaries.

The U.S. economy runs a large negative trade balance with the rest of the world through its imports of vast quantities of raw materials and manufactured goods. It also is the world's leading destination for international migration; over 1 million people a year immigrate to the United States.

Although immigration is not as important in China, that country has made vast strides in recent years in opening its economy to the rest of the world. As a result, it has become one of the world's major exporters of manufactured goods and a major recipient of overseas capital flows.

Global economic factors have had their effects on India as well; its industries are becoming more open to the world market after decades of strong protection. Although immigration flows have only a small effect on India's overall population trends, capital flows and remittances from Indians abroad are playing an increasingly important role in the economy.

Study Findings

The vastly different characteristics of the six study regions provide a wide gamut for viewing the role of population as both an independent variable and a dependent variable. Population interacts with other factors in society through cultural, political, or economic institutions to affect land use and the environment. But just as surely, those factors, the environment, and changing land use patterns cause changes in the size, growth rate, and distribution of population itself.

The predominantly rural sites of Kerala and Haryana in India and the Jitai Basin in China have had markedly different population trends. In recent years Kerala and the Jitai Basin have experienced declines in fertility and considerably lower population growth. The lower population growth has accompanied the conversion of agricultural land to less labor-intensive uses, whether it be the conversion of rice paddy to coconut or rubber plantations in Kerala or the transformation of marginal hillside cultivation to pine forests in the Jitai Basin. Haryana, by contrast, has been a major agricultural success story, but one where continued high fertility and ecological constraints threaten many of the gains from that success.

In Kerala, the emphasis on education and social well-being has led to an exceptionally high level of health care and education for women and men. The high standard of health care is reflected in the low infant mortality rates and high levels of life expectancy (Zachariah et al., 1994). The high levels of female education have led to much lower levels of fertility than in the rest of India (Jeffrey, 1987).

Of great importance are the effects of higher education on out-migration. The supply of human capital in Kerala seems to be too high for the amount of available financial capital (Madhavan, 1985). As Chapter 5 on Kerala points out, this situation has led to high levels of unemployment. Consequently, a substantial portion of the well-educated workforce has moved to the Gulf states or to other parts of India to find employment suitable to their skills, leading to net out-migration of about three per thousand persons a year. Although the traditional measures of personal income place Kerala in the lower half of Indian states, such measures do not capture the extensive flow of remittances back into the state from the highly skilled workforce of emigrants (Madhavan, 1985).

The far-reaching land reform of recent decades in Kerala has had a more direct effect on land use change and population redistribution. It has reduced the average size of landholdings which, when combined with the increased skill levels and alternative opportunities for the recently educated population, has made paddy cultivation both uneconomical and undesirable. Moreover, Kerala has been the scene of substantial internal migration, with marked increases in the population in the highlands (associated with large-scale rubber cultivation) and the continued conversion of land to residential uses to meet the preference for single-family housing.

In China's Jitai Basin, the influence of government policy on population change has been even more direct. The shift in government fertility policies from pro-natalist to the more recent one-child family program has had direct effects on population growth. The one-child policy, applicable to the urban population and some rural areas, led to moderate fertility declines. As the rate of population growth declined, the intensity of cultivation declined. That decline, together with government efforts to encourage reforestation, led to the conversion of land from cultivation to forests (Li, 1990).

Since 1980, the economic liberalization that led to economic growth in coastal cities and the acceptance of floating populations has led to the large-scale, de facto migration of young adults to the cities of Shanghai and Guangzhou and their surrounding economic zones. As Chapter 8 on the Jitai Basin details, this floating population cannot legally migrate permanently and must return regularly to its household registry locations within the Jitai Basin. As this population has grown, continual seasonal migration has led to an influx of money, technology, and knowledge into the province and has increased the economic well-being of those remaining behind.

In contrast to the relative stagnation of agricultural production in Kerala and the Jitai Basin, Haryana owes much of its increase in per capita income to the introduction of improved agricultural technology—particularly new genetic strains of crops associated with the Green Revolution. The increased agricultural production, however, has been accompanied by considerable environmental consequences—salinization, aquatic weed infestation, and pesticide pollution (Repetto, 1994). The increased affluence has been influential in lowering the mortality rate.

Yet increased affluence has not been accompanied by significant improvements in the status and educational level of women (see Chapter 6 on Haryana). The fertility level remains high, and the crude annual birth rate and the rate of natural increase are above the national average. Although Haryana has a small net out-migration, population growth is still high (Table 2-1). One consequence of this high growth rate is a marked decline in the net sown area per agricultural worker, from 3.0 hectares in 1971 to 2.0 in 1991, with similar declines in the average size of landholdings.

The predominantly urban sites in the study—the Pearl River Delta, South Florida, and Chicago—have the higher migration rates (Chicago, until recently) characteristic of areas with high economic growth, but they also have the lower fertility levels typical of developed economies and of urban areas in general.

A closer look at the Pearl River Delta (described in Chapter 9) reveals the conflicting sides of the Chinese economic and demographic policies also at work in the Jitai Basin. Shenzhen, Guangzhou, and the other special economic zones of the Pearl River Delta are displaying the amazing economic growth produced by two decades of market-oriented development (Ma and Lin, 1993). Demographic policies, on the other hand, have led to a reduction in the rate of natural increase in the population of the Pearl River Delta. Because the one-child family policy is strictly enforced in urban areas and because economic imperatives in these areas lead to increased female participation in the labor force, fertility has declined sharply. Left to its own internal population growth, the Pearl River Delta could not meet the labor demands of its dynamic economy.

The demand for labor has been met through legal, formal changes of residence for a portion of the population, but mostly by the influx of the "floating population" described earlier. The national and regional authorities have permitted this "temporary" migration to meet the major labor needs of the dynamic urban economies. Although an attempt has been made to control and register the movement of the floating population (especially in Shenzhen City), official counts may miss some undocumented migrants and the numbers are likely higher than reported. The growing attraction of the population to the Delta and away from the more rural parts of the country has been instrumental in major land use changes as agricultural uses of the land have given way to industrial, commercial, and residential development.

In the counties of South Florida, fertility rates are low in global terms but relatively high when compared with those of other developed areas. Both domestic and international migration to the area continues to stimulate population growth, although at a much slower rate than in the early part of the twentieth century. Chapter 10 on South Florida describes various stages of land use change and population settlement from the frontier days before 1900 to the present, drainage and land conversion activities during 1900–1930, the postwar economic boom and flood control projects of 1950–1970, and the more recent periods of environmental protection and restoration of natural habitats. The government played a key role in the land use conversions both in the early drainage activities and in the later preservation and restoration activities. Although suburbanization of the South Florida population continues and growth is occurring farther and farther from the urban centers, tough zoning measures and federal ownership of large portions of the original Everglades have preserved a vast low-density area near the built-up urban areas.

The city of Chicago and the surrounding region grew rapidly from the mid-1800s to the mid-1900s. During that period and into the last half of the twentieth century, the expanding growth of Greater Chicago resulted in the widespread conversion of agricultural land to urban and suburban uses. Although fertility rates were high during the late 1800s, the major factor was massive in-migration from the east and later from the rural parts of the Midwest as agricultural employment gave way to manufacturing and service-based employment. Chapter 11 on Chicago chronicles this growth and Chicago's transformation from a frontier town to a major agrarian and then commercial center. It also depicts its rapid suburbanization in recent years and the transformation of large parts of the immediate countryside from agricultural to residential and commercial uses.

CONCLUSION

The case studies described here and elsewhere in this volume do not support a view of the world in which changes in land use and environmental degradation stem solely from the numerical population. As demonstrated in each of the study regions, the human population exercises its influence more by its actions than by its numerical presence. In fact, the most egregious omission in a formula such as I = PAT is the role of society and its institutions—economic, political, and cultural. In the study regions, it is precisely these societal factors that most affect population, consumption, land use, and the environment. In each case study the nature and influence of social, economic, and political factors may have been different, but they were always profound.

Economic development seems to be the prime mover in population change—first in declines in mortality, later in fertility declines, and even later in increased population mobility and urbanization. Government policies can be effective as well—for example, public health campaigns to reduce mortality, strong national family planning programs, and strict regional and local zoning and land use restrictions that influence population distribution.

Much of population theory deals with closed systems, but in today's world there is no such thing. Population can have an effect on the environment at great distances, and flows of population and goods across boundaries can permit localized higher densities, while the concentration of population into urban areas may have the effect of decreasing density over much larger areas that are losing population to the cities.

REFERENCES

Banister, J. 1985. China's Changing Population. Washington, D.C.: U.S. Census Bureau.
Bongaarts, J. 1996. Population pressure and the food supply system in the developing world. Population and Development Review 22(3):483–503.
Boserup, E. 1965. The Conditions of Agricultural Progress. London: Allen and Unwin.
Cooney, R. S., and J. Li. 1994. Household registration type and compliance with the "one child'" policy in China, 1979–1988. Demography 31(1):21–32.
Davis, K. 1945. The world demographic transition. Annals of the American Academy of Political and Social Sciences 237:1–11.
Ehrlich, P. R. 1968. The Population Bomb. New York: Ballentine Books.
Feeney, G., and Y. Jianhua. 1994. Below replacement fertility in China? A close look at recent evidence. Population Studies 48(3):381–394.
Goldstein, S. 1990. Urbanization in China, 1982–87: Effects of migration and reclassification. Population and Development Review 16(4):673–701.
Holdren, J. P., and P. R. Ehrlich. 1974. Human population and the global environment. American Scientist 62:282–292.
Jeffrey, R. 1987. Governments and culture: How women made Kerala literate. Pacific Affairs 60(3):447–472.

Jolly, C. L., and B. B. Torrey 1993. Population and Land-use in Developing Countries. Washington, D.C.: National Academy Press.

Keyfitz, N. 1996. Population growth, development, and the environment. Population Studies 50(3):335–359.

Li, J-N. 1990. Population effects on deforestation and soil erosion in China. Population and Development Review 16:254–258.

Lipton, M. 1989. Response to rural population growth: Malthus and the moderns. Population and Development Review 15(supplement):215–242.

Ma, L. J. C., and C. Lin. 1993. Development of towns in China: A case study of Guangdong Province. Population and Development Review 19(3):583–606.

Madhavan, M. C. 1985. Indian emigrants: Numbers, characteristics, and economic impact. Population and Development Review 11(3):457–481.

Meyer, W. H., and B. L. Turner II. 1992. Human population growth and global land-use/cover change. Annual Review of Ecology and Systematics 23:39–61.

Repetto, R. 1994. The "Second India" Revisited: Population, Poverty, and Environmental Stress over Two Decades. Washington, D.C.: World Resources Institute.

Simon, J. 1981. The Ultimate Resource. Princeton: Princeton University Press.

U.S. Census Bureau. 2000. International Data Base. May 10, online at *www.census.gov/ipc/www/idbnew.html*

Zachariah, K. C., et al. 1994. Demographic Transition in Kerala in the 1980s. Thiruvananathapuram: Centre for Development Studies.

Zeng, Y. 1996. Is fertility in China in 1991–92 far below replacement level? Population Studies 50(1):27–34.

3

Land Use Change in Space and Time

The regions of India, China, and the United States described in this volume are each unique, as all places are.[1] But do they have common discernible patterns of land use change that may provide insights into the dynamics of how people and places interact? The Tri-Academy Project examined and compared the timelines, patterns, and associated attributes of land use change in six study regions—Kerala, India; Haryana, India; Jitai Basin, China; Pearl River Delta, China; South Florida, USA; and Chicago, USA. In doing so, project researchers achieved a closer look at the intertwined fates of the forestland, grassland, wetland, agricultural land, and built-up land in those regions. The transformation from less intensively modified forests, grassland, and wetland, to land uses with greater human modification, such as agricultural fields and urban settings, is the most usual trajectory but not the only one (Arizpe et al., 1994). A comparison of these and other transformations provides the foundation for the analysis of population/land use dynamics described in this chapter. The goal of this analysis, as with other land use change studies, is to contribute to the integration of the natural and social sciences, the linkage of science to policy, and the development of pathways to sustainable development. (Turner, 1991; Fresco et al., 1997).

---

[1] In the following quote substitute "population/land use studies " for "history": "Cross-national comparative history can undermine two contrary but equally damaging presuppositions—the illusion of total regularity and that of absolute uniqueness. Cross-national history, by acquainting one with what goes on elsewhere, may inspire a critical awareness of what is taken for granted in one's own country, but it also promotes a recognition that similar functions may be performed by differing means" (Frederickson, 1998).

Using the common variable data set developed by the Tri-Academy Project, researchers examined the fate of forests, grassland, and wetland in the six study regions and tracked the nature of changes in agricultural areas and cropping patterns and of changes in urban or built-up areas. Among other things, the data allowed them to test the common perceptions that less intensively managed lands such as forests are declining ubiquitously and that built-up areas are rapidly expanding everywhere. The study focused, in particular, on the interrelated effects of population and land use against the backdrop of changing government policy. Population pressures influence land use, and changes in land use may affect social relations. Some types of land use policies also may attract or discourage settlement. Where data were available, this study also explored the environmental and social impacts that may accompany land use changes.

LAND USE CLASSIFICATION SCHEME

Each country in the Tri-Academy Project has its own land use classification scheme for data collection and planning purposes. Land use has been measured in the study regions by means of a variety of methods, including surveys, statistical reporting, air photogrammetry, and satellite data analysis. Thus the first task was to rationalize the national schemes into a consistent classification that would allow comparison across regions (see Table 3-1). The forest category includes both unmanaged and planted forests; the grassland/wetland category includes rangeland and pastures; the agriculture category includes plantation, grain, and horticultural cropping systems; and the built-up category includes urban areas and land used for transportation and communications. Grassland, rangeland, and wetland were combined because they represent more extensively managed short vegetation types than the plantation, grain, and horticultural crops represented in the agriculture category. The garden land found in the Chinese classification system denotes perennial crops such as orchard crops and tea and is included in the agriculture category of the Tri-Academy classification.

TABLE 3-1 Tri-Academy Project Land Use Classification Scheme

Class	Definition
Forest	Less intensively managed and planted forests
Grassland/wetland	Grassland, rangeland, and wetland
Agriculture	Plantation, grain, and horticultural cropping systems
Barren/wasteland	Unused
Built-up	Urban areas, land used for transportation and communications
Water	Lakes and rivers

The intent of the Tri-Academy classification scheme was to seek commonalities across the case study regions in terms of functionality given the often sparse and disparate land use data available. More detailed classifications that involve, for example, the quality of forest regrowth in China, are beyond the scope of the project. Although the coarse aggregation of land use categories made formal comparisons difficult, it did allow identification of common and contrasting factors and themes among the regions.

The total area and percentages of land in each category over time are shown in Table 3-2. The land use data shown are for geographical regions comprised of groups of districts or counties within provinces or states, except for Haryana, where state-level data are provided. The land use data provided for Kerala are aggregates of that available for the Alleppey, Kottayam, and Idukki districts.

Over the course of the study, several issues related to data and land use classifications arose. For example, land used for transportation and communications in China is included in the urban category. In South Florida, the grassland land use category includes wetland as well as rangeland. Another issue was that official data sometimes do not reflect actual conditions. In Kerala, the official data indicated no change over certain decades in forestland, whereas researchers noted a substantial decline. In other sites, particularly in China, a reported increase in the urban population was not necessarily caused by the movement of people but by a redefinition and reclassification of towns and villages. Length of data records varied considerably, but all regions are represented for the period 1975–1995. Finally, the percentage of total area classified according to land use has changed over time in some of the regions, most noticeably in the Jitai Basin. The data in the tables and figures in this chapter are based on the common variable database developed by the study participants. The data may differ slightly from the more detailed information or land use classification schemes used in the case studies.

The study regions vary considerably in land area and population (Figure 3-1).[2] Areas range from 0.965 million hectares for Chicago to 4.421 million hectares for Haryana. In 1950, South Florida had the smallest population (0.76 million) and the state of Kerala had the largest (13.55 million). Forty years later, in 1990, the Jitai Basin had the smallest population (2.35 million), and Kerala was still the most populous of the six regions (29.10 million—see Chapter 2 for a more complete discussion of demographics of the study areas).

Because the land areas and total populations of the study regions vary considerably, population density was used to compare land use

---

[2]For Kerala, population and area data are given at the state level; land use data are for three districts: Alappuzha (Alleppey), Kottayam, and Idukki.

TABLE 3-2 Common Variable Database of Land Use Change, Six Study Regions, Various Years

Study Region	Year	Geographic Area (million ha)	Forest (%)	Grassland/ Wetland (%)	Agricultural Land (%)	Barren/ Wasteland (%)	Built-up Areas (%)	Water Areas (%)	Total Area Classified (%)
Kerala, India	1960	0.813	30.7	.7	62.0	3.7	2.9	.0	100.0
	1970	0.813	31.2	.5	63.5	1.0	3.8	.0	100.0
	1980	0.917	29.4	.3	61.1	2.2	4.0	3.1	100.0
	1990	0.871	30.9	.2	60.1	1.9	3.6	3.2	100.0
Haryana, India	1970	4.421	2.2	1.2	80.6	4.1	7.0	.0	95.1
	1980	4.421	3.0	.7	81.5	1.7	8.3	.0	95.2
	1990	4.421	3.8	.5	80.9	2.2	7.6	.0	95.0
	1995	4.421	2.5	.5	81.5	2.1	9.1	.0	95.7
Jitai Basin, China	1965	1.251	41.8	—	17.1	—	—	4.0	62.9
	1981	1.251	33.6	20.1	15.9	20.8	4.2	5.4	100.0
	1986	1.251	44.7	15.3	15.8	13.5	5.3	5.3	100.0
	1994	1.251	51.6	10.8	15.7	9.7	6.7	5.6	100.0
Pearl River Delta, China	1973	1.722	29.6	12.3	38.0	5.0	2.4	12.6	99.9
	1982	1.722	32.3	3.0	34.6	5.8	7.5	16.8	100.0
	1995	1.722	37.0	.2	34.7	.7	15.7	12.8	101.1
South Florida, USA	1900	2.712	31.9	60.1	.0	.0	.0	2.9	95.0
	1953	2.712	22.9	59.7	6.9	.0	2.4	2.8	94.7
	1973	2.712	20.7	42.5	20.5	.0	8.1	2.8	94.6
	1988	2.712	15.6	39.3	21.4	.4	13.8	9.5	100.0
Chicago, USA	1900	.965	4.0	—	90.0	—	6.0	—	100.0
	1955	.965	4.0	—	84.0	—	12.0	—	100.0
	1972	.965	6.3	.9	55.7	2.7	33.0	1.4	100.0
	1992	.965	11.6	4.2	47.8	.3	33.5	2.6	100.0

NOTE: Geographic area and land use data for Kerala are for the three districts of Alappuzha (Alleppey), Kottayam, and Idukki.

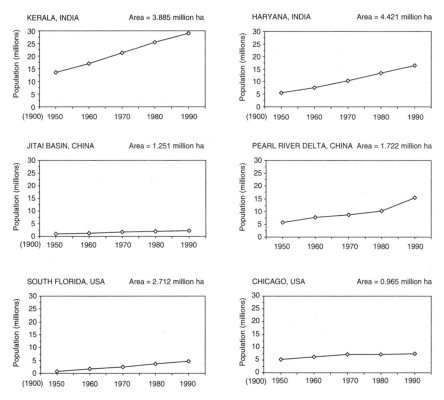

FIGURE 3-1 Population of the six study regions, 1950–1990.

changes with population trajectories (see Table 3-3 for the population densities of the six study regions from 1950 to 1990). Over the period 1950–1990, one study region in each country had relatively low population density (Haryana, Jitai Basin, South Florida) and one had relatively high population density (Kerala, Pearl River Delta, and Chicago). South

TABLE 3-3 Population Density, Six Study Regions, 1950–1990 (persons per hectare)

Study Region	1950	1960	1970	1980	1990
Kerala, India	3.488	4.350	5.495	6.551	7.490
Haryana, India	1.282	1.717	2.346	3.042	3.723
Jitai Basin, China	.807	1.015	1.303	1.655	1.879
Pearl River Delta, China	3.293	4.454	4.971	5.959	8.926
South Florida, USA	.280	.597	.900	1.324	1.715
Chicago, USA	5.439	6.537	7.355	7.531	7.676

Florida had the lowest population density over time. In 1950 Chicago had the highest population density, but it was surpassed by the Pearl River Delta in 1990. All regions show increases in population density over the period 1950–1990, but South Florida, Haryana, and the Pearl River Delta had the most dramatic changes over time. For example, in 1950 the Pearl River Delta ranked third in population density; in 1990 it ranked first.

PATTERNS OF LAND USE CHANGE

Similarities and differences in the patterns of land use are discernible when the land use data are plotted as timelines of change over the period 1900–1995 (Figure 3-2). This section uses such timelines, data on popula-

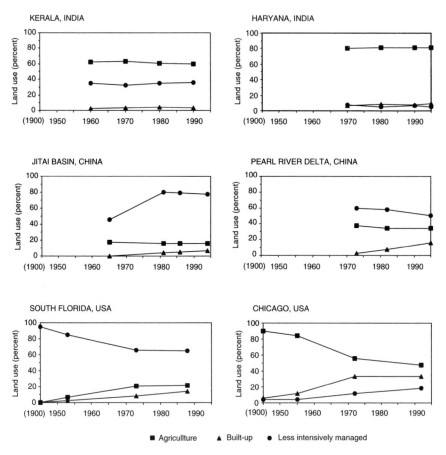

FIGURE 3-2 Land use in the six study regions, various time periods. NOTE: "Less intensively managed" category includes forests, grassland/wetland, barren/wasteland, and water.

tion density, and supporting information from the case studies to address four questions about land use patterns in the study regions:

1. *Are less intensively managed lands declining in the study areas?* There is a widespread perception that as populations expand, they encroach progressively on less intensively managed lands (forests, grassland, and wetland), and convert them to agricultural and built-up areas. This perception is tested by examining the fates of these land use types in the six study regions.

2. *What is the pattern of change in agricultural land?* It is commonly believed that the agricultural area of a region first expands to provide food for local population growth and then contracts as urban areas spread. Is this trajectory evident in the study data?

3. *What is the dynamic of change for subsistence and market crops?* As regions develop, it is often assumed that subsistence crops give way to market crops. If so, how are such changes related to the trajectories of agricultural land change discussed above? What do the study data reveal about increases in crop productivity and their relationship to expansion or contraction of agricultural land area?

4. *What has happened to built-up areas?* Built-up areas are perceived to be "taking over" less intensively managed and agricultural lands. Is this true in the study regions? What is the rate of change in built-up areas in the six regions?

1. Are Less Intensively Managed Lands Declining?

The answer to this question depends on a comparison of trends in forest areas, grassland, and wetland with trends in population density. These land use categories include managed land uses such as agroforestry and pastures, but they may be used to indicate trends in areas that have undergone less-intensive use by humans.

Contrary to common perceptions, the recent official data indicated that forested areas in the six study regions have changed minimally or have increased in most areas, even while population density has increased in all areas (Figure 3-3). More specifically, for the period 1970 to the present, the study's common data set shows that forestland has not declined dramatically and is even increasing in the two study regions of China. After a sharp decline from 1900 to 1950, South Florida shows only a small decline in forestland over the later period. In Kerala, the official published data show little change in forested areas, but other sources show a significant decline. In contrast to forests, grassland and wetland areas are declining in several of the study regions: Jitai Basin, Pearl River Delta, and South Florida (Figure 3-4).

In Kerala, the official data show that the forested area remained constant over the period 1970–1995, at about 30 percent, despite state-level

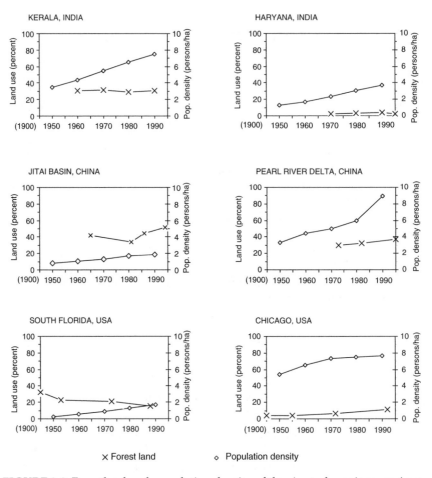

× Forest land   ◇ Population density

FIGURE 3-3 Forestland and population density of the six study regions, various time periods. NOTE: For Kerala, population density is at the state level; land use change is for the Alappuzha (Alleppey), Kottayam, and Idukki Districts.

population density increasing by more than a third. However, the study participants point out that the land use data may not reflect actual conditions (see Chapter 5). Topographical maps from the early part of the century, LANDSAT satellite images from 1973, and India remote sensing (IRS) images since 1981 indicate a substantial decline in forest vegetation cover over time. Chattopadhyay (1985) estimates that forest vegetation covered 44.4 percent of Kerala in 1905, 27.7 percent in 1965, 17.1 percent in 1973, and 14.7 percent in 1983. Field-level observations also indicate that

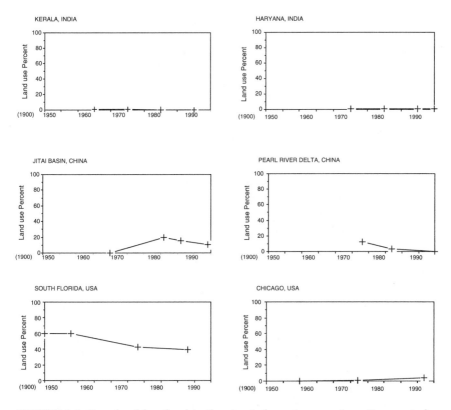

FIGURE 3-4 Grassland/wetland in the six study regions, various time periods. NOTE: For Kerala, land use change is for the Alappuzha (Alleppey), Kottayam, and Idukki Districts.

government incentives and the resulting migration into forested areas resulted in the conversion of forest areas into cropland.

In the arid and semiarid state of Haryana, virtually all land was converted to agriculture before the 1970s (see Chapter 6). Forest, which covers only about 3 percent of the land area, actually increased slightly during the study period. Meanwhile, from 1950 to 1990 population density almost tripled. Although the small increase in area under forest cover in the 1980s is an indication of efforts to promote environmental conservation, Haryana's percentage of land under forest cover remains far below the Indian national average of 33 percent. The national Ninth Five-Year Plan (1997–2002) specifies that not less than 2 percent of the land area in each district should be classified as forest cover. In Haryana, major land use classifications were remarkably static over the period 1971–1990, implying that the most important land use changes were modifications rather than conversions.

In the Jitai Basin region of China, forests have been increasing since the 1980s. The original vegetation was subtropical mixed broadleaf and needleleaf forest, located on low to moderate slopes. Over the past 50 years, much of the original forest was destroyed by human activities and later replaced by secondary woods and shrubs (see Chapter 8). Between 1950 and 1978, a great deal of forest was cut down to serve as fuel for steel production, to clear fields for agriculture, and to provide firewood for domestic purposes. In Taihe County, the forest cover decreased from 48.7 percent in 1956 to 44.4 percent in 1961 to 31.3 percent in 1978, which caused soil erosion and loss of biodiversity. In the early 1980s the distribution of forestland to individual ownership added incentive for cutting. Since the 1980s the central government has regulated forest cutting and encouraged the return of marginal cultivated land to forestland. Thus forestland in the Jitai Basin increased from 0.42 million hectares in 1981, to 0.56 million hectares in 1986, to 0.64 million hectares in 1993, and it now covers more than 50 percent of the total area.

The Pearl River Delta has long been exploited for agriculture and settlement because of its level terrain, high land quality, and convenience for transportation (see Chapter 9). Thus in this region deforestation of the original subtropical and tropical vegetation has been greater than in other parts of Guangdong Province. Forests covered only about 30 percent of the Pearl River Delta until very recently. Since 1950 population density has increased from 3.3 persons to 8.9 persons per hectare because of the massive and rapid economic development in the region, particularly since 1980. The forest area now appears to be increasing, however, because of replanting policies. The reported percentage of grassland/wetland area has declined from over 10 percent in the early 1970s to nearly zero in the 1990s, although this latter percentage appears to be extremely low.

In South Florida, longer-term data reveal that forestland has been declining gradually since 1900 as population density in the region has grown from very low levels, 0.3 persons per hectare in 1950, to 1.7 persons per hectare in 1990. Total forest cover declined from 31.9 percent in 1900 to 15.6 percent in 1988. The pine forest that once covered the eastern coastal ridge has disappeared except for one patch preserved within the boundaries of Everglades National Park (see Chapter 10). The land in either grassland or wetlands also has declined—from 60.1 percent in 1900 to 39.2 percent in 1988. The extensive Everglades marsh, built through peat depositions over the past 5,000 years and once covering 12,000 square kilometers, has been reduced by 50 percent in this century to its present 6,000 square kilometers. Total land in the less intensively managed categories of forest and grassland/wetland has dropped dramatically in the region, from 92.1 percent to 54.9 percent since 1900.

In the Chicago study region, most of the land to the west is well-watered grassland; the land to the east was timberland, but it was cleared for farms by early in the nineteenth century (see Chapter 11). The land north of Chicago also was wooded, but by 1900 most of the usable timber had been cut and the lumber business in the region shrank. The cut timberland was converted primarily to farming and grazing. Like in other regions, however, recent data (1955–1992) reveal that forest and grassland/wetland areas in the Chicago region have increased, to over 10 percent and 4 percent, respectively. Restoration of wetland may account for some of latter increase. These increases in less intensively managed land have occurred as population density has leveled off to about 7.5 persons per hectare.

In summary, a comparison across regions confirms that forestland had indeed declined up to 1970, but that, according to the official data, forested areas have been stabilizing or even increasing in many of the study regions since that time, even as population density has continued to rise. The current stability in forestland may stem in part from significant declines early in the century, when most expansion for agriculture took place. Some of the Tri-Academy study regions probably have experienced less change in forested areas because of a long history of dense population. A concern, however, is that official data may not reflect actual forested areas in some study regions.

The Jitai Basin, where forests are increasing significantly as a result of active government policy intervention encouraging reforestation, illustrates the importance of government intervention in the maintenance and growth of less intensively managed areas. Similarly, in South Florida a dominant force in land use change has been the federal government's efforts to reclaim the wetland environment of the Kissimmee River. Yet in several of the study regions, including the Jitai Basin, Pearl River Delta, and South Florida, grassland and wetland are declining. Thus it appears that grassland and wetland may now be more at risk of conversion than forested areas.

2. What Is the Pattern of Change in Agricultural Land?

During the period 1975–1995, when comparable data are available for all six regions, agricultural land in the study regions remained remarkably constant, despite increases in population density in all regions (Figure 3-5). Even in Haryana, India, which is still in the process of adopting the set of agricultural management techniques known as the Green Revolution, agricultural land cover appears to have reached the limit of expansion and was even beginning to decline slightly in the most recent decade (1980–1990) included in the study (see Chapter 6). Since 1971 agricultural land in Haryana has remained basically static at about 80 percent of total area. As land cover categories, cultivable wasteland and fallow land, other than current fallow, have virtually disappeared in Haryana.

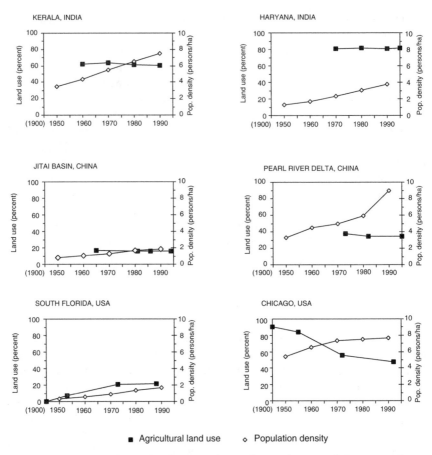

FIGURE 3-5 Agricultural land use and population density of the six study regions, various time periods. NOTE: For Kerala, population density is at the state level; land use change is for the Alappuzha (Alleppey), Kottayam, and Idukki Districts.

In Kerala, agricultural land accounted for about 60 percent of total area over the period 1960–1990, as represented by the three districts aggregated in the Tri-Academy common variable data set. This steady percentage of agricultural land is similar to that throughout the state of Kerala over the same period, indicating that spatial expansion of agricultural area has probably reached its limit despite increases in population density.

In the Pearl River Delta, farmland declined by over 10 percent in the decade between the early 1970s and the early 1980s. As the special economic zones were created, industrial and commercial development came to an area that had been one of the prime "rice bowls" of China. Vast amounts of highly productive cropland were lost as population density increased rapidly. Since the early 1980s, agricultural land overall has remained static because of the increasing cultivation, on the more marginal upland sites, of horticultural crops for consumption in the cities of Shenzhen and Guangzhou. Agricultural land use in the Jitai Basin has been steady at about 16 percent of total land area since 1965.

Chicago and South Florida, where changes in agricultural land are the most striking, demonstrate two contrasting land use-population density trajectories. The Chicago study covers the longest period, beginning with the almost complete conversion to agriculture by the 1870s and ending with the virtual disappearance of farmland within the city's borders and in the surrounding suburbs by the present day. In this case, the most rapid declines in agricultural land, which occurred from the 1950s to the 1970s, were accompanied by the greatest increases in population density. Agriculture continues to play a role in the larger region, however, because of the highly fertile soils. In 1992, 48 percent of the total area was still in farms, producing corn for feedlots elsewhere in the Midwest. By contrast, in South Florida increases in agricultural land and population density have gone hand in hand. Agricultural land grew from nearly zero in 1900 to about 20 percent by the early 1970s as the Everglades wetlands were gradually drained for sugarcane and other crop production. Population density tripled from 0.3 to 0.9 persons per hectare from 1950 to 1970. Since the early 1970s, the percentage of agricultural land has remained stable, and population density has continued to grow, reaching 1.7 persons per hectare in 1990.

3. What Is the Dynamic of Change for Subsistence and Market Crops?

In general, subsistence crop areas have decreased over time, and areas sown to market crops have increased in most of the study regions. Haryana is a major Green Revolution site that now provides rice and wheat for all of India. Total agricultural area has not changed greatly in Haryana, but the area sown to pulses (edible legumes), which are subsistence crops, decreased by 10 percent in the 1960s and by an additional 12 percent in the 1980s (see Table 6-9 in Chapter 6). The absolute area as well as the proportion of cropped area allocated to traditional crops such as jowar, bajra, maize, barley, and gram also declined. By contrast, the area allocated to Green Revolution crops—rice, wheat, and cotton—increased. Rice and wheat production climbed by 9 percent in the 1960s and by 2 percent in the 1980s. Oilseeds, another market crop in Haryana, declined slightly (by 1 percent) in the 1960s, but increased by 9 percent in the 1980s. Most of these changes have occurred as a result of crop switching as opposed to putting more land under cultivation.

In Kerala, the land devoted to rice and tapioca (cassava), both subsistence crops, increased by 14 percent and 50 percent, respectively, over the 20-year period from 1956 to 1976, but declined by 50 percent and 57 percent over the most recent two decades (see Table 5-5 in Chapter 5). Market crops in Kerala, represented by coconut and rubber, increased in area—coconut by 50 percent and rubber by 107 percent—between 1957 and 1976 and by 45 percent and 117 percent between 1975 and 1997. Export crops such as pepper, ginger, coffee, cashew, and fruits also have increased in area. The year 1975 is considered to be a major turning point in the cropping pattern, because the area used for rice cultivation reached its peak, followed by a clear shift away from food crops. Sugarcane and tea areas also have declined. These declines have stemmed from the far-reaching land reform of recent decades that reduced the average size of landholdings. The smaller landholdings, combined with the higher skill levels and alternative opportunities for the recently educated population, made paddy cultivation both uneconomical and undesirable.

In the Pearl River Delta, farmland area decreased and garden area increased in the 1980s, indicating a shift toward horticulture to supply the rapidly expanding urban areas of Shenzhen and Guangzhou; much less rice is now grown in the Delta. In the Jitai Basin, areas of tea and citrus, high-value market crops, increased dramatically between 1965 and 1987.

By contrast, the U.S. study regions, Chicago and South Florida, have continuously and primarily produced market crops, but the kinds of crops grown have changed significantly. The Chicago study region experienced the wheat boom of 1920, a sharp decline in area sown to oats after 1950, and the general ascendancy of corn in recent decades. In South Florida, pineapples were grown in the early decades of the 1900s, but they have now virtually disappeared. Citrus and sugarcane have gained in prominence.

4. What Has Happened to Built-up Areas?

India, China, and the United States have very different approaches to structuring development and even to defining built-up areas, making direct comparisons of trends difficult. Given that caveat, however, it appears that changes in built-up areas appear to track changes in population density more closely than do changes in other land use categories (Figure 3-6).

Over the last 30 years, Shenzhen has been transformed from a small fishing village in the Pearl River Delta into a major economic center. As a result, Shenzhen and other newly designated cities are part of a dramatic increase in the built-up area (now approaching 20 percent of total area) of the Pearl River Delta; population density has increased from just below five to almost nine persons per hectare. In the more rural Jitai Basin,

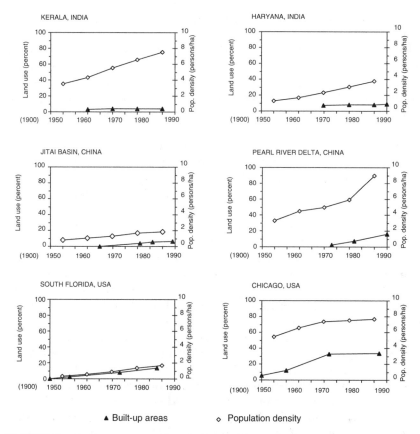

FIGURE 3-6 Built-up areas and population density of the six study regions, various time periods. NOTE: For Kerala, population density is at the state level; land use change is for the Alappuzha (Alleppey), Kottayam, and Idukki Districts.

urban land has expanded steadily in areas adjacent to existing urban sites, from very little built-up land in 1965 to 6.7 percent in 1994.

By contrast, the built-up areas of Haryana and Kerala in India appear to be relatively stable, although there is some potential for encroachment by New Delhi into the Haryana region. Haryana is less urbanized than many developed states of India: only one-fourth of its population resides in urban areas. There have been small increases, however, in areas devoted to nonagricultural uses (housing, industrial estates, and infrastructure such as roads) as a result of increased urbanization, growth in manufacturing, and the government policy of creating development zones.

Kerala, characterized by small, well-distributed urban centers rather than one large city, displays a unique rural–urban continuum. Traditionally dispersed linear settlements developed along the ridges and upper slopes of the highland region, and the intervening valleys between the two ridges were used for seasonal agriculture and primary sector activities. Communication networks, such as roads and highways, originally developed along the ridges. As population density and home building grows throughout Kerala, rural–urban distinctions are blurring, even though the expansion of designated urban areas is mostly stagnant or slow.

In South Florida, growth in built-up area tracks growth in population density. The amount of built-up land remained relatively low through the end of World War II, but then began to grow rapidly. This development first took place on the Atlantic coast along a 160-kilometer region running north–south, and somewhat later on the western coast along the Gulf of Mexico. Today, over 14 percent of the total area of South Florida is urban. This percentage is significant because approximately two-thirds of the study region is publicly owned land that cannot be developed. Unlike the customary sequence in which less intensively managed land use categories are converted first to agricultural land and then to urban uses, here suburban growth is transforming forestland, grassland, and wetland directly as population density continues to rise.

In Chicago, the first major period of urban land use expansion occurred in the early 1900s. The rapid suburbanization that followed World War II dramatically increased the amount of built-up land; population density increased concurrently. Much of the conversion occurred through the loss of agricultural land in areas outside of Cook County. Since the mid-1970s, urban growth within the study area has been essentially stagnant: the proportion of built-up area has held steady at about 33 percent. Growth in population density also has slowed. Thus Chicago might be designated a "mature" urban area.

PROCESSES OF CHANGE

Findings from the case studies in response to the four questions posed reveal that forested areas generally seem to be steady or even increasing in most sites, while grassland and wetland areas are declining. Government policies play an important role in protecting and enhancing these less intensively managed land uses. Agricultural land areas in most of the study regions have not changed substantially in the last 30 years, although cropping patterns have altered dramatically, moving away from subsistence crops to more marketable crops. In the regions studied, the major transformations in the use of agricultural land occurred in the earlier periods. As subsistence farming is replaced by market-oriented production, food consumption patterns also tend to change. More and more varied food usually becomes available as transportation and infrastructure systems improve with development and as rising incomes permit more variety in diets. Built-up areas, though differently defined, are increasing in almost all the case study regions, but at the expense of grassland and unused land rather than agricultural areas.

As these land use changes have been under way, all the study regions have undergone increases in population density. Increases in this single demographic measure do not appear to be strongly linked with change in forest or agricultural land, but the growth in population density does appear to be closely linked to changes in built-up areas as defined in the study regions.

At a more subtle yet still significant level, these land use trends also illustrate important shifts in the process of land utilization within the study regions. All sites appear to be at or approaching a steady state in their major land uses. The shifts now occurring appear to be driven in part by market forces and public policies and reflect the processes of land use intensification and changes in cultural and ecological values rather than significant changes in major land use categories. For example, while the amount of agricultural land in the study regions remained relatively stable in area, the land in all regions was used more intensively or for higher-value activities. In the Jitai Basin, land was increasingly utilized for higher-value export crops such as citrus and other fruits. At other sites, such as in the United States, intensification has resulted in significant subregional shifts in land use. Agricultural lands were converted to urban land uses, and more distant lands with native cover were developed agriculturally.

All study regions witnessed a decline in land with low-intensity uses, particularly grassland and wetland. Although not a primary focus of this study, this shift has probably led to a drop in wildlife habitat, biodiversity, and natural flood control throughout the six study regions. By contrast, most regions also saw an increase in the amount of forestland. While initially this increase might seem to conflict with the trend of loss in some less intensively managed land uses, it is evident that the forest utility in all cases was explicitly defined with respect to human uses and mandated by policy instruments. Forests are used to control soil erosion, provide fuelwood, and, in limited examples, for recreation. Satellite measurement techniques are being used in several of the study regions for monitoring and analyzing changes in forest areas and other land cover types (Liverman et al., 1998).

The shifts in land use processes illustrate the construction of increasingly human-dominated landscapes at each of the study sites, where land value and use are defined largely by human societal needs. This finding is congruent with the trajectory of increasing population density at all sites. The shifts and constructions in land use and the concurrent demographic changes are explored in more detail in the chapters on the individual study regions.

REFERENCES

Arizpe, L., M. P. Stone, and D. C. Majors, eds. 1994. Population and Environment: Rethinking the Debate. Boulder: Westview Press.

Chattopadhyay, S. 1985. Deforestation in parts of Western Ghats region (Kerala). International Journal of Environmental Management 20:219–230.

Fredrickson, G. M. 1998. The Comparative Imagination: On the History of Racism, Nationalism, and Social Movements. Berkeley: University of California Press.

Fresco, L., R. Leemans, B. L.Turner II, D. Skole, A. G. vanZeijl-Rozema, and V. Haarmann, eds. 1997. Land Use and Cover Change (LUCC) Open Science Meeting Proceedings. LUCC Report Series No. 1. International Geosphere-Biosphere Programme and the International Human Dimensions Programme. Institut Cartografic de Catalunya, Barcelona.

Liverman, D., E. F. Moran, R. R. Rindfuss, and P. C. Stern, eds. 1998. People and Pixels: Linking Remote Sensing and Social Science. Washington, D.C.: National Academy Press.

Turner, B. L., II. 1991. Thoughts on linking the physical and human sciences in the study of global environmental change. Research and Exploration 7(2):133–135.

4

Findings and Observations of the Tri-Academy Project

Using insights gained from the case studies and the cross-study comparisons, this chapter responds directly to the three research questions posed in Chapter 1 and describes the project's findings, acknowledging, however, that the complex interactions of population and land use involve a variety of social and economic processes. Many studies, including two publications of the U.S. National Academy of Sciences, Population and Land Use in Developing Countries (1993) and Population Growth and Economic Development: Policy Questions (1986), describe this complexity. The findings presented here are an attempt to identify factors common to the study regions in the three countries. The case studies provide many examples of specific interactions among population, technology, consumption, and changes in land use. Some of these examples are used here in the responses to the three research questions posed earlier; fuller analyses are found in the chapters devoted to specific study regions.

RESEARCH QUESTIONS

1. What is the nature of the significant population and land use transformations in the study regions?

In each of the study regions, population rose during the period 1950–1990. Most of the increases could be attributed to births minus deaths, but in the Pearl River Delta and South Florida, the rate of migration (or immigration) was higher than the natural increase. Every region also experienced an identifiable change in land use patterns, some proportionate to the population increase and some not. In some regions such as the Pearl River Delta and South Florida, the change was reflected in the more basic indices such as hectares of agricultural land converted to built-up land or decline in grassland and wetland. In other regions, such as Haryana and Kerala, a closer look at the movements of people within the region and shifts in crops grown is required. When population changes and land use changes are taken together, it may be said that every site underwent a transformation during the study period.

Kerala, a poor region with a highly developed social system, is among the leaders in India in health, education, and social indicators (see Chapter 5). Many of the men and women educated in the system emigrate to the Persian Gulf countries and elsewhere, but their remittances (salary sent back to the home country, usually to family) fuel economic development in Kerala. A recent transformation was triggered by the expulsion of many expatriates from the Gulf region in the early 1990s. At the time, the changes in the Indian government's real estate and commodity pricing policies encouraged internal migration to the highland areas and a switch from grain to cash crops.

The transformation in Haryana coincided with the introduction of Green Revolution technologies that increased agricultural productivity and attracted large numbers of migrants from other parts of India (see Chapter 6). The sectoral change in land use was small, but farmers moved toward income-producing cash crops and away from the local production and consumption of traditional staple crops. The government amplified this trend by favoring the semiarid Green Revolution areas with infrastructure projects at the expense of the arid zones.

Before the 1950s, China's Jitai Basin in Jiangxi Province was a relatively rural area known for its agriculture and handcraft; transport was largely provided by its the river system (see Chapter 8). In the late 1950s, however, the region became the laboratory for a succession of central government economic policies that nearly destroyed the economy and severely damaged the environment. Reform in 1978 led to economic development and provided an outlet for out-migration to the Pearl River Delta that ultimately brought remittances back to the Jitai Basin. Today, the environment is being restored and new investments from returning migrants are stimulating the local economy.

The Pearl River Delta, the historic frontier of China, had few industries and a low growth rate until 1978, when it was declared a special economic zone (see Chapter 9). To stimulate economic growth, the government allowed foreign investment and the conversion of collective farms to industrial uses, with individual farmers permitted to retain some of the proceeds. Housing was built in anticipation of the influx of laborers from other regions, and rules regulating migration were suspended. Rapid urbanization followed. In the Pearl River Delta, land use change, insti-gated by central government policies, preceded and helped to foster a rapid increase in population.

Modern South Florida is the product of substantial migration from the northern U.S. states and a flood of immigrants from Central and South America and the Caribbean Basin (see Chapter 10). Presently, agricultural development in the region is limited by the uniquely strict environmental laws that prohibit settlement in the interior Everglades ecosystem that covers nearly half the region. As a result of these conditions, the transformation in South Florida was sensitive to government land use policies. A key element of this transformation was the shift in agriculture from producing for local demand to accommodating national and international markets.

A small city of 5,000 in 1840, Chicago grew at a rate of over 10 percent a year until 1900 (see Chapter 11). In its first transformation, Chicago changed from a small city that served as the center of agroindustry for an immense area of the Midwest to, by 1900, the world's greatest rail center and the country's second largest city. In its second transformation, the city became less tied to the surrounding agricultural lands, and by the 1980s and 1990s it had become a service industry center. This transforma-tion was accompanied by the large-scale movement of population from the city to suburban areas.

Urbanization was a facet of change in all of the study regions. In Kerala, the number of towns doubled from 1951 to 1991, and in the Pearl River Delta, not only did the population of towns and cities increase, but the built-up area of Shenzhen City, in particular, increased sixfold from 1982 to 1990. The rate of expansion of the urbanized area of Chicago grew by nearly a factor of three between 1955 and 1972.

These transformations and land use changes had, in turn, broad so-cial and environmental impacts in the study regions. The effects of these changes on certain social groups—upland and lowland groups, landless people, women, and the rural poor—differed. For example, in Chapter 7 of this volume, Sumati Kulkarni documents for Kerala and Haryana the greater economic marginalization of women that has gone hand in hand with land use transformations. In Kerala, because labor-intensive rice cul-tivation has declined, women have found their position in the rural labor market weakened. In Haryana, the scene of a tremendous increase in productivity and where rice has emerged as a cash crop, women do have a greater role in productive work. Yet as the mechanized and livestock-related jobs held by men have gained in prestige and income in Haryana, the position of women continues to deteriorate. Women's work remains less recognized in Haryana, and differentials between men and women in wages—and even life expectancy—persist.

As for the environmental impacts of transformations and land use change, soil salinity and erosion, a decline in water quality, and loss of biodiversity were documented in the Tri-Academy case studies. For example, from 1966 to 1983 in Haryana the area under irrigation almost doubled, resulting in rising water tables and waterlogging in the canal-irrigated and low-lying areas in the east-central part of the state. In southwestern Haryana, which is suffering from saline and saline-sodic groundwater, falling water tables and salinization are direct threats to the future of agriculture. In Kerala, soil erosion has accompanied the shift to export crops. But Kerala enforces national environmental regulations and has enacted land use regulations aimed at protecting wetland and prohibiting the direct conversion of paddy fields to settlements.

An interesting illustration of the range of forces driving the impact of population change on land use is evident in the intensification of agriculture in the Pearl River Delta (Turner et al., 1994). Prior to 1981, growing industrial emissions of sulfur dioxide and nitrogen oxide had led to acidification of soils and reduction of soil quality in the area. But with the development of orchards and market gardens and their associated technologies, farmers began to return organic matter to the soil even as control of emissions began to take effect.

Other examples of the effects of land use change on the environment are found throughout this report. The deforestation generated in the Jitai Basin by the Great Leap Forward and its emphasis on steel production fueled by forest products was accompanied by increased soil erosion and a decline in overall land quality. In the Pearl River Delta, increased industrial and urban expansion has led to dramatic changes in water and air quality. And in the coastal region of South Florida, loss of biodiversity and hydrological function accompanied the massive draining of the Everglades to expand agricultural and residential lands and to protect them from flooding.

Yet another example illustrates the complex relationship between population growth and the environment. The city of Zhuhai, located in one of the special economic zones designated by the Chinese government in the Pearl River Delta, has benefited from its status and special policies for stimulating economic growth since August 1980. During 1990–1995, its average gross domestic product (GDP)—the value of industrial and agricultural products, net government revenue, and savings per capita— in Zhuhai municipality was significantly higher than those of the other five municipalities in the Delta area not included in the special zone. Zhuhai also has become a local model for controlled development in the environmental pollution arena. By all available measures, environmental pollution in the Zhuhai municipality appears to be significantly less than in the other five municipalities. This result apparently stems from actions taken by the municipal government of Zhuhai, led by an active mayor, which has strongly emphasized the importance of environmental protection, made a substantial investment in processing wastewater and residue, and required all new projects to conform to a high standard of environmental protection. Moreover, the population growth of Zhuhai is dominated by migration, and the annual rate of increase of total population between 1990 and 1995 was 7.9 percent, compared with 4.9 percent for the other five municipalities in the region. This is not the negative correlation between population growth and environmental quality that one might expect.

2. To what extent have local population growth and consumption directly influenced the changes in land use?

The population of all the study regions is increasing (see Figure 3-1 in Chapter 3 for population trends for 1950–1990), but the population growth in South Florida is the most dramatic, sixfold in 40 years. Haryana and the Pearl River Delta are the next fastest-growing regions, with population almost tripling over the period 1950–1990. Elsewhere, Kerala and the Jitai Basin both showed steady growth—more than doubling over the same period. Only Chicago grew relatively slowly, just over 40 percent during the 40-year period. From 1980 to 1990, the Pearl River Delta was the fastest-growing study region, at a rate of almost 50 percent for the decade.

What are the dynamic relationships between population and land use in the six study regions (see Figures 3-3, 3-5, and 3-6 in Chapter 3)? In Kerala, the more basic measures of land use change are nearly insensitive to the fast-rising population. Likewise, in Haryana the percentage of agricultural land has remained stable in the face of the increasing population, indicating large increases in population density in relation to arable land. In the Jitai Basin, as population slowly increased, forestland fell initially, then rose in response to environmental policy changes at the expense of barren wasteland and grassland. The Pearl River Delta saw its proportion of built-up land grow faster than population during the early 1980s; forests also increased while grassland, barren land, and water declined. Population increases in South Florida are associated with significant declines in natural areas—grassland, wetland, and forest—and with increases in built-up areas, especially since the 1950s. This process is now being reversed by plans for government restoration and extended protection of the Everglades natural area. In Chicago, the population was stable in the 1970s and 1980s, but agricultural land declined and forest and grassland increased in response to parkland and reforestation policies.

Figures 3-3, 3-5, and 3-6 in Chapter 3 suggest that population density correlates poorly with specific land use changes in the study regions. As noted in Chapter 1, all the regions have high population densities. Complicating the analysis is the question of whether population growth or land use change is the independent variable—or indeed whether the relationship is dominated by other factors. In other words, a rapidly growing population can be associated with economically motivated land use change, as in the Pearl River Delta, or with slow and higher-order change, such as choice of crops planted rather than gross area cultivated, as in Haryana. In the complex South Florida case, countervailing policies such as drainage and flood control together with the establishment of national parks, water conservation areas, and strict zoning have confined most population growth to within a few miles of the coasts. In the Pearl River Delta, land use or technological change generally preceded and attracted in-migration. Land use change at other sites appears to be more in response to other economic forces or government actions than to population growth.

Shifts in people's consumption patterns stemming from affluence and technology may be associated with increased demands on the land. For example, consumption changes as people move from rural to urban settings and—in Haryana—as local farmers shift from grains to cash crops. Only in the Jitai Basin were changes in crop or livestock production—but not gross agricultural area—related to changes in consumption. None of the study regions produces agricultural products exclusively for the local population; each produces its share of cash crops. Therefore, to the extent that land use responds to consumption, this demand originates in large part outside the study area.

Every study region also has been touched by technological change, but in very different ways. Perhaps the classic example of the influence of technology on land use change is found in Haryana, a Green Revolution site. The state has undergone dramatic changes in land use as a result of the introduction of new, high-yielding wheat and rice varieties and the accompanying development of infrastructure for irrigation and for providing chemical inputs. Such advances have dramatically modified the agricultural system away from its reliance on millets and pulses. Although the Green Revolution has had a positive impact on the economy of Haryana and given the state a crucial role in the food security of the nation, Green Revolution technology has had a negative effect on the environment by bringing about profound changes in Haryana's land and water quality through a complex set of interacting biophysical and socioeconomic factors.

Another aspect of technological change is the technology-based industrial development that has played a major role in transforming the Pearl River Delta, once one of the "rice bowls" of China, into an urbanized landscape. This transformation has been amazingly rapid. In the span of 15 years, the modest town of Shenzhen became a big city with over 600 high-rise buildings. A major highway now links Shenzhen and Guangzhou, and furniture and other factories line the highway for miles. Per capita energy consumption in the Delta's Guangdong Province almost doubled between 1985 and 1996, whereas energy use per capita in neighboring Jiangxi Province was much lower and growing much more slowly. The Pearl River Delta experience can be likened to that of Chicago, where railroads were among the initial transforming elements. In the Delta, however, the land use transformation was much more rapid.

A different role was played by technology in South Florida. In the late 1940s, after a series of disastrous floods, the U.S. Army Corps of Engineers applied then-current environmental technologies to control flooding in the Everglades. This intervention laid the groundwork for the settlement pattern that has been sustained until the present, restricting the densely populated areas to the two coasts and leaving the central region almost uninhabited. Today, many of the antiflooding measures are being reversed to protect and restore the Everglades itself.

The case studies indicate that technologies influence land use in no simple way and that the impact of technology is not directly related to affluence. The most environmentally benign uses of technology are found in the poorest study region (reforestation in the Jitai Basin) and in one of the richest (restoration of the Everglades in South Florida), while the most destructive were the Great Leap Forward in the Jitai Basin and some effects of the Green Revolution in Haryana. The results seem to indicate that technology has a variety of influences on population and consumption patterns and their association with changes in land use. The direction of the relationship is unclear, however, and demands yet another tier of explanation.

3. From a comparison of the case studies, what can be learned about the general nature of the forces driving the transformations and about the influence of government policies on population growth and mobility, land use, and economic development?

The case studies reveal two fundamental forces that influence both population shifts and land use transformation: government policy and globalization and migration.

Government Policy

A hypothesis that arises in all case studies is that land use change is more consistently tied to government policies, directly or indirectly, than to other, more "natural" forces such as population growth or rising affluence and consumption. Policies that have affected land use include environmental policies, population policies, foreign investment regulations, economic price controls on agricultural inputs and outputs, resettlement incentives, taxation, privatization, and reforestation programs.

The Pearl River Delta was transformed more by the Chinese government's decision to open up that area to foreign investment than by any intrinsic pressure of population or consumption. The landscape of South Florida was largely determined by the U.S. government's environmental policy, which directly constrained the forces of population pressure; by immigration policies, particularly those for Cuban immigrants; and by state income tax laws, which encouraged population growth. Kerala's unique combination of social, education, land reform, and commodity pricing policies transformed both its agriculture and its rate of population growth. A variety of agricultural policies, including investments in research at the national and international levels, pricing policies, subsidies for infrastructure development, and centers for the distribution of new cultivars, all contributed to increases in agricultural productivity in Haryana. By contrast, government policy was less influential in the Chicago region; private capital financed the physical and commercial development of Chicago well into the twentieth century. After World War II, however, government did play a role in the growth of the metropolitan area, directly through the federal highway system and indirectly through government housing and financing policies, including tax deductions for mortgage loan interest and real estate taxes.

Perhaps the starkest example of the role policy has played on land use is the decadal transformation of the Jitai Basin. The central government of China promulgated land reform policies between 1950 and 1957 that stimulated farmers to place more land under cultivation. The adoption in 1958 of the Great Leap Forward, a policy to encourage steel production, spurred the cutting down of large areas of forest for fuel. The years 1966–1976 saw the effects of land reform policy that emphasized the need to "put grain production first." The result was a vast expansion of rice paddy fields. Then in 1982, the "household responsibility system" of forestland ownership transferred day-to-day control of land in the Jitai Basin from public to private hands. This policy resulted in further losses of forestland. Finally, over the last two decades policies to encourage reforestation succeeded in increasing forest area in the region.

Globalization and Migration

No study region has been unaffected by globalization and increasing economic integration. Globalization, defined as the influence of markets—labor markets, commodity markets, manufactured goods markets—remote to the region, has had a major effect on the movement of people and use of land in each study region. Thus the demand that stimulated the conversion of farmland in the Pearl River Delta to built-up land, particularly for industrial uses—factories and workers' houses—did not originate largely within the Pearl River Delta itself but in other parts of the country and the world. The demand from the West for electronic and textile products was more influential than local demand for food and housing. In Haryana, the national need for grain production promoted the adoption of Green Revolution agricultural technologies. This transformation resulted in dramatic increases in agricultural exports from the state and attracted laborers from other parts of India with their own demand for food, even as subsistence crop production declined significantly. Likewise in Kerala, rice land was converted to rubber and coconuts despite the rising rice-consuming population. Land use in large stretches of South Florida was influenced by the Cuban revolution; the U.S. government boycott of Cuban sugar resulted in the dramatic increase in sugar production in the region.

The other face of globalization is the movement of people. A closer look at the in- and out-migration patterns of the study regions reveals that many have counterpart regions that serve as a destination and source of migrants. For example, many workers from the less-developed Jitai Basin migrate to the special economic zone of the Pearl River Delta. Kerala provides workers to regions both within and outside India, and the pace of migration has accelerated as the educated unemployed leave in search of employment opportunities. Over half the emigration from Kerala is to foreign countries, with the Middle East accounting for over half of all destinations. In earlier years Chicago was the destination of many immigrants from Central Europe, along with heavy migration from the east and rural Midwest of the United States. South Florida is today a strong magnet for immigrants from South and Central America and the Caribbean, as well as the elderly from the northern states.

On a national scale, all three countries are strongly affected by globalization. The U.S. economy runs a large negative trade balance with the rest of the world, importing vast quantities of raw materials and manufactured goods. It is also the world's leading destination for international immigration, receiving over a million people a year. Although international immigration is not as important for China, that country has made vast strides in recent years in opening its economy to the rest of the world. It has become one of the world's major exporters of manufactured goods and a major recipient of overseas capital flows. Global economic factors have affected India as well; its industries have become more open to the world market after decades of strong protection. Although immigration flows to India have only a small effect on population trends, capital flows and remittances from Indians abroad play an increasingly important role in the economy.

FINDINGS

The case studies in this investigation do not support the view that land use change and environmental degradation are determined by the size of the local population. In today's world there are virtually no closed systems. Demands by large populations can have an effect on the environment at great distances, and flows of population and goods across boundaries can permit higher local densities to be supported. Despite rising population levels, environmental restoration activities are under way in all six regions.

In summary, three general findings emerged from the six study regions.

1. *The Intertwined Effects of Population, Consumption, and Technology.* As noted, the population of each study region is increasing. Migration, as opposed to natural population growth, is the dominant source of these increases in the Pearl River Delta and South Florida, two of the three fastest-growing regions. The effect of local consumption on land use patterns often is less important than that of external consumption. In all regions, the area devoted to subsistence crops has decreased over time and the area sown in market crops has increased. In some regions, local consumption has changed in response—for example, meat, milk, and fish consumption has risen in the Jitai Basin and grain consumption has fallen in Haryana. In the study regions, the impact of technology on the environment was found to be positive or negative, depending on the time and the situation. In Haryana and the Jitai Basin, technological change led to environmental degradation, but more recently in Florida and the Jitai Basin it permitted restoration of natural areas. Green Revolution technology has played a major role in transforming the nature of agricultural land use.

2. *Stability and Change in Land Use.* Contrary to common perceptions, forest areas seem to be stable or even increasing in the study regions of high population density. Grassland and wetland areas, by contrast, are declining and may be more at risk of land use transformation. From 1970 to 1995, total agricultural land in most study regions did not undergo major changes, even though the populations of the regions did grow significantly. Thus population increases are not uniformly associated with decreases in agricultural land areas. Recovery and restoration of land are possible with appropriate and effective land use policies; however, the ecological and political settings in which they occur may be complex. As for the people themselves, land use change has affected the social groups within regions differently.

What most strikes the eye of the visitor to these regions is the remarkable growth in certain built-up areas in places like the Pearl River Delta. In the corridor of development between Hong Kong and Guangzhou, the conversion of farmland to residential, commercial, industrial, and transport uses is extraordinary. Yet even there, the relationship between population growth and consumption is not clear. Many of the new residences are empty, built in anticipation of—and as an attraction to—workers drawn to the economic zone by the land use changes.

3. *The Importance of Government Policy.* Of the various factors mentioned in this report, government policy generally appears to have the greatest single effect on land use change. In the study regions, the effects of government policies are amplified by the fact that no region is a closed system; people, capital, and goods flow across all boundaries. As a result, external forces sometimes have the dominant effect on land use changes. The case studies also revealed that policies often are not motivated by the pressure of population growth and that some policies result in land use changes that provoke increased migration or movement of people. Policies in the study regions that have had a major effect on land use change include: price controls on agricultural inputs and outputs, infrastructure support, taxation, privatization, and reforestation programs. Economic policies have been especially important in the Chinese regions and in Kerala; infrastructure support was important in Haryana and South Florida.

BEYOND THE CASE STUDIES

In an increasingly globalized world, places are linked more strongly over greater distances. Understanding the role of government action is critical to understanding how global forces reshape regions and countries. Government policies can offset or mitigate the effects of natural population growth on land use, or they can force or encourage land use changes first, which in turn causes movement of people. At best, policy becomes an important mechanism through which jurisdictions can channel global forces and define opportunities for growth. At worst, global flows of people and capital cause unintended consequences that subvert the intention of government action. Any understanding of the interaction between land use and population in any place will hinge on taking into account external and global forces.

These observations suggest that any case studies of the interactions between population and land use should fully incorporate the national and international contexts of the region or regions under study, as well as their linkages with agents and institutions at other spatial scales. Conversely, the relative impact of global forces on regions, including their influence on local decisionmaking, also must be assessed. Multiple-site case studies will be critical to defining comparative baselines and understanding cross-cutting issues. The effectiveness of single-site, context-rich studies will be limited unless careful attention is paid to the cross-border flows of people, goods, pollutants, and finances. Satellite data offer great potential for complementing national-scale data, as well as field censuses and ethnographic studies, in order to document changing land cover and land use in multiple regions over time. Agencies that provide national and international land use data will play a key role in creating useful frameworks for data exchange and research collaborations.

These findings also have important implications for local sustainability initiatives. A broader perspective will help local governments and institutions better define the true drivers of local environmental change and encourage them to design policies that could foster sustainable development. For example, the water restoration projects currently proposed for Haryana will succeed only after a reevaluation of and shift in India's national food supply policies. Similarly, any attempt to increase or limit agricultural development in South Florida must take into account the U.S. government's Cuba policy and domestic environmental politics. Recognition of the importance of these kinds of spatial linkages can be a significant step toward more effective environmental management—an idea that may have already found its voice in the injunction of many environmental activists to "think globally, act locally." The word globalization has, of course, become something of a cliche. But the study described here of six very different regions in India, China, and the United States suggests its importance to any analysis of population and resource issues and to the evaluation of policies designed to achieve sustainability.

REFERENCE

Turner, B. L., II, W. B. Meyer, and D. L. Skole. 1994. Global land use/land cover change: Towards an integrated program of study. Ambio 23(1):91–95.

PART II

India

Indian Case Studies: An Introduction

P. S. Ramakrishnan
School of Environmental Sciences,
Jawaharlal Nehru University

With its rapidly growing population touching the 1 billion mark, its food security a concern, and its other developmental needs begging answers, India has seen its land use dynamics undergo rapid changes during the last few decades. The complex connections between the country's population and land use dynamics are compounded by a high level of heterogeneity in ecological conditions, extreme socioeconomic differences, and linguistic and cultural diversity within the societal structure. These differences appear in the two study sites chosen for India: the state of Kerala in southwestern India and the state of Haryana in the northwestern part of the country.

The two study sites were selected in order to examine a variety of contrasting ecological and social characteristics (see map). Kerala, in the humid tropics, has a very high population density. The population itself is characterized by large-scale out-migration from the region, the smallest population growth in the country, a dependence on food imports from outside the region, the highest level of literacy in the country, and a large middle class. Furthermore, in Kerala the weaker sections of society and women in particular enjoy a high degree of empowerment. By contrast, Haryana, located in a semiarid/arid environment, has wider disparities between the rich and the poor, one of the highest population growth rates in the country, a very low literacy rate, and a relatively low level of gender empowerment. Benefiting from its location in the Green Revolution belt of the country, Haryana, as a major exporter of food to the rest of the country, contributes substantially toward self-sufficiency in food at the national level.

KERALA

The state of Kerala, a narrow strip of land on the Arabian Sea, has three distinct topographic zones—a coastal lowland, the Western Ghats highland to the east, and the midland zone in between—and elevations of up to 2,694 meters above mean sea level. The lowland region (at sea level) is well known for its extensive rice and coconut cultivation and the highland for its forests and plantation crops such as tea, coffee, rubber, and cardamom. The undulating midland zone, which makes up about 42 percent of Kerala's total land area, has a variety of annual and perennial cropping systems.

Rainfall in Kerala is confined to the southwest monsoon (June–September) and the northeast monsoon (October-November) periods. The mean annual temperature ranges between 25°C and 31°C in the lowlands and midlands, with cooler temperatures in the mountains.

The present state of Kerala was formed in 1956 by merging two more densely populated states—Travancore in the south and Cochin (which had a long history of progressive social policies), now the central region—with the more sparsely populated Malabar District in the north which was part of the Madras Presidency during British rule. The three regions therefore have somewhat different political histories. Of the three, Malabar is the more underdeveloped.

Although Malayalam is the official state language, Tamil- and Kannada-speaking linguistic minorities reside in the border areas. Of the major religious groups, Hindus form the majority (about 57 percent), followed by Muslims (about 23 percent), and Christians (about 19 percent).

The last few decades have seen drastic demographic and land use changes in the state, particularly in the Malabar region because of the migration into the area. Migration from the lowlands to the highlands within the same region also has been significant. Out-migration from the state to other parts of the country and to Middle Eastern countries is another factor affecting land use dynamics, and indeed the economy of the state itself through the funds sent home (remittances) by those who left.

Rapid urbanization and sharp shifts in land use from annual to perennial cropping systems have stemmed partly from population dynamics (determined largely by demographic structure and gender-related factors) and partly from government policies. A recent major change has been the shift from wet rice cultivation to plantation crops such as rubber and coconut. But with the decline in the area under rice, women's position in the rural market has been weakened, and they find themselves somewhat marginalized.

HARYANA

The state of Haryana was created in 1966 when the then-composite state of Punjab was reorganized on a linguistic basis. The additional presence of Hindu and Sikh populations originally from Pakistan has contributed to the sociocultural diversity of the region. Like Kerala, Haryana is one of India's smaller states; it covers an area of 44,212 square kilometers and has a population of about 16.5 million. On the basis of physiography and drainage, the state can be divided into an eastern semiarid but well-irrigated plain, a western arid plain which has severe wind erosion, sand dunes, and a deeper water table, and a southern plain which has the rocky outcrops of the Aravalli hill range.

In contrast to Kerala, the climate of Haryana is continental, with a hot, dry summer from March to June, a rainy monsoon season from July to September, and a cold winter from October to February. Winter rains are scanty but important for the winter crops. The deep, loamy alluvium of the semiarid part of the state supports a variety of crops such as wheat, maize, pulses, millets, sugarcane, and cotton under irrigated conditions. The sandy and sandy loam seric soils of the arid zone are largely planted in millets and pulses, grown under rainfed conditions.

The rice–wheat rotation predominates in the Haryana region, as well as in the rest of the Indo-Gangetic plains. Rice is sown during the warm monsoon season, and wheat is the crop of the winter months. The last few decades in Haryana have seen extensification, intensification, and diversification in the cropping patterns for cereal crops, oilseeds, and cotton, largely as a result of government policies, although economics also has been an important driver of change. The adverse environmental consequences of these pressures on the land have been felt most in the arid zones of the state. Intensification of agriculture has led to a declining water table and salinization in both the semiarid and arid regions, but more so in the latter.

Another important land-based activity in the state is livestock—cows and buffaloes for milk production, goats and sheep largely for meat and some wool. Indeed, Haryana is a major dairy center, and the local consumption levels and exports have contributed to the health of the people and the economy of the state. Because the land needed for fodder production has to be apportioned from the cropland area, this dimension has had its own impact on land use dynamics, apart from the land degradation caused by overgrazed pastures.

Haryana's literacy rate is lower than that of Kerala and is only a little above the national average of 52 percent. Patriarchy has deep roots in Haryana. Women there, in contrast with those in Kerala, may have a greater role in land use-related work, but they remain subordinate to men in all areas of life. Moreover, the custom of early marriage and high fertility rates, although affected somewhat favorably by rapid economic development, particularly in urban centers, still persist among the rural population—a big contrast from the situation in Kerala.

In short, the Indian study sites offer contrasting ecological, social, economic demographic, and gender dimensions of the problems associated with land use dynamics. Kerala is characterized by a high level of human resource development and faces the problems associated with population pressure and rapidly changing demographic features. Haryana, though very prosperous economically, is weighed down by issues centered on human resource development.

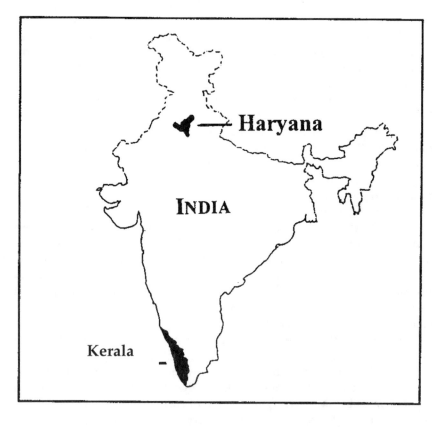

Indian Study Regions

5

Population and Land Use in Kerala

P. S. George
Centre for Development Studies,
Thiruvananthapuram, Kerala
S. Chattopadhyay
Centre for Earth Science Studies,
Thiruvananthapuram, Kerala

The state of Kerala, located in the southwestern corner of the Indian Peninsula, came into existence in 1956. It was formed by merging the three administrative units of Travancore in the south, Cochin in the central region, and the Malabar District in the north. Malayalam, a South Indian Dravidian language with Sanskrit influence, is the state language. Travancore and Cochin had a long history of progressive social policies followed by enlightened monarchs; the Malabar District was a part of the Madras Presidency under British rule.

GEOGRAPHY, SOILS, AND CLIMATE

Kerala has an area of 38,864 square kilometers, roughly the size of Switzerland. It lies between 8° 18' and 12° 48' north latitude and 74° 52' and 77° 22' east longitude. It is bounded on the east by a geological escarpment running roughly northwest to southeast parallel to the coast known as the Western Ghats, on the west by the Arabian Sea, on the south by the state of Tamil Nadu, and on the north by the state of Karnataka (Figure 5-1).

Located in the southwestern fringes of the Western Ghats, Kerala is characterized by an asymmetrical topography. Its landform is dominated by undulating, subdued hills and steep scarp slopes, and its altitude ranges from below mean sea level to 2,694 meters above mean sea level. Kerala's location and altitudinal variations have endowed the state with a wide range of agroecological conditions.

80 GROWING POPULATIONS, CHANGING LANDSCAPES

The state has three distinct elevation zones known as the lowland, midland, and highland regions (Figure 5-2). The lowland region, ranging from nearly level to gently sloping, is a strip of land running along the coast bordering the Arabian Sea, and it occupies approximately 10 per-

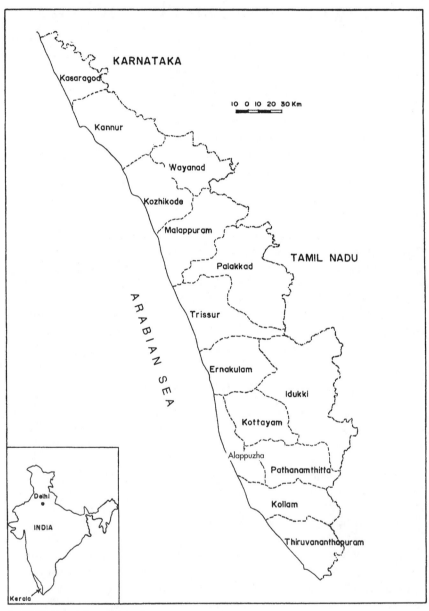

FIGURE 5-1 Map of Kerala.

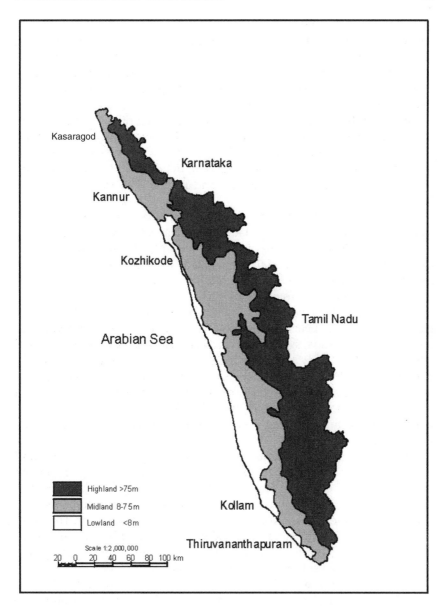

FIGURE 5-2 Three natural elevation zones, Kerala. SOURCE: Resource Atlas, Centre for Earth Science Studies, Thiruvananthapuram.

cent of the total area. This region is characterized by marine landforms consisting of beach ridges and beaches with swamps and lagoons. The lowland region is well known for its backwaters with extensive rice fields and coconut plantations.

The midland region, with altitudes ranging from 7.5 to 75 meters above mean sea level, is made up primarily of valleys. Flat-bottomed valleys and gently to moderately sloping areas account for 42 percent of the landmass. The terrain is undulating, with numerous rivers, small hills, and valleys. A variety of seasonal, annual, and perennial crops are grown in its mainly lateritic soil.

In the highland region, with its ranges of steep hills, altitudes range from 75 to 750 meters above mean sea level. This region constitutes about 43 percent of the state's landmass; it is covered with forests and drained by small streams. The soil varies widely in depth and texture. Plantation crops, including tea, coffee, rubber, and cardamom, are grown in the highlands.

Kerala has distinct biophysical characteristics that vary across the state and contribute to its population and land use dynamics. Based on these characteristics, the state can be divided into six major zones—lowlands and coastal plains, Malabar midlands, Palghat region, southern midlands, foothills, and eastern highlands. For administrative purposes the state is divided into fourteen districts.

Laterite and lateritic soils cover around 60 percent of the total geographical area. The beaches, subdued sand dunes, level lands with valleys, submerged lands, swamps, and marshes are characterized by coastal alluvium that is sandy to clayey loam in texture. They are moderately well drained, although some areas experience excessive drainage due to loose sandy deposits. The soils in river valleys are loamy in texture and are well drained. The hills and upland soils, composed of laterite and laterite-derived materials are deep, well-drained loams and clays with a fairly high gravel content.

Kerala's climate may be characterized as tropical—that is, hot and humid. The mean monthly relative humidity varies between 85 percent and 95 percent from June through September; it is about 70 percent in January. The southwest monsoons bring rainfall in June through September and the northeast monsoons in October through November. The mean annual rainfall is approximately 2,900 millimeters, with a range of 651–5,883 millimeters. The mean annual number of rainy days is 126, with a range of 45–172 days. July is the rainiest month of the year.

During the period 1956–1993, the mean annual temperature varied from 25.4°C to 31°C in the midland region. The diurnal variation fell within the range of 5°C–7°C because the state is situated between the sea and mountains. The temperature remained around 30°C during the summer months of April and May and decreased during July and August because of high rainfall during the southwest monsoons. The temperature was lower in the high mountain regions, falling below 15°C in the northeastern district of Idukki.

DEMOGRAPHY

In 1991 the population of Kerala was about 29 million; between 1901 and 1991 the population had increased approximately fivefold. Over the 40 years between 1901 and 1941, the 1901 population of 6.4 million doubled; it then doubled again after only 30 years, between 1941 and 1971. The intercensal growth rate, which includes both natural increase and net migration, was high—2.31 percent—between 1961 and 1971; it then declined to 1.75 percent between 1971 and 1981 and to 1.32 percent between 1981 and 1991. The population density of Kerala increased from 165 persons per square kilometer in 1901 to 747 persons in 1991. The female population outnumbered the male population throughout the century; the number of females per thousand males increased from 1,004 in 1901 to 1,036 in 1991.

The rate of natural increase was less than 2 percent before 1941 and after 1981 and greater than 2 percent during the three decades between 1941 and 1971. Until 1941 Kerala was characterized by a net influx of migrants, but later the situation was reversed, with more people migrating out of Kerala. The emigration rate was 0.22 percent between 1971 and 1981, when approximately 250,000 persons left Kerala for employment in the Middle East. This trend continued during the 1980s, with a net migration rate of 0.31 percent.

Fertility and Mortality Rates

The birth and fertility rates of Kerala have declined consistently over the last 40 years (see Table 5-1 for a summary of the state's birth, fertility, death, and infant mortality rates, as well as life expectancy). The crude birth rate (CBR) per thousand persons declined from 43.9 during 1951–

TABLE 5-1 Demographic Indicators, Kerala, 1951–1993 (annual average per thousand persons)

Period	Crude Birth Rate	Crude Fertility Rate	Crude Death Rate	Infant Mortality Rate	Expectation of Life at Birth Male	Expectation of Life at Birth Female
1951–1961	43.9	5.6	19.7	128	46	50
1961–1971	37.1	5.0	12.2	66		
1971–1981	28.1	3.4	8.6		62	65
1990	19.0	2.1	5.9	17	68	72
1993	16.6	1.7		13	69	74

SOURCES: All data except 1993 crude birth rate obtained from: Government of Kerala. Economic Review. Thiruvananthapuram: State Planning Board (various issues); 1993 crude birth rate obtained from Sample Registration System.

1961, to 28.1 during 1971–1981, to 16.6 in 1993 (an estimate obtained from the Sample Registration System). Kerala's fertility rate, especially marital fertility rate, was one of the highest in India in the 1950s and 1960s. More recently, however, a relatively high age at marriage and improvements in the education level and status of women have kept the total fertility rate (TFR) and birth rate under control (see Table 5-1).

According to census estimates, the annual crude death rate per thousand persons declined from 19.7 during 1951–1961 to 8.6 during 1971–1981. (The rate for a 10-year period is the simple average of the annual rate for each of the 10 years.) The Sample Registration System has placed the crude death rate for the first half of the 1990s at around 6 per thousand. The infant mortality rate in Kerala has undergone a remarkable decline—from 128 per thousand live births for 1951–1961 to 13 in the early 1990s.

Expectation of life at birth is an important indicator of the overall health of the population. Kerala has seen significant improvements in the life expectancy of both males and females. Male life expectancy increased from 46 years during 1951–1961 to 68 years in 1990. Over the same interval, female life expectancy increased from 50 years to 75 years.

Urban Growth

The 1991 census found the urban population of Kerala to be 7.7 million, or more than one-fourth of the state's population (Table 5-2). In 1901 urban dwellers accounted for only 7 percent of the population. Urban growth exceeded 5 percent in the decades 1941–1951 and 1981–1991. The number of towns increased over four times between 1901 and 1951 and more than doubled again by 1991.

TABLE 5-2 Indicators of Urbanization, Kerala, 1901–1991

Year	Share of Urban Population (percent)	Urban Growth Rate (percent)	Urban–Rural Growth Difference	Number of Towns
1901	7.1			21
1911	7.3	1.54	0.4	27
1921	8.7	2.98	2.2	44
1931	9.6	3.46	1.4	53
1941	10.8	3.05	1.6	62
1951	13.5	5.27	3.4	94
1961	15.1	3.99	1.8	92
1971	16.2	3.57	1.1	88
1981	18.8	3.75	2.2	106
1991	26.4	6.09	2.2	197

SOURCE: Government of Kerala. Economic Review. Thiruvananthapuram: State Planning Board (various issues).

Migration

Kerala has a reputation for providing migrants to regions both inside and outside the country. The pace of migration accelerated over the last decade primarily for two reasons. First, the educated unemployed are moving out of the state in search of employment opportunities. Second, farmers are moving from land-scarce regions to regions that offer greater potential for cultivation.

Because the rise in job expectations resulting from increased education levels has not corresponded to an increase in employment opportunities within the state, Kerala suffers from very high unemployment. Indeed, approximately 10 percent of the India's total unemployed population is from Kerala. Unemployment, then, has led to large-scale migration both within and outside the country. Over half the migration from Kerala is to foreign countries. Based on a 1992–1993 survey, the state Department of Economics and Statistics estimated that of the almost 1.2 million migrants from Kerala, some 56 percent migrated to the Middle East and other foreign countries and 44 percent to other parts of India (Government of Kerala, 1997).

SOCIAL STRUCTURE

Over the twentieth century Kerala maintained a literacy level well above the national average. By 1991 it had achieved the highest literacy rate in India—89.8 percent (Table 5-3). The 1991 female literacy rate of 86.2 percent was more than double the national average of 39.3 percent. The total state expenditure on education in 1996–1997 was Rs. 18 billion, of which 49 percent was spent on primary education, 30 percent on secondary education, and 21 percent on university and technical education.

The religious composition of Kerala is more balanced than that of the nation as a whole. According to the 1991 census, Hindus made up 57 percent of the population, Muslims 23 percent, and Christians 19 percent (Table 5-4). Apparently, there has been a differential growth rate of popu-

TABLE 5-3 Literacy Rates, Kerala and India, 1901–1991 (percent)

	Kerala			India		
Year	Male	Female	Total	Male	Female	Total
1901	19.2	3.2	11.1	9.8	0.6	5.4
1951	49.8	31.4	40.5	25.0	7.9	16.7
1961	55.0	38.9	56.8	34.4	12.9	24.0
1971	66.6	54.3	60.4	39.5	18.7	29.5
1981	87.7	75.7	70.4	46.6	24.7	36.0
1991	93.6	86.2	89.8	64.1	39.3	52.2

SOURCE: Census of India and Kerala (various years).

TABLE 5-4 Major Religions, Kerala, 1981 and 1991 (percent)

	1981	1991
Hindu	58.2	57.3
Muslim	21.2	23.3
Christian	20.6	19.3

SOURCE: Census of Kerala, 1981 and 1991.

lation among religious groups. Between 1981 and 1991 the shares of Hindus and Christians in the total population declined slightly, while that of Muslims increased.

Kerala's notable accomplishments in the health standards of its population are reflected in the state's low infant mortality rate, low maternal mortality rate, and high life expectancy. Contributing factors are an extensive network of health infrastructure, high female education levels, and general health consciousness and awareness. During 1996–1997 the immunization coverage for pregnant women was 87 percent; for infants it was 100 percent coverage against typhoid, tetanus, polio, and tuberculosis and 99 percent coverage against measles. Both state and private medical institutions provide allopathic, ayurvedic, and homeopathic care. Between 1997 and 1998 the total state expenditure on medical and public health was Rs. 5.6 billion, indicating an annual per capita state expenditure of Rs. 175. About 45 percent of the rural population and 70 percent of the urban population have access to protected water supplies.

ECONOMIC STRUCTURE

State income for 1996–1997 was estimated at Rs. 74 billion at constant prices (1980–1981 price level) and Rs. 285 billion at current prices. Between 1980 and 1997 the state income at constant prices indicated an annual growth rate of 5.8 percent and at current prices a growth rate of 10.4 percent. During this period, per capita income grew at an annual rate of 4.4 percent at constant prices and 8.9 percent at current prices. Also during this period there was a marked decline in the contribution of the primary sector to the net domestic product and a marked increase in the contribution of the tertiary sector.

Of the total number of working factories registered in Kerala in 1996, 3 percent were in the public sector and 96.8 percent were in the private sector. Of the total number of workers employed in the factories, 26.7 percent were employed in the public sector and 73.2 percent were employed in the private sector. Kerala has a strong traditional industries sector. The manufacture of matting and rope from coir, a type of coconut fiber, is the major traditional industry, providing employment for about 390,000 workers. The handloom industry employs another 200,000 workers. Cashew processing is a major seasonal industry.

In the absence of direct estimates, indicators such as the percentage of population living below the poverty line, the distribution of households according to expenditure and class, and distribution of landholdings are used as variables for estimates of income distribution. According to Key Indicators of Rural Development, published in 1996 by the government of Kerala, the proportion of population living below the poverty line in Kerala declined from 46 percent in 1977, to 26.1 percent in 1984, to 16.4 percent in 1988.

CHANGES IN LAND USE

In view of the wide variation in physical settings and development patterns in Kerala, aggregate data at the state level do not capture the dynamic processes involved in the state's land use transformation. More useful are in-depth field studies from different ecological settings and the available field-level studies on migration and land use changes in different parts of the state. From these studies emerges a scenario depicting the conversion of rice land to other uses, deforestation, migration, and urban expansion.

Kerala has witnessed major changes in its land use pattern. The most important are the shrinking area devoted to cultivating food crops and an increase in the rate of deforestation. The land area used for rice cultivation declined from 876,000 hectares in 1975 to 431,000 hectares in 1996, with the result that local rice production barely meets one-third of the total consumption requirements of the state. Although no official estimate of deforestation in Kerala is available, it is widely known that in certain regions large-scale conversion of forest area has occurred, contributing to concerns about sustainable land use.

The official claim that the forested area of Kerala did not change between 1960–1961 and 1995–1996 may not reflect actual conditions. In the absence of recurrent surveys of the area classified as forest, the official estimates continue to indicate no change in area. However, topographical maps available since 1900 and LANDSAT images (1973 and 1983) indicate a substantial decline in forest vegetation cover over time (Chattopadhyay, 1985). The 1905 estimate of 44.4 percent area under forest vegetation had declined to 27.7 percent by 1965, to 17.1 percent by 1973, and to 14.7 percent by 1983. Field-level observations also indicate the conversion of forestland to cropland, a development arising from government policies that encouraged agricultural production and migration from coastal to upland regions.

Shifts in Cropping Patterns

When the state of Kerala was formed in 1956, the total cropped area was over 2 million hectares. Rice was the dominant crop, accounting for about 35 percent of the cropped area, followed by coconut, accounting for 21 percent (Table 5-5). In 1996, when the total cropped area was just over 3 million hectares, coconut was the primary crop, followed by rubber and then rice. Between 1957 and 1997 the area of rice cultivation declined by 44 percent, while the areas planted with coconut and rubber increased by 117 percent and 450 percent, respectively, both surpassing rice in hectares. The cultivation of tapioca also declined—from 10 percent of the total cropped area in 1957 to less that 5 percent in 1996.

The year 1975 is considered a major turning point in cropping patterns; the area used for rice cultivation reached its peak that year (Figure 5-3). After 1975 there was a clear shift away from food crops, mainly rice and tapioca, in favor of tree crops such as rubber and coconut and some of the export-oriented crops such as pepper, ginger, and coffee. As a result, coconut, pepper, coffee, rubber, cashews, and fruits increased in area, while cereals, sugarcane, and tea declined in area. These shifts have significant implications for the food security of the state, which already depends on outside supplies to meet more than half the its food requirements.

Rice lands are converted into coconut gardens by one of two ways.

TABLE 5-5 Changes in Cropping Patterns between 1957 and 1996, Kerala

	Area (thousand hectares)			Percent Change	
	1957	1975	1996	1957–1975	1975–1996
Total cropped area	2,211	2,933	3,067	32.6	4.6
Rice	767	876	431	14.2	−50.8
Other cereals and pulses	28	45	29	−22.4	−35.5
Sugarcane	9	8	6	−11.1	−25.0
Pepper	91	108	173	18.7	60.2
Areca nut	50	77	73	54.0	−5.2
Cashew	44	109	100	147.7	−8.3
Cardamom	28	54	43	92.9	−20.4
Ginger	9	12	14	33.5	16.7
Banana and plantain	42	52	72	23.8	38.5
Tapioca	214	327	142	52.8	−56.6
Coconut	463	693	1,005	49.7	45.0
Tea	40	38	37	−5.0	−2.4
Coffee	17	42	82	147.0	95.2
Rubber	100	207	450	107.0	117.4

SOURCE: Government of Kerala. Economic Review. Thiruvananthapuram: State Planning Board (various issues).

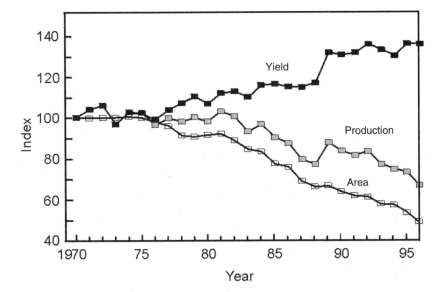

FIGURE 5-3 Rice area, production, and yield, Kerala, 1970–1995. SOURCE: Government of Kerala. Economic Review. Thiruvananthapuram: State Planning Council (various issues).

The first method involves planting coconut saplings on the bunds (embankments) of the rice fields. Then, gradually, farmers widen the bunds and plant additional rows of coconut saplings until the entire field is converted into a raised coconut garden. In the second method, farmers create mounds within the paddy fields at regular intervals and plant them with coconut saplings. As these plants reach a certain stage in their growth, more mounds are created until the whole plot is converted into a coconut garden. Both methods are irreversible.

As noted, Kerala has experienced a drastic decline in the area used to cultivate rice, from approximately 29 percent of total cropped area in 1974 to 15 percent in 1997. In turn, the contribution of the rice crop to the state's income fell from 19 percent in 1984 to 10 percent in 1995. This downward trend was quite steady over these years. Because yield increases during this period did not match the decrease in area, total production also declined. The impact of this downward trend on food security, employment opportunities, and ecology has raised serious concerns.

The conversion of land used for rice cultivation to seasonal and perennial crops reflects a shift in cropping pattern, whereas the conversion of rice land to nonagricultural uses indicates changes brought about by population pressures and infrastructure development. When rice land was converted to nonagricultural uses, 44 percent was used for buildings and courtyards, 15 percent for roads and railways, and 10 percent for canals and storage tanks.

In 1990 Gopinathan and Sundarasan reported on a survey of 5,700 households in the Thiruvananthapuram and Malappuram Districts of Kerala to determine why farmers converted rice land to other uses (Tables 5-6a and 5-6b). The primary reason given was the unprofitable nature of rice cultivation. Between 1979 and 1989, 50 percent of farmers in Thiruvananthapuram discontinued rice cultivation; in Malappuram, 82 percent. In both of these regions, rice was primarily replaced by coconut, followed by rubber. A large increase in the cost of rice cultivation without a corresponding increase in output price, coupled with an unfavorable price change of rice compared with other crops, were identified as the major factors influencing the shift to other crops. Labor management problems and the conversion of land to nonagricultural purposes also influenced the shift away from rice cultivation.

An earlier analysis by Unni (1983) of the factors responsible for the shift from rice to coconut cultivation during the 1960s and 1970s revealed that rice prices had fluctuated during that period while coconut prices increased consistently. Rice cultivation also required higher labor and fertilizer inputs than coconut cultivation, thus placing rice cultivation at a disadvantage compared with coconut cultivation.[1] In short, the relative profitability of rice cultivation had declined in favor of coconut cultivation.

Sivanandan (1985), George (1982), Panikar (1980), and Kannan and Pushpangadan (1988) also identified increased cost of cultivation and reduced profitability as the major factors influencing the shift from rice to other crops. Indeed, changes in average farm prices (at current rupees) between 1970 to 1996 indicate that among the major crops grown in Kerala, rice registered the lowest price increase (Table 5-7). The available empirical evidence thus clearly indicates that the price changes of rice relative to those of other crops, higher cultivation costs, labor-management issues, and the shift of land to meet population needs, such as housing and infrastructure, were some of the factors that induced conversion of rice land. Moreover, state policies on land and labor created an environment that promoted the policy requiring commercial crops. For example, the state's requirement that the title to land be confirmed facilitated the commercialization of land and thereby brought about a fundamental change in the customary modes of land tenure. For farmers, this development included a movement away from rice cultivation and toward commercial crop production (Uma Devi, 1984).

---

[1]The total labor input per hectare of rice cultivation is substantially higher than the labor input in coconut cultivation. The annual labor input for 1 hectare of rice has been estimated at 160 man-days; for coconut, only 75 man-days.

TABLE 5-6a Crop Shifts, Thiruvananthapuram and Malappuram Districts, 1979–1989

Crop	Thiruvananthapuram District		Malappuram District	
	Percent of Farmers Discontinuing Crop	Percent of Farmers Introducing Crop	Percent of Farmers Discontinuing Crop	Percent of Farmers Introducing Crop
Rice	50.0	0	81.5	0
Tapioca	46.4	1.2	8.5	0
Banana/plantain	0	7.2	6.6	5.1
Coconut	0	52.0	0	83.0
Rubber	0	29.8	0	8.5
Pepper	0	4.8	0	0
Others	0	1.2	0	0
No shift	3.6	3.6	3.4	3.4

SOURCE: Gopinathan, C., and C. S. Sundaresan. 1990. Cropping Pattern Changes and Employment Effects in Selected Districts of Kerala. Thiruvananthapuram: Centre for Management Development.

TABLE 5-6b Farmers' Reasons for Shifting from Rice Cultivation to Other Crops, by Period of Conversion (percent)

Reason	Before 1968	1968–1982	1983–1992	Total
Uneconomic paddy cultivation	41.4	75.8	75.8	71.2
Lack of irrigation facility	55.3	15.5	9.6	18.0
Building construction	2.0	5.5	10.5	7.5
Public purposes	1.3	2.1	2.6	2.2
Total	100	100	100	100
Total respondents	760	2,190	2,750	5,700

SOURCE: Gopinathan, C., and C. S. Sundaresan. 1990. Cropping Pattern Changes and Employment Effects in Selected Districts of Kerala. Thiruvananthapuram: Centre for Management Development.

TABLE 5-7 Farm-Level Price of Important Agricultural Commodities, Kerala, 1970–1996 (current rupees)

Commodity	Unit	1970 (Rs.)	1996 (Rs.)	Percent Increase
Rice	100 kg	90.25	607	570
Coconut	100 numbers	56.68	480	760
Tapioca	100 kg	20.59	300	1,357
Banana	100 numbers	16.69	161	865
Pepper	100 kg	616.90	8,780	1,320
Ginger	100 kg	271.98	4,214	1,450
Cashew	100 kg	139.80	2,730	1,850
Rubber	100 kg	429.68	4,900	1,040

SOURCE: Government of Kerala. 1997. Statistics for Planning. Thiruvananthapuram: Department of Economics and Statistics; and Economics Review.

The government's differential tax structure on wetland, gardens, and wasteland also encouraged a shift away from paddy. For the purpose of taxation, land in Travancore had been classified as wetlands, garden, and wasteland. The tax on rice land was 20 percent of gross income, on land cultivating coconuts 1.5 percent, and on land used for rubber cultivation 2 percent (Narayanan, 1994).[2] Even though the land used for the cultivation of plantation crops other than coconut was not suitable for the cultivation of rice, the policy of lightly taxing plantation farmers and heavily taxing rice farmers meant subsidizing the former at the cost of the latter (Uma Devi, 1984).

The policy of differential taxation was meant to promote market-oriented cultivation, especially aimed at outside markets. The commercial crop sector of Travancore responded positively to the stimulus by developing a lucrative export market, based on comparatively high prices (Panikar et al., 1978). Thus the exports from Travancore increased, yielding an ever-increasing trade surplus over the decades. Given the relative prices of principal imports and exports and the prevailing foreign trade arrangements, the allocation of agricultural resources to nonfood crops seemed advantageous for Travancore. Furthermore, the extensive marginal land brought under cultivation at this time was not suited for rice cultivation.

Clay mining also has reduced the availability of land for rice cultivation (Resmi, 1996). After the topsoil has been removed for four to five years, land used for clay mining can seldom be used for growing rice cultivation. The loss of rice fields to clay mining also results in a decline in the groundwater recharging capacity of the area. Moreover, mining clay upstream and in the middle area of irrigation projects adversely affects water retention capacity. Clay mining therefore often has several unfavorable economic and ecological effects (Resmi, 1996).

Migration and Land Use Change

In 1991, the lowland of Kerala accounted for 10 percent of the state's total area and 18 percent of its population, the midland 72 percent of area and 77 percent of population, and the highland 18 percent of area and 6 percent of population (Table 5-8). Since 1901, the population shares of the lowland and midland regions have declined and that of the highland region has increased. Migration and deforestation are probably related to these trends.

Although migration to other states and countries is very important to Kerala's economy in terms of remittances, its impact on land use has not

---

[2]The rates of taxation on wetland, gardens, and rubber land are available in Volume 4 of the *Travancore Land Revenue Manual* (Government of Travancore, 1940).

TABLE 5-8 Distribution of Area and Population in the Three Natural Regions of Kerala (percent)

Characteristic	Lowland	Midland	Highland
Share of area	10.1	71.9	18.0
Share of 1901 population	20.0	78.2	1.8
Share of 1991 population	18.2	75.9	5.9
Population growth, 1901–1991	305.8	331.7	1,342.8

SOURCE: Centre for Earth Science Studies (CESS). 1997. Analysis of the Environmental Impact of the Lowland to Highland Migration in the Western Ghat Region: Kerala. Thiruvananthapuram.

been analyzed.[3] It has been clearly established, however, that interregional migration has had a major impact on land use patterns. Two distinct patterns of interregional migration with major implications for land use have emerged: (1) migration from the district of Travancore to the district of Malabar, and (2) intradistrict movement from the midland to highland regions of Travancore.

Travancore–Malabar Migration

The movement of population from Travancore to Malabar began in the 1930s. Many of the migrants who settled primarily in the hilly tracts of Malabar were small farmers from Travancore. The majority were Christians belonging to the Syrian Catholic denomination. From the 1920s to the 1960s Travancore experienced a much greater rate of population increase than did the Malabar region (Table 5-9), but the proportion of arable land under cultivation was lower in Malabar than in the Travancore region, providing a strong attraction for migrant farmers. As a result, beginning in the 1960s the population growth rate of Malabar caught up with and surpassed that of Travancore.

In addition to population pressure, the commercialization of agriculture was an important factor influencing migration. Many farmers in the midland region in Travancore had begun to grow commercial crops by the turn of the century, but the depression of the 1930s had placed small farmers under heavy debt. The unoccupied, hilly tracts of Malabar thus provided the promise of fertile ground for the farmers from Travancore. Furthermore, the inheritance system of the Syrian Christians, which allowed the partitioning of land among sons, provided farmers with the incentive to dispose of small, inherited tracts of land in Travancore in

---

[3]The information available on remittances is sketchy. One estimate has placed them at over Rs. 100 billion. The state economy does, however, experience temporary setbacks during years of large-scale return migration such as 1991 and 1997.

TABLE 5-9 Comparative Growth Rates of Population and Land
Utilization, Travancore and Malabar, 1911–1991 (percent)

Year	Population Growth during Decade		Cultivated Land as a Percent of Arable Land	
	Travancore	Malabar	Travancore	Malabar
1911–1921	13.9	2.8	73.7	59.7
1921–1931	24.8	14.0	79.7	61.1
1931–1941	19.1	11.2	96.3	64.9
1941–1951	24.0	21.1	98.1	66.0
1951–1961	31.1	22.4	98.4	70.5
1961–1971	22.1	30.7	98.5	74.6
1971–1981	15.3	25.4	98.5	80.2
1981–1991	7.8	20.4	98.6	86.2

SOURCES: Tharakan, P. K. M. 1976. Migration of Farmers from Travancore to Malabar,
1930 to 1960: An Analysis of Economic Causes. M.Phil. thesis. Jawaharlal Nehru University,
New Delhi; and Government of Kerala. Statistics for Planning. Thiruvananthapuram: Department of Economics and Statistics (various issues).

order to acquire more profitable land in Malabar. Because land prices
were somewhat high in Travancore and relatively lower in Malabar, migrants managed to acquire there larger areas of land as well as monetary
compensation.

The peasant migration acquired momentum in the 1940s and continued during the 1950s and 1960s. When the Travancore–Malabar migration began, Malabar had a static subsistence economy, with traditional
food crops occupying more than half the cropped area (Joseph, 1998). The
migrants adopted a strategy of clearing the land and, at first, growing
seasonal subsistence crops. They then gradually moved on to growing
perennial commercial crops. In most cases, the migrants acquired cultivable wasteland or forestland and converted it to land suitable for cultivation. In a survey of 341 farmers migrating to Malabar between 1940 and
1980, Joseph (1998) found that of the land they acquired, approximately
55 percent was cultivable wasteland, 38 percent forestland, and the remaining 7 percent cultivated land (Table 5-10). Migration thus opened up
new initiatives for full utilization of the agricultural potential of Malabar.

Highland Migration

Peasant migration from Travancore to Malabar was widespread before Kerala became a state in 1956; the population shift within Travancore
to its highland region, particularly the Idukki District, occurred around
1956. Several economic and political forces favored the shift. For example,
under its "Grow More Food" campaign, the government granted exclu-
sive cultivation rights in the forest area of the Idukki District. Although

TABLE 5-10 Nature of Land Acquired by Migrant Households, Malabar, 1940–1980

Years of Migration	Number of Households	Nature of Land Acquired (hectares)			
		Cultivated	Cultivable Wasteland	Forest	Total
<1940	7	—	2.8	20.2	23.0
1941–1945	6	2.4	20.0	10.1	32.5
1946–1950	63	9.7	97.1	406.35	13.1
1951–1955	33	2.0	105.4	17.8	125.2
1956–1960	81	8.3	239.2	67.8	315.3
1961–1965	64	29.3	159.2	32.6	221.1
1966–1970	56	35.0	161.7	25.1	221.8
1971–1975	18	12.5	34.4	2.8	49.7
1976–1980	13	14.2	31.8	2.8	48.8
Total	341	113.4	851.6	585.5	1,550.5
(percent)		(7.3)	(54.9)	(37.8)	

SOURCE: Joseph, K. V. 1998. Migration and land use: A case study of migration from Travancore to Malabar. Background paper no. 4, Population and Land Use Study, Centre for Development Studies, Thiruvananthapuram.

this step was taken to increase food production in the 1960s, large-scale rubber cultivation later was implemented in the area.

The major influx of migrants to Travancore's hilly region occurred between 1940 and 1960. Over a wider period, 1901–1991, it recorded a population growth rate of 1,343 percent, against the state average of 345 percent. The maximum growth rate was recorded in the 1950s. Migration attraction indices computed for all districts in Travancore using four variables—per capita availability of land, extent of wasteland, extent of forest cover, and cropping intensity—indicate that Idukki ranks the highest in all variables among the districts.

Migration contributed to a change in the ratio of females to males in the highland districts of Wayanad and Idukki (Figure 5-4). Although the ratio of females to males was greater than one for Kerala generally, the ratio of females to males was lowest—966 and 975 females per thousand males, respectively—in the Wayanad and Idukki Districts, where the in-migrant population was mostly male.

Deforestation

Migration may have contributed to Kerala's balanced regional development by improving the productive capacity of the highland region and it may have enhanced the incomes of small farmers, but it also led to ecological imbalance in the high ranges because of the link between the influx of farmers and deforestation.

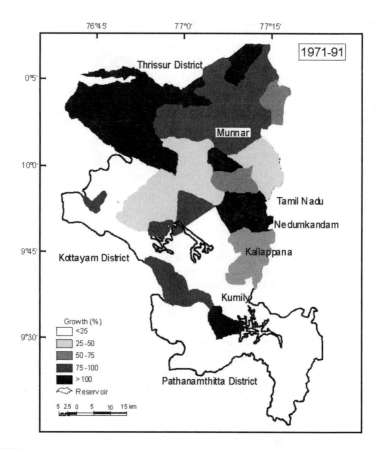

FIGURE 5-4 Population growth, Idukki District, 1971–1991.

Kerala has witnessed large-scale deforestation during this century. According to Narayanan (1996), four major state initiatives favored deforestation. The first one occurred toward the end of the nineteenth century when a Royal Proclamation aimed at encouraging the establishment of plantations guaranteed settlers the tax-free use of government forestland for 10 years and imposed only light taxation thereafter. Although the benefits were initially realized by large capitalists, small farmers were later also attracted to the forestland. Second, the "Grow More Food" campaign of the mid-1940s opened up forestland for the cultivation of food crops. Third, a colonization program of the state government prior to the reorganization of the states opened up new settlements in deforested areas. And, fourth, major investments in power generation and irrigation projects in the postindependence era entailed deforestation to make way for reservoirs and infrastructure such as roads.

Although the official estimates of forest area do not reflect this decline because of the reporting system used, studies based on satellite imagery have revealed a substantial decline in forest area. According to one estimate by the Center for Earth Science Studies, the area under forest in Kerala, expressed as a percentage of the total geographic area, declined from 36 percent to 12 percent between 1965 and 1990. Apparently, up until 1960 migrants to Idukki acquired land through deforestation. But over time the share of deforested land in the total land acquired declined, and from 1980 on land was acquired mainly through purchases from earlier settlers (Table 5-11). Over the same period, the decline of forestland in the Wyanad and Idukki Districts, with the greatest concentration of migrants, was about 40 percent.

In a study of several villages in the Idukki District, Jeena (1997) observes that the changes in land use pattern between 1940 and 1990 occurred in two stages. In the first stage deforestation resulted from the expansion of cultivated area to forestland, fueled by government policies set in place in the 1940s. The second stage corresponded to the introduction of rubber cultivation to the area in the 1960s, based on its high profitability and adequate incentives for commercial plantation crops.

Old Survey of India maps, LANDSAT images from 1973, and IRS (Indian Remote Sensing) images from 1992 reveal a progressive decline in natural vegetation cover in the Idukki District from 88 percent in 1905 to 20 percent in 1992. The area devoted to agricultural plantations and settlements has increased from 16 percent (based on a survey carried out from 1913 to 1928) to 43 percent (based on an analysis of satellite images from 1992)—see Table 5-12. (Because of the dispersed nature of settlements, it is not possible to distinguish settled areas from agricultural plantations in the satellite data.) Increases in the area classified as water bodies stem from the impoundment of the Idukki and Idamalayar reservoirs. The Idukki reservoir generates most of the hydroelectric power produced in Kerala.

TABLE 5-11 Nature of Acquisition of Land by Settlers in Idukki Villages

| | Percent of Land Acquired by | |
Years of Migration	Deforestation	Purchase
Before 1950	100.0	0
1950–1960	100.0	0
1960–1970	36.4	63.4
1970–1980	19.1	80.9
After 1980	0	100.0

SOURCES: Sample survey results reported in Jeena, T. S. 1997. Internal Rural Migration and the Impact of Deforestation on Cropping Patterns in Kerala. M.Phil. thesis. Jawaharlal Nehru University, New Delhi.

TABLE 5-12 Temporal Variation in Land Use in Idukki District (percent)

Land Use Category	Period I, 1913–1928	Period II, 1954–1970	Period III, 1992	Change between I and II	Change between I and III	Change between II and III
Forest, including degraded forest and forest plantations	82.10	65.00	54.00	–17.10	–28.10	–11.00
Agricultural plantations and settlements	16.30	33.40	43.38	+17.10	+27.08	+9.98
Water bodies	1.60	1.60	2.62	0	+1.02	+1.02

NOTE: Period I corresponds to the survey carried out during 1913–1928, period II during 1954–1970, and period III in 1992.

SOURCE: Centre for Earth Science Studies (CESS). 1997. Analysis of the Environmental Impact of the Lowland to Highland Migration in the Western Ghat Region: Kerala. Thiruvananthapuram.

Deforestation is associated with several undesirable conditions. In the highlands of Kerala with its rugged topography and heavy rainfall, forests reduce the peak flow and prolong the duration of flow, thereby reducing surface runoff. Deforestation causes rapid runoff from catchment areas, as well as frequent flash floods in downstream areas. When annual crops such as cassava are grown on the deforested land, soil erosion occurs on slopes, which in turn increases the silt carried by rivers and reduces the storage capacity of reservoirs. Erosion of the topsoil also leads to reduced soil quality and low productivity over time. Some of the landslides in the Idukki District during recent years are thought to be the result of deforestation and the changing cropping patterns.

Urbanization

In Kerala the trend toward urbanization differs from that in the rest of India in several aspects. The state is dominated by small, well-distributed urban centers rather than one large megacity. Moreover, Kerala displays a unique rural–urban continuum. Traditionally, dispersed linear settlements developed along the ridges and upper slopes and the intervening valleys between ridges were used for seasonal agriculture or primary sector activities. The valleys also served as water cushions during monsoons.

In 1981 Kerala had an urban population of only 19 percent, compared with a national average of 23 percent. Ten years later the urban population of Kerala accounted for 26 percent of the total population, compared with a national average of 25 percent. The area under urban administration in 1991 accounted for 8.65 percent of the geographical area, compared with 2.66 percent in 1961 (CESS, 1997). District-wise, with the exception of the Ernakulam and Kannur Districts, the spatial expansion of urbanization is either stagnant or slow. In 1961 Alappuzha (Alleppey) District ranked first among all the districts in urbanization—7.79 percent of its total area was classified as urban. The situation remained unchanged up to 1981, and an additional 12.54 percent of the total district area came under urban administration in 1991. The town of Alleppey has been an important port in recent history and has played a significant role in the local economy.

The impacts of urbanization on land use are felt widely. On the one hand, the spatial expansion of urban centers brings more rural area under urban administration. On the other hand, land use within the urban centers undergoes various changes. An analysis of the land use dynamics of the city of Thiruvananthapuram illustrates these changes. The analysis was carried out using the land use and land type data extracted from Survey of India topographical maps and IRS images with a scale of 1:50,000. Spatial analysis of the data was carried out using a geographic information system (GIS).

Thiruvananthapuram, formerly known as Trivandrum, covers an area of 326 square kilometers. The capital of modern Kerala, Thiruvananthapuram also was the capital of the historic state of Travancore. By the turn of the nineteenth century, it had a population of 57,882, which had grown to 524,006 in 1991. The original settlements were in low-lying sandy areas.

In Thiruvananthapuram land use changes over the years were instrumental in changing the landscape ecology, which had far-reaching consequences for the environment. The more major land use changes were in residential areas, where, given the preference of the local populace to live in single-family housing, significantly more land was required to house the population than in other parts of the country. A comparison of the land use data for Thiruvananthapuram for 1961 and 1976 reveals that the areas classified as wetland, rice fields, and parks and open spaces declined cumulatively from 36.5 percent in 1961 to 17.45 percent in 1976 (Table 5-13). A more recent survey by Chattopadhyay and Jayaprasad (1991) revealed that wetland made up only 5 percent of the region. This decline continues despite restrictions imposed by the government against conversion of wetland, which have been earmarked as the "Green Belt."

In urban areas generally, the urban influence is spreading to surrounding rural areas, and the rural–urban distinction is diminishing at a fast pace. In the Thiruvananthapuram City Region, for example, rice fields accounted for 11 percent of the total area in 1966 (Figure 5-5) but only 6 percent in 1991 according to satellite image data. The spatial distribution

TABLE 5-13 Land Use Change, Thiruvananthapuram City Corporation, 1961 and 1976 (percent)

Land Use Category	1961	1976	Change
Residential	46.00	59.00	+13.04
Wetland/rice fields	24.00	9.60	−14.40
Park and open space	12.50	7.85	−4.65
Public and semigovernment land	5.30	8.86	+3.56
Roads and streets	4.50	7.33	+2.83
Other (industrial, etc.)	7.70	7.32	−0.42

SOURCE: Chattopadhyay, S. 1985. Deforestation in parts of Western Ghats region (Kerala), India. International Journal of Environmental Management 20:219–230.

indicates that conversion of rice land to urban uses is greatest within and near the city. In the coastal plain, however, the decline is less, primarily because wetland in the region has been acquired by the government and is therefore protected—at least temporarily.

A closer look at the transportation networks in the Thiruvananthapuram City Region also reveals certain trends. Roads and highways were originally developed along the ridges, and today the main routes are following this pattern, developing along the ridges, whereas branch routes cut across or run along the valleys. The National Highway (NH 47) passes through the area, cutting across the city for a length of 32 kilometers. The rice fields located near the national highways, state highways, and minor roads are more prone to conversion than ones in outlying areas. The satellite images clearly show that land use within the urban area and the adjoining rural areas are undergoing significant changes.

ENVIRONMENTAL ISSUES

Kerala is well known for having a cleaner environment than the other states of India. Environmental pollution is an emerging problem, however. This section focuses on the growing problem of water pollution and, more generally, the policy measures that have been implemented at the national level to deal with environmental protection.

Water Pollution

Kerala's major industries are dumping an estimated 500,000 cubic meters of effluents containing a variety of pollutants into the rivers of Kerala every day. Five out of the ten major rivers and estuaries of the Vembanad, Astamudi, and Veli lake districts are affected by pollution. Although no detailed study has been carried out for the entire state, site-specific analyses, especially of water quality, have been conducted over

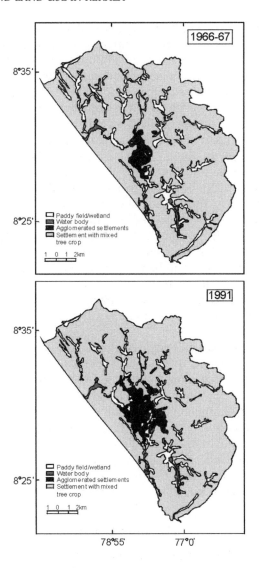

FIGURE 5-5 Land use, Thiruvananthapuram City Region, 1966–1967 and 1991.

the past few years. These studies indicate that the pollution problem is closely associated with land use practices.

The Centre for Earth Science Studies, under the aegis of the national Department of Ocean Development, regularly monitors coastal waters at various locations. Its research has found high concentrations of dissolved and particulate cadmium and mercury in water samples collected from the coastal waters at Kochi (formerly Cochin) and Veli (Pillai et al., 1994). Dissolved oxygen levels and biological oxygen demand (BOD) levels also indicate environmental degradation.[4] Pollution in the Vembanad estuary is attributed to industrial and urban effluents from the city of Kochi and adjoining areas. As a major port and industrial center, this region is subject to heavy anthropogenic pressure. An estimated 3.5 billion liters of domestic sewage is produced daily in the urban areas of Cochin. Approximately 90 percent of this sewage is untreated and discharged into surrounding bodies of water (Kumaran, 1994). High concentrations of phosphates, nitrates, and ammonia are causing eutrophication of the Vembanad lakes. Water bodies in and around Thiruvananthapuram also are affected by urban and industrial discharges.

Backwaters and rural estuaries in Kerala experience varying degrees of pollution. Apart from urbanization and industrialization in the lowlands and coastal plains, the common practice of coconut retting contributes to the degradation of ambient water quality. Coconut retting is the process through which coconut husk is immersed in brackish water before fiber is extracted from the husk. Hydrogeochemical analysis of selected rivers in rural areas also indicates the presence of fecal coliform bacteria.

Finally, because Kerala's freshwater environment is optimal for growing rice, rice is cropped three times annually, requiring heavy use of fertilizers. The residual nitrates have contributed to water quality problems. Pollution attributed to fertilizer and pesticide residues is reported in the Alappuzha-Kottayam area, and the algal blooms observed in rice fields are possibly associated with an increase in nitrate levels (Mary Kutty, 1996). Moreover, there is evidence that postharvest soils carry residual nitrates and phosphorus. Given Kerala's achievement in various sectors, the contamination of water in both rural and urban areas is a matter of serious concern.

Policies and Regulations

Protection of the environment is part of the Indian cultural heritage. Some species of plants are worshiped, as evidenced by the sacred groves found throughout India which are considered divine property and are protected by fencing. Reinforcing these traditional practices, Articles 48 A and 51 A (g) of the constitution of India decree that the "state shall endeavor to protect and improve the environment, and to safeguard the forests and wildlife in the country," as well as "to protect and improve the

---

[4]Biological oxygen demand (BOD) is a measure of water quality. An increasing BOD corresponds to deteriorating quality.

natural environment, including forests, lakes and rivers, and wildlife, and to have compassion for the living creatures." To combat the enormous damage already inflicted on the environment, the national government has implemented various regulations, including the following (Government of India, 1992):

- Wildlife (Protection) Act, 1972, amended in 1983, 1986, and 1991;
- Water (Prevention and Pollution Control) Act, 1974, amended in 1988;
- Water (Prevention and Pollution Control) Cess Act, 1977, amended in 1991;
- Forest (Conservation) Act, 1980, amended in 1988;
- Air (Prevention and Pollution Control) Act, 1981, amended in 1988;
- Environment (Protection) Act, 1986;
- Motor Vehicle Act, 1938, amended in 1988;
- Public Liability Insurance Act, 1991; and
- A Notification on Coastal Regulation Zone, 1991.

The Forest (Conservation) Act of 1980 seeks to prevent diversion of forestland to any other purpose. The act was amended in 1988 to ensure ecological balance in soil, water, and biomass management while meeting the requirements of the rural and tribal populations, increasing productivity, ensuring efficient use of forest products, and limiting the involvement of the population. In addition to enforcing these regulations, Kerala has enacted certain rules for land use practices. For example, the direct conversion of paddy fields to settlements is not permitted, and the construction of settlements in wetland areas (green belts) is prohibited.

CONCLUSION

Conversion of rice land, migration, deforestation, and urban expansion are the major land use/population issues in Kerala. On its agricultural lands, Kerala has witnessed major changes in cropping patterns, especially a substantial decline in the area used for rice and cassava cultivation and an increase in coconut and rubber cultivation. State policies on taxation, coupled with lax enforcement of regulations prohibiting the conversion of rice land to other purposes, have accelerated the process of rice land conversion. In addition, incentives for expansion and the high profitability of rubber production have contributed toward expanded cultivation of rubber.

The conversion of rice land to other uses has increased Kerala's dependence on other states to meet its rice requirements. Rice is a labor-intensive crop, and a decline in the area devoted to its cultivation has adverse impacts on employment opportunities, income distribution, and food consumption. Because rice straw is the main source of roughage for feeding cattle, a reduction in rice cultivation also leads to reduced availability of cattle feed.

Population pressures, unemployment, and state policies in Kerala have encouraged large-scale internal migration, which has resulted in rapid deforestation of the regions to which people moved. The consequences of deforestation include frequent flash floods and landslides, soil erosion, and silting of reservoirs, all capable of causing serious ecological and environmental problems. Population growth also has led to the conversion of rice land to, among other things, clay mining for brick making. Clay mining contributes to a decline in the groundwater recharging capacity and in the water-retention capacity of the soil.

Urbanization in Kerala differs from that in the rest of India, because the state is dominated by small, well-distributed urban centers rather than a large megacity. Moreover, Kerala displays a unique rural–urban continuum. The local populace prefers to live in single-family housing, and thus significantly more land is required to house the population than in other parts of the country.

Lack of employment opportunities for a large number of educated hopefuls and the shortage of arable land have provided strong incentives for interregional, interstate, and international migration. Thus the state economy has become somewhat dependent on remittances. The use of remittances for nonproductive activities, especially acquisition of consumer items manufactured outside the state, has earned Kerala a reputation as a consumer state. In the absence of major investments in productive sectors, it is likely that the state will remain a net consumer in the future.

REFERENCES

Centre for Earth Science Studies (CESS). 1997. Analysis of the Environmental Impact of the Lowland to Highland Migration in the Western Ghat Region: Kerala. Thiruvananthapuram.

Chattopadhyay, S. 1985. Deforestation in parts of Western Ghats region (Kerala), India. International Journal of Environmental Management 20:219–230.

Chattopadhyay S., and B. K. Jayaprasad. 1991. Evaluation of paddy field in Thiruvananthapuram City. Report submitted to the Trivandrum Development Authority, Centre for Earth Science Studies, Thiruvananthapuram.

George, P. S. 1982. Agricultural price movements in Kerala. In: Agricultural Development in Kerala, P. P. Pillai, ed. New Delhi: Agricole Publishing Academy.

Gopinathan, C., and C. S. Sundaresan. 1990. Cropping Pattern Changes and Employment Effects in Selected Districts of Kerala. Thiruvananthapuram: Centre for Management Development.

Government of India. 1992. National Conservation Strategy and Policy Statement on Environment and Development. New Delhi: Ministry of Environment and Forest.

Government of Kerala. 1996. Key Indicators of Rural Department. Thiruvananthapuram: Department of Rural Development.

Government of Kerala. 1997. Economic Review. Thiruvananthapuram: State Planning Board.
Government of Travancore. 1940. Travancore Land Revenue Manual. Thiruvananthapuram.
Jeena, T. S. 1997. Internal Rural Migration and the Impact of Deforestation on Cropping Patterns in Kerala. M.Phil. thesis. Jawaharlal Nehru University, New Delhi.
Joseph, K. V. 1998. Migration and land use: A case study of migration from Travancore to Malabar. Background paper no. 4, Population and Land Use Study, Centre for Development Studies, Thiruvananthapuram.
Kannan, K. P., and P. Pushpangadan. 1988. Agricultural stagnation in Kerala: An exploratory analysis. Economic and Political Weekly 23(39):A120–A128.
Kumaran, P. 1994: Urban pollution in Kerala with specific reference to Kochi. International Congress on Kerala Studies 5(abstracts):175, 176.
Mary Kutty, A., C. M. Joy, and T. Joseph. 1996. Potential effect of fertiliser residues on algae of Kuttanad. Pp. 59–60 in Proceedings of the Eighth Kerala Science Congress. Thiruvananthapuram.
Narayanan, N. C. 1994. Issues in Sustainable Land Use. M.Phil. thesis. Jawaharlal Nehru University, New Delhi.
Narayanan, N. C. 1996. Land use intervention in the highland tracts of Kerala and sustainable livelihoods: A case study of Adivaram. Photocopy.
Panikar, P. G. K. 1980. Recent trends in area under production of rice in Kerala. Working Paper 116. Centre for Development Studies, Thiruvananthapuram.
Panikar, P. G. K., et al. 1978. Population growth and agricultural development: A case study of Kerala. Paper prepared for the United Nations Population Fund (UNFPA), New York.
Pillai, R., V. Rema Devi, V. Saravanan, and P. P. Ouseph. 1994. Distribution of heavy metals and nutrients in the nearshore sediments and waters along the southwest coast of India. Pp. 91–93 in Proceedings of the Sixth Kerala Science Congress. Thriuvananthapuram.
Resmi, P. B. 1996. Environment and Sustainable Development: The Case of Brick Industry in Kerala. M.Phil. thesis. Jawaharlal Nehru University, New Delhi.
Sivanandan, P. K. 1985. Kerala's Agricultural Performance: Differential Trends and Determinants of Growth. M.Phil. thesis. Jawaharlal Nehru University, New Delhi.
Uma Devi, S. 1984. Impact of Plantations on Kerala's Economy with Special Reference to Rubber: Some Historical and Quantitative Aspects. Ph.D. dissertation. University of Kerala, Thriuvananathapuram.
Unni, J. 1983. Changes in cropping pattern in Kerala: Some evidence on substitution of coconut for rice. Economic and Political Weekly 18(39):A100–A107.

6

Population and Land Use in Haryana

Prem S. Vashishtha
Agricultural Economics Research Centre, University of Delhi
R. K. Sharma
Agricultural Economics Research Centre, University of Delhi
R. P. S. Malik
Agricultural Economics Research Centre, University of Delhi
Seema Bathla
Institute of Economic Growth, Delhi

Scientists and policymakers are concerned about the world's growing population. For them, two key issues are food security—the ability of nations to feed their growing numbers of citizens—and the sustainability of agricultural systems in the face of intensified cultivation, the rising use of chemical inputs, and the increasing pressure on already scarce water resources. Because the relationships among population growth, land use, and sustainability of resources are complex, exploration of these relationships must depend on detailed, region-specific studies and cross-regional comparisons.

This study examines the relationships among land use, population growth, and consumption in Haryana, a landlocked state in northwest India. It borders on the states of Uttar Pradesh in the east, Himachal Pradesh in the northeast, Punjab in the north, and Rajasthan in the west, and the territory of Delhi in the south (Figure 6-1). With a geographical area of 44,212 square kilometers and a population of 16.5 million in 1991, Haryana constitutes 1.3 percent of India's geographical area and 1.9 percent of its population. The capital of Haryana, Chandigarh, is shared by the neighboring state of Punjab.

Except for some low hills in the north and south, Haryana is flat. The state has no perennial river except for the Yamuna, which flows along its eastern side. Haryana has a subtropical monsoon climate with meager, aberrant rains, hot summers with excessive sunshine and intense heat, and cold winters. The minimum temperature in January is 1°C, and the maximum in the summer months is 48°C. The average annual rainfall varies across districts, from a minimum of 42 centimeters in Hissar to a

108   GROWING POPULATIONS, CHANGING LANDSCAPES

FIGURE 6-1 Districts of Haryana.

maximum of 156 centimeters in the district of Ambala. The average annual rainfall is 59 centimeters.

Based on its agroclimatic conditions, Haryana can be divided into two homogeneous regions: the eastern semiarid zone and the western arid zone. These regions show marked differences in patterns of land use, especially in the agricultural sector, and in levels of development. Intensity of land use in the two regions does not differ significantly, yet agriculture in the semiarid region is dominated by the cultivation of high-yielding, high-value crops such as rice and wheat, which accounted for 58.3 percent of the gross cropped area in 1991–1992. By contrast, in the same year a large proportion of the cropped area (63.4 percent) in the arid zone was allocated to lower-yielding, lower-value crops such as bajra (millet), pulses, oilseeds, and cotton.[1] As a result, the per-hectare quantity and value of output in the two regions differ significantly.

[1]This contrast was even sharper in 1971–1972 when bajra (millet), pulses, oilseeds, and cotton together occupied 72.6 percent of gross cropped area in the arid zone and 34.2 per-

Haryana has well-developed agricultural and industrial sectors, and its economy is growing rapidly—per capita income is the third highest among the sixteen major states in India. Haryana's outstanding agricultural development has been attributed primarily to the Green Revolution. Initiated over the period 1967–1978, it resulted in the intensification and expansion of agriculture in many developing countries and was very successful in India. Major aspects of the Green Revolution were the expansion of farmland and the adoption of double-cropping systems (two crop seasons per year) and seeds that had been improved genetically—that is, high-yielding varieties (HYV) of wheat, rice, corn, and millet. These practices continue to shape land use in Haryana today.

This study examines changes in land use in the arid and semiarid agroecological regions of Haryana and the extent to which such changes are consistent with the goals of sustainable development. More specifically, it explores land use patterns in the context of the roles of population, technology, prices, and public policies, and analyzes the ecological consequences, particularly on water resources, of the intensification of agriculture. This study also examines socioeconomic indicators to determine whether the success brought by advanced agricultural technology has been translated into social benefits. Finally, it looks at the role of Haryana in providing food security for the nation, contrasting the demand for agricultural commodities for local consumption with the demand from markets outside the region.

HARYANA: A DEMOGRAPHIC PROFILE

Two important forces driving changes in land use in Haryana are the size and growth rate of its population. These forces and their relationship to migration, land availability, and urbanization are examined in this section.

Population

Haryana experienced a low population growth rate throughout the first half of the twentieth century, but it is currently contributing to India's population expansion by an annual growth rate of 2.5 percent. In fact, Haryana is one of the fastest-growing states in India, despite its relatively high per capita income and commendable economic progress (Table 6-1). In 1991 Haryana's total population was 16.5 million, or about 2 percent of India's 850 million people. The population of Haryana tripled over the period 1951–1991, from 5.6 million to 16.5 million. Although the annual

cent in the semiarid zone. Rice and wheat together accounted for only 12.6 percent and 40.2 percent of gross cropped area in the arid and semiarid zones, respectively.

TABLE 6-1 Population Size and Growth Trends, India and Selected States, 1901–1991

State	Population Size (thousands)				Annual Growth Rate (percent)		
	1901	1951	1971	1991	1901–1951	1951–1971	1971–1991
Bihar	27,311	38,782	50,719	75,021	0.70	1.34	1.96
Haryana	4,623	5,674	10,036	16,464	0.41	2.85	2.47
Kerala	6,396	13,549	21,347	29,099	1.50	2.27	1.55
Punjab	7,545	9,161	13,551	20,282	0.39	1.96	2.02
Tamil Nadu	19,253	30,119	41,199	55,859	0.89	1.57	1.52
Uttar Pradesh	48,628	63,220	88,342	139,112	0.52	1.67	2.27
India	238,396	361,088	548,160	846,303	0.83	2.09	2.17

SOURCE: Srinivasan, K., ed. 1996. Population Policy and Reproductive Health. New Delhi: Population Foundation of India.

growth rate has declined from 2.85 percent for the period 1951–1971 to 2.47 percent for the period 1971–1991, the latter growth rate is still much greater than the national annual growth rate of 2.17 percent for the same period. The rapid decline in mortality in the last half-century is commonly ascribed to improvements in nutrition and sanitation in some urban areas and better health care.

Haryana's crude annual birth rate for the period 1991–1996 was 31.9 per thousand persons compared with 29.2 for India (Table 6-2). Its death rate for the same period was 8.6 per thousand persons, which is lower than the national average of 9.8. Combining these rates results in a natural growth rate for 1991–1996 of 23.3 per thousand persons for Haryana compared with 19.4 for India.

Life expectancy at birth in Haryana is 59.5 years for females, 61.5 years for males. The state ranks third among the major states in life expectancy for males, after Kerala (65.9 years) and Punjab (63 years). Its life expectancy for females, however, is unimpressive; Haryana ranks eighth among the major states.

The increase in population has led to greater population density, because the land area remains unchanged. The population density of Haryana rose from 227 persons per square kilometer in 1971 to 372 in 1991, an increase of 64 percent. This density is much higher than the 1991 national average of 257 persons per square kilometer. Although the rate of increase of population density has been declining since the 1950s, it is projected to rise in the twenty-first century—to as high as 455 persons per square kilometer in the year 2001 and 530 by the year 2011 (Table 6-3). Such high densities, in spite of the decline in population growth rates witnessed in recent years, stem from the high population growth main-

TABLE 6-2 Natural Growth Rate of Population, Haryana and India, 1951–2016

Year	Crude Birth Rate (number of live births per thousand persons) (1)	Crude Death Rate (number of deaths per thousand persons) (2)	Natural Growth Rate (increase per thousand persons) (3) = (1) − (2)
Haryana			
1951–1961	—	—	—
1961–1971	44.00	16.90	27.10
1971–1981	42.10	9.90	32.20
1981–1991	36.50	11.30	25.20
1991–1996	31.90	8.60	23.30
1996–2001	24.00	7.75	16.25
2001–2006	22.75	7.09	15.66
2006–2011	21.98	6.90	15.09
2011–2016	21.01	6.85	14.15
India			
1951–1961	41.70	22.80	18.90
1961–1971	41.20	19.00	22.20
1971–1981	36.90	17.70	19.20
1981–1991	33.90	12.60	21.30
1991–1996	29.20	9.80	19.40
1996–2001	24.10	8.99	15.11
2001–2006	22.84	8.27	14.57
2006–2011	22.27	7.80	14.48
2011–2016	21.41	7.48	13.94

NOTE: State-level estimates of crude birth rate and crude death rate for 1951 were unavailable.

SOURCES: All figures for 1971–1991: Nutrition Foundation of India. 1992–1993. National Family Health Survey-Haryana. New Delhi: Nutrition Foundation of India; all figures for 1996–2016: Population Projections—India and the States, 1996–2016, Census of India, 1991; 1951 and 1961 crude birth and death rates for India: Pathak, K. B. 1996. Fertility and mortality transition in India: Policy perspectives and priorities. In: Population Policy and Reproductive Health, K. Srinivasan, ed. New Delhi: Population Foundation of India.

tained in earlier decades. Therefore, the pace at which population pressures on the land are increasing is a matter of great concern.

Migration, Land Availability, and Urbanization

Migration is an important component of Haryana's demographic character. According to the census of India, the number of in-migrants to Haryana was 1.26 million in 1971, 1.51 million in 1981, and 1.84 million in 1991, for a compound growth rate of 1.90 percent a year (Table 6-4). In-migrant workers in the categories of cultivators and agricultural wage

TABLE 6-3 Population Density and Growth Rates, Haryana and India, 1951–2011

Year	Haryana Population Density (number of persons per square kilometer)	Haryana Change in Population Density (percent)	Haryana Compound Annual Growth Rate of Population Density (percent)	India Population Density (number of persons per square kilometer)	India Change in Population Density (percent)	India Compound Annual Growth Rate of Population Density (percent)
1951	128			111		
1961	172	34.17	2.98	134	21.41	1.96
1971	227	31.73	2.79	167	24.10	2.18
1981	292	28.78	2.56	208	25.02	2.26
1991	372	27.40	2.45	257	23.51	2.13
1996	420	12.69	2.42	284	10.39	2.00
2001	455	8.45	1.63	308	8.37	1.62
2011	530	16.56	1.54	359	16.45	1.53

SOURCES: Figures for 1996, 2001, and 2011: Population Projections—India and the States, 1996–2016 and Census of India, 1991. Other figures: Statistical Abstract of India (various issues).

TABLE 6-4 Number and Growth Rate of In-migrants,[a] Haryana, 1971 and 1991

	All (workers + nonworkers)	Workers	Cultivators	Agricultural Laborers
1971				
Haryana	1,261,140	519,145	110,880	50,715
Arid region	370,005	148,125	45,295	25,535
Semiarid region	891,135	371,020	65,585	25,180
Central tract	498,980	222,745	51,310	18,285
Southern tract	392,155	148,275	14,275	6,895
1991				
Haryana	1,835,796	564,533	81,851	54,927
Arid region	510,941	131,752	39,326	25,351
Semiarid region	1,324,855	432,781	42,525	29,576
Central tract	746,488	236,982	29,700	20,507
Southern tract	578,367	195,799	12,825	9,069
Compound Annual Growth Rate: 1971–1991 (percent per annum)				
Haryana	1.90	0.42	–1.51	0.40
Arid region	1.63	–0.58	–0.70	–0.04
Semiarid region	2.00	0.77	–2.14	0.81
Central tract	2.03	0.31	–2.70	0.58
Southern tract	1.96	1.40	–0.53	1.38

[a]Refers to people residing in Haryana whose last place of residence was outside Haryana (all durations)—that is, in-migration is net of migration across districts within Haryana.

SOURCE: Prepared by the author based on data from: Census of India 1971, Haryana, Series 6-Haryana, Part II-D, Migration Tables; Census of India 1991, Haryana, Series 6-Haryana, Part II-D, Vol. 1, Migration Tables.

earners grew at a rate of –1.51 percent and 0.40 percent a year, respectively, over the period 1971–1991. Overall, in-migrants account for 12.57 percent and 11.15 percent of Haryana's population in 1971 and 1991, respectively (Table 6-5).

The employment of a substantial proportion (24–31 percent) of in-migrants in cultivation and agricultural wage earning has contributed to a decline in net sown area per capita, thereby increasing the population pressure on land for the livelihood of the rural population. For the period 1971–1991, the net sown area per primary sector worker declined from 2.99 hectares to 2.03 hectares, and the decline in net sown area per capita of rural population was even greater—from 0.43 hectares to 0.29 hectares

114

GROWING POPULATIONS, CHANGING LANDSCAPES

TABLE 6-5 Population and Availability of Agricultural Land, Haryana, 1971 and 1991

Indicator	Unit	1971	1991	Absolute Change, 1971–1991
Population	number	10,036,808	16,463,648	6,426,840
Rural	number	8,263,849	12,408,904	4,145,055
Urban	number	1,772,959	4,054,744	2,281,785
Share in total population				
Rural	percent	82.34	75.37	–6.96
Urban	percent	17.66	24.63	6.96
Workers in total population engaged as				
Cultivators	number	1,302,608	1,829,530	526,922
Agricultural laborers	number	430,312	896,782	466,470
Net sown area (NSA)	thousand hectares	3,565.40	3,575.00	9.60
Landholdings	number	998,704	1,529,779	531,075
Households	number	1,530,180	2,614,725	1,084,545
Rural	number	1,222,415	1,882,390	659,975
Urban	number	307,765	732,335	424,570
NSA per rural population	hectares	0.43	0.29	–0.14
NSA per primary sector worker	hectares	2.99	2.03	–0.96
NSA per landholding	hectares	3.57	2.34	–1.23
NSA per rural household	hectares	2.92	1.90	–1.02
In-migrant[a] population	number	1,261,140	1,835,796	574,656
Share of in-migrants[a] in total population	percent	12.57	11.15	–1.42
Share of in-migrant[a] workers engaged as				
Cultivators	percent	21.36	14.50	–6.86
Agricultural laborers	percent	9.77	9.73	–0.04
Household industry workers	percent	2.62	1.69	–0.93

[a]Refers to people residing in Haryana whose place of last residence was outside Haryana (all durations)—that is, in-migration is net of migration across districts within Haryana.

SOURCES: (1) Census of India, 1971 & 1991, Series VI, Part II-D, Migration Tables, Haryana for migrant population data; (2) Census of India, 1971 & 1991, Series VI, Part V-A & B, Vol. 1, General Economic Tables, Haryana; (3) Statistical Abstract of Haryana (various issues) for rural and urban population, net sown area, landholding, and household data; (4) the rest of the figures were generated by the author from these categories.

(Table 6-5). In addition, the number of landholdings increased at the rate of 2.15 percent a year, resulting in net sown area per rural landholding declining from 3.57 hectares to 2.34 hectares, a decline of 2.10 percent a year.

Haryana, with only one-fourth of its population residing in urban areas, is less urbanized than many developed states of India. However, urbanization is on the rise: the urban population, which constituted approximately 10 percent of the net population before 1951, had grown to 18 percent by 1971 and 25 percent by 1991 (Table 6-5). The increasing rate of urbanization is clearly revealed by the difference in the growth rates of the rural and urban populations. Between 1971 and 1991 the urban population of Haryana grew at an average rate of 4.22 percent a year, while the rural population grew at an average rate of 2.05 percent a year.

The urban density of Haryana in 1991, at 5,309 persons per square kilometer, was greater than that in almost all states of India. From 1981 to 1991 urban density increased by 40 percent. According to the 1991 census, approximately 60 percent of Haryana's urban population is concentrated in metropolitan areas with populations equal to or above 100,000. Nearly 40 percent of the rural population is concentrated in villages with populations under 5,000.

CHANGES IN LAND USE

This section describes the history of agricultural development in Haryana since 1950, reports the results of a state-level analysis of changes in land use, examines how cropping patterns have changed over time, and compares the practices and effects of the Green Revolution in the two major agroecological regions of the state.[2]

Agricultural Development of Haryana since 1950: Five Phases

Haryana is primarily an agricultural region; more than 80 percent of its area is classified as net sown area. Since 1950 agriculture has been the main driver of the state's economic development. Haryana's agricultural development can be broken down into five phases that will help to illuminate changes in the state's land use patterns.

• *Phase I (1951–1966): Population Pressure and Extensive Cultivation.* Although Haryana's population grew slowly during the first half of the twentieth century (0.41 percent a year), population pressure began to intensify after 1950; from 1951 to 1966 the population increased at a rate of 2.85 percent a year. Agriculturally, this phase was characterized by extensive cultivation, facilitated by the more widespread use of irrigation through the canal system. Increased population pressures led to expansion of the net sown area—from 3 million hectares in 1950 to 3.4 million in 1960—primarily to meet the food requirements of the fast-growing population (Table 6-6).

---

[2]For land use data on major regions in the area, see J. F. Richards et al. 1994. Historic Use and Carbon Estimates for South and Southeast Asia, 1880–1980. Environmental Sciences Division Publ. No. 4174. ORNL/CDIAC-61 NDP-046, Oak Ridge National Laboratory.

TABLE 6-6 Sown Area, Irrigated Area, and Adoption of High-yielding Varieties, Haryana, 1950–1996

Indicator	Unit	1950	1960	1966	1971	1981	1991	1996
Gross irrigated area (GIA)	thousand hectares	657	1,205	1,736	2,200	3,500	4,340	4,673
Gross cropped area (GCA)	thousand hectares	3,470	4,583	4,599	5,000	5,800	5,600	5,976
GIA as percentage of GCA	percent	18.93	26.29	37.75	44.00	60.34	77.50	78.20
Net irrigated area (NIA)	thousand hectares	n.a.	1,007	1,293	1,565	2,248	2,666	2,760
Net sown area (NSA)	thousand hectares	2,982	3,400	3,422	3,600	3,700	3,500	3,586
NIA as percentage of NSA	percent	n.a.	29.62	37.80	43.47	60.76	76.17	76.97
Cropping intensity	percent	116.36	134.79	134.40	138.89	156.76	160.00	166.64
Area under high-yielding varieties of:								
Rice	thousand hectares				70	441	475	498
	percent				24	87	75	60
Wheat	thousand hectares				796	1,437	1,760	1,863
	percent				68	92	98	95

SOURCE: Statistical Abstract of Haryana (various issues).

With the adoption of the double-cropping system, cropping intensity increased from 116 percent in 1950 to 135 percent in 1960. Public investments in canal irrigation systems also played an important role in creating favorable physical conditions for the intensification of agriculture. The net irrigated area, as a percentage of net sown area, increased from 30 percent in 1960 to 38 percent in 1966 (Table 6-6). During this early phase, canals irrigated most of the net irrigated area; wells irrigated a smaller portion.

• *Phase II (1966–1971): Spread of the Green Revolution.* After India faced a severe food crisis in the mid-1960s, the issue of food security assumed utmost priority. The national government implemented measures to facilitate the adoption of the new Green Revolution technology and to procure food from surplus areas such as Haryana, Punjab, and western Uttar Pradesh.[3] Diffusion of Green Revolution technology was facilitated by the creation of infrastructure, including private investment in irrigation sources, and government regulation of wheat prices.

These activities benefited the economy of Haryana. The government expedited creation of the necessary infrastructure by increasing the number of regulated markets and opening branches of commercial banks outside large towns. Surplus supplies of wheat were sold mainly to public procurement agencies, and any remaining was sold in the open markets. Government intervention in the food market ensured that producers would receive fair prices and prevented wheat prices from crashing at the regional level.

During this phase the Green Revolution played a prominent role in land use change in Haryana. With the implementation of Green Revolution technology and the introduction of the high-yielding crop varieties over the period 1966–1971, the net sown area expanded by 5 percent and the irrigated area by 21 percent (Table 6-6).

• *Phase III (1971–1981): Consolidation of the Wheat Revolution and Beginning of the Rice–Wheat Rotation.* Three aspects of this phase are noteworthy. First, the area allotted for rice cultivation increased throughout Haryana—from 291,000 hectares in 1971 to about 505,000 hectares in 1981 (Table 6-7). Second, groundwater exploitation began in both the semiarid and arid regions, and the number of tube wells rose. Third, with continuation of the price support system for wheat and rice, the rice-wheat crop rotation became a lucrative proposition for the farmers.

• *Phase IV (1981–1991): Intensive Cultivation and Depletion of Natural Resources.* In the 1980s new environmental problems emerged in agriculture, including those related to groundwater depletion and soil degrada-

---

[3]In 1971 government agencies procured 709,000 tonnes of wheat from Haryana, or 29.5 percent of Haryana's wheat production and 13.9 percent of the total wheat procured at the national level.

TABLE 6-7 Area Under Cereal Crops, Haryana, 1971–1991

	Rice			Wheat			Bajra (Millet)		
	1971	1981	1991	1971	1981	1991	1971	1981	1991
Area under crop (thousand hectares)	291	504.6	637	1,117	1,561.9	1,805.8	882.1	851.9	556.6
Percent of gross cropped area	5.8	8.7	11.4	23.3	26.8	32.4	17.5	14.6	10

SOURCE: Statistical Abstract of Haryana (various issues).

tion. Tanwar (1994) has pointed out that during the 1980s about 60 percent of the area of Haryana faced a declining water table. Thus overutilization of groundwater was a major concern. The decline was more conspicuous in areas where freshwater was available (approximately 40 percent of the land area of the state). Almost 50 percent of the state area depended on groundwater that was marginal in quality; 9 percent depended on water that was brackish (Tanwar, 1995).

• *Phase V (1991–1997): Stagnating Yield Levels and Depletion of Natural Resources.* During the 1990s the highly intensive cultivation in Haryana began to face a crisis situation. The yields of major cereal crops were either stagnating or declining, and little increase in the rice yield had been observed since 1991 (Figure 6-2). Although the value of wheat per hectare continued to increase in the 1990s, the value of rice per hectare showed a decline over the same period (Figure 6-2). Both agricultural scientists and policymakers became very concerned about the situation (ICAR, 1998).

Another concern is soil degradation. According to the National Bureau of Soil Survey and Land Use Planning (NBSS&LUP), which classifies soil by its physical and chemical degradation, one-third of the land area of Haryana has degraded soil, of which 23 percent suffers from medium-level degradation and 5 percent from high-level degradation (Table 6-8). Chemical degradation, probably from the excessive use of chemical fertilizers and pesticides, accounts for 6 percent of soil degradation.

State-level Analysis

The Statistical Abstract of Haryana describes five broad land use categories: (1) forest; (2) land not available for cultivation; (3) other uncultivated land, excluding fallow; (4) fallow land; and (5) net sown area (Table 6-9). These categories are cumulatively referred to as the "reported area."

Net sown area has remained static at 81 percent of total area since 1971, indicating that the potential for expansion of cultivation was al-

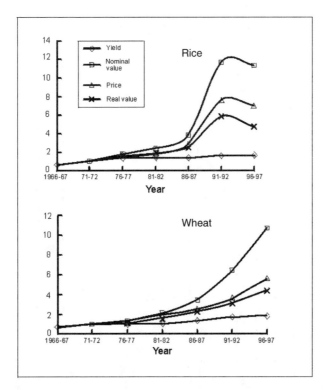

FIGURE 6-2 Indices of yield, value, and price of rice and wheat, 1966–1997.
NOTE: Nominal value (rupees/hectare at current prices) is computed from yield and price and converted to "real value" (rupees/hectare at constant 1981–1982 prices) using NSDPagr as a deflator. All four categories were then measured relative to their 1971–1972 levels.
SOURCES: Statistical Abstract of Haryana (various issues); Agricultural Prices in India, Ministry of Agriculture, Government of India (various issues).

ready exhausted more than 20 years ago. A related yet striking feature of the land use pattern in Haryana is the very small proportion of the reported area under forest cover, 2.3 percent in 1970 and 2.5 percent in 1995. Such low forest cover values indicate extensive use of land for cultivation. Although the area under forest cover increased slightly in the 1980s from efforts to promote environmental preservation, Haryana's percentage of land under forest cover remains far below the national norm of 33 percent. The Ninth Plan (1997–2002) of India specifies that not less than 2 percent of the land area of each district should be classified as forest cover.

A combination of government policies, population pressures, and available technological options are responsible for other types of changes

TABLE 6-8 Severity of Soil Degradation, Haryana

Type of Soil Degradation	Class of Severity Area (hectares)				As Percent of Total State Area			
	Low	Medium	High	Total	Low	Medium	High	Total
Physical degradation[a]								
Water erosion		305,273	9,894	315,167		6.90	0.22	7.13
Water erosion and stoniness		23,023	13,408	36,431		0.52	0.30	0.82
Wind erosion		392,235	143,993	536,228		8.87	3.26	12.13
Wind erosion and stoniness		2,609		2,609		0.06		0.06
Flooding	89,550	52,539	4,336	146,315	2.03	1.19	0.10	3.31
Water erosion and salinity		26,740		26,740		0.60		0.60
Wind erosion and salinity		90,119	2,270	92,389		2.04	0.05	2.09
Flooding and salinity		33,580	22,491	56,071		0.76	0.51	1.27
Chemical degradation[b]								
Salinity and sodicity	124,636	92,637	38,381	255,654	2.82	2.10	0.87	5.78
Total	247,766	1,007,666	212,172	1,467,604	5.60	22.79	4.80	33.19

[a]Refers to displacement of soil material principally by wind and water.
[b]Refers to internal soil deterioration resulting from the accumulation of chemical substances such as salt and loss of nutrients.

SOURCE: National Bureau of Soil Survey and Land Use Planning. 1996–1997. Soil of India. NBSS Publication 44, Series 3.

TABLE 6-9 Land Use Patterns, Haryana, 1970–1995

Category	Area (thousand hectares)				Percent of Reported Area			
	1970	1980	1990	1995	1970	1980	1990	1995
1. Forest	99.1	132.0	169.0	110.0	2.3	3.0	3.9	2.5
2. Not available for cultivation	489.5	434.0	417.0	494.0	11.1	9.9	9.5	11.2
2.1 Nonagricultural uses	308.8	369.0	338.0	400.0	7.0	8.4	7.7	9.1
2.2 Barren and uncultivated	180.7	75.0	97.0	94.0	4.1	1.7	2.2	2.1
3. Other uncultivated land, excluding fallow	98.0	60.0	48.0	51.0	2.2	1.4	1.1	1.2
3.1 Permanent pastures and grazing	54.2	30.0	23.0	24.0	1.2	0.7	0.5	0.5
3.2 Under trees, crops not included in NSA	2.6	0	4.0	4.0	0.1	0	0.1	0.1
3.3 Cultivable waste	41.2	30.0	21.0	23.0	0.9	0.7	0.5	0.5
4. Fallow land	149.8	177.0	169.0	156.0	3.4	4.0	3.9	3.5
4.1 Other than current fallow	0.3	0	0	0	0	0	0	0
4.2 Current fallow	149.5	177.0	169.0	156.0	3.4	4.0	3.9	3.5
5. Net sown area (NSA)	3,565.4	3,602.0	3,575.0	3,586.0	81.0	81.8	81.7	81.5
Total, all categories (1+2+3+4+5)	4,402	4,405	4,378	4,398	100	100	100	100

SOURCE: Statistical Abstract of Haryana (various years).

in land use. For example, an increase in the area devoted to nonagricultural uses is the direct result of increasing urbanization, industrialization, and the state government's policy of creating industrial estates.[4] The area under nonagricultural uses increased from 309,000 hectares in 1970 to 338,000 hectares in 1990, a change that can be attributed to increased land use for housing, industrial estates, and infrastructure (such as roads).

By contrast, barren and uncultivated land, land used for grazing and as permanent pasture, and cultivable wasteland have all decreased. The decrease in land area in the "barren and uncultivated" category (it declined from 4.1 percent of the reported area in 1970 to 2.2 percent in 1990) is a result of land reclamation policy. The availability of technology for reclaiming land affected by severe salinity and sodicity has made such reclamation feasible and financially viable. Reclamation of barren land for cultivation has in part mitigated the negative effects of the expansion of the area under nonagricultural uses.

The decline in area classified as permanent pastures and grazing land is a direct result of the increased population pressure from both humans and animals. Permanent pastures and grazing land declined by 30,000 hectares between 1970 and 1990. As a proportion of reported area, they declined from 1.2 percent in 1970 to only 0.5 percent in 1990. Fallow lands increased by about 20,000 hectares from 1970 to 1990, while net sown area declined by about 25,000 hectares (a small proportion of the total) in the 1980s, possibly indicating the retirement of cultivated land deficient in soil nutrients or suffering from increased salinity. Unacceptable salinity levels may be related to the combined effects of inappropriate agricultural practices, lack of proper drainage, and exploitation of groundwater.

Cropping Patterns

Changes in land use over a period of time can be classified as: (1) conversion of land from one use category to another (for example, land is shifted from agricultural uses to nonagricultural uses; (2) changes in land use within a given land use category (for example, agricultural land is shifted from one crop to another); and (3) changes in land use intensity (for example, a farmer grows more than one crop a year, resulting in increased cropping intensity). These three types of land use change may occur concurrently; they are not necessarily sequential in nature.

Over the past three decades Haryana has undergone these three types of change in land use to varying degrees. In addition to the changes from one category of land use to another over the years, significant shifts also

---

[4]The best-known examples are the big industrial estates created in Faridabad and Gurgaon by the government of Haryana.

have occurred within categories of land use. The most notable of these have been within the agricultural sector. For example, the absolute area and proportion of cropped area allocated to traditional crops such as jowar, bajra, maize, barley, and gram have declined, and the area allocated to rice, wheat, and cotton has increased. While some of these increases in area have stemmed from the increased availability of cropped area, most of the changes have resulted from crop switching.

Significant changes in cropping patterns have been implemented in Haryana over the years. The proportion of cropped area allocated to cereals increased from 45 percent in 1960 to more than 57 percent three decades later (Table 6-10). The proportion of area allocated to oilseeds and cotton also increased over this period, while that allocated to sugarcane declined very slightly. Finally, there has been a notable decline in the proportion of area allocated to pulses, from 33 percent in 1960 to 7 percent in 1990.

As a result of shifts in cropping area and technological progress, wheat production increased from 2.4 million tonnes in 1971 to 6.5 million tonnes in 1991 (Table 6-11). Likewise, rice production increased from 536,000 tonnes in 1971 to 1.8 million tonnes in 1991. Pulse production, however, declined—from 682,000 tonnes to 273,000 tonnes over the same period.

In Haryana, where more than 80 percent of the total reported area is utilized by cropping systems, farmers individually own and operate small

TABLE 6-10 Shifts in Cropping Patterns, Haryana, 1960–1990 (thousand hectares)

Area allocated to:	Year			
	1960	1970	1980	1990
Cereals	2,039.9	2,750.3	3,232.1	3,187.5
	(45.33)	(54.48)	(55.48)	(57.23)
Pulses	1,504.4	1,205.1	1,115.5	389.1
	(33.43)	(23.87)	(19.14)	(6.99)
Oilseeds	203.5	175.6	216.5	701.3
	(4.52)	(3.48)	(3.72)	(12.59)
Cotton	108	241.7	329.5	505.8
	(2.40)	(4.79)	(5.66)	(9.08)
Sugarcane	138	114.4	145.1	160.9
	(3.07)	(2.27)	(2.49)	(2.89)
Other	506.2	560.9	787.3	625.4
	(11.25)	(11.11)	(13.51)	(11.22)
Cropped area	4,500	5,048	5,826	5,570
	(100)	(100)	(100)	(100)

NOTE: Figures in parentheses are percentage of each crop in the gross cropped area.

SOURCE: Statistical Abstract of Haryana (various years).

TABLE 6-11 Cereal Production, Haryana, 1971 and 1991 (thousand tonnes)

	Year		
Crop	1971	1991	Percent Change
Wheat	2,402	6,496	170
Rice	536	1,803	236
Coarse grains	923	506	–45
Total cereals	3,861	8,805	128
Pulses	682	273	60
Foodgrains	4,545	9,078	100

SOURCE: Statistical Abstract of Haryana (various years).

parcels of much of the available land. While conversion of the agricultural land to purposes other than agricultural is generally not permitted, farmers do make almost all the other decisions related to crop production and allocation of land.

Effects of the Green Revolution on the Arid and Semiarid Regions

Haryana is a relatively small state in area, but, like other states, its climate, rainfall, soils, and infrastructure development vary widely across districts. Because these factors have a significant impact on the economy of each administrative unit, a study that correlates population and land use at the district level is useful. Such a study does have its limitations, however, because district boundaries have changed over time for administrative purposes without regard for agroclimatological and ecological differences.

The districts of Haryana can be classified into two main agroecological regions: arid and semiarid (Table 6-12). The semiarid region is further subdivided into the central and southern tracts. These regions differ in cropping patterns, level of agricultural technology, and infrastructure development. A more disaggregated analysis can be carried out at the regional level using the detailed agroclimatic/ecological characteristics furnished by the National Bureau of Soil Survey and Land Use Planning (1992) and presented by Vashishtha et al. (1999). However, a grouping of districts into arid and semiarid regions is more helpful in understanding broadly the nature of the forces driving land use change. Values of certain parameters computed for the arid and semiarid regions on the basis of aggregation of districts into two regions are not perfectly accurate. Yet the benefit of offering an intertemporal comparison far outweighs the loss of marginal accuracy (see Vashishtha et al., 1999).

Certain shifts in cropping pattern, however, have occurred in both regions. The semiarid region, with its more favorable conditions for agri-

TABLE 6-12 Classification of Districts by Agroecological Region, Haryana

Region	Soils and Climate	Districts
Arid	Hot arid with desert and saline soils	Mahendragarh, Hisar, Rewari, Bhiwani, Sirsa
Semiarid	Hot semiarid with alluvium-derived soils	Central tract: Karnal, Jind, Kurukshetra, Panipat, Sonipat, Kaithal, Ambala, Yamunanagar Southern tract: Rohtak, Faridabad, Gurgaon

NOTE: The physical boundaries of districts have been divided and reorganized, and new districts have been created over time. In 1971 Haryana had 12 districts, and that figure was used as the base of the intertemporal comparison of change in various parameters at the district level. Central tract areas have intensive irrigation facility. Part of the district of Ambala is a hilly tract. Southern tract areas have poor drainage and waterlogging and are affected by soil salinity.

SOURCE: Prepared by the author on the basis of detailed information provided by: National Bureau of Soil Survey and Land Use Planning. 1992. Agro-Ecological Regions of India. Indian Council of Agricultural Research, Nagpur.

culture, more than doubled its area under rice cultivation from 1971 to 1991—from 272,000 hectares to 574,000 hectares—as the rice–wheat crop rotation became more widespread. Even in the arid region, which is less favorable for agriculture, the area devoted to rice cultivation increased from 19,000 hectares in 1971 to 64,000 hectares in 1991 (Table 6-13). In both regions the area under wheat, the dominant cereal in the state, increased substantially between 1971 and 1991. The area under coarse cereals (bajra) went down drastically.

TABLE 6-13 Area Under Cereal Crops by Region, Haryana, 1971–1991 (thousand hectares)

	Rice			Wheat			Bajra (millet)		
Region	1971	1981	1991	1971	1981	1991	1971	1981	1991
Arid	19.2	41.2	63.6	237.8	396.9	560.7	521.1	535.4	399.5
	(0.9)	(1.6)	(2.6)	(11.7)	(14.9)	(22.9)	(25.6)	(20.1)	(16.3)
Semiarid	271.8	463.4	573.7	939.2	1,165	1245.1	361	316.5	157.1
	(9.0)	(14.6)	(18.4)	(31.2)	(36.8)	(39.9)	(12)	(10)	(5)

NOTE: Figures in parentheses are the percentage each crop occupies of the gross cropped area.

SOURCE: Prepared by the author based on district-level data obtained from Statistical Abstract of Haryana (various issues).

Expansion of irrigated area and a price policy favoring oilseeds and cotton were common factors in the pattern shifts. In the arid region both oilseeds and cotton gained at the cost of pulses, while in the semiarid region only oilseeds replaced pulses. Higher prices as well as the technological thrust to raise productivity for oilseeds were mainly responsible for making this crop more profitable. As for pulses, although prices rose significantly over the period 1971–1991, the lack of technological breakthroughs in yield kept it a low-priority crop, even in the arid region.

One marked difference in the cropping patterns of the two regions is that the semiarid region uses a much higher percentage of area for water-intensive crops (Table 6-14). For example, in 1991 in the arid region cereals accounted for about 43 percent of the gross cropped area (GCA), pulses 11 percent, oilseeds 18 percent, and cotton 18 percent. By contrast, in 1991 in the semiarid region cereals accounted for 68 percent of the GCA, pulses 4 percent, oilseeds 9 percent, and cotton 2 percent. Rice cultivation occupied only a small portion of the GCA—3 percent—in the arid region in 1991 and 18 percent of the GCA in the semiarid region (Table 6-13). The expansion of area used for cultivating rice in the semiarid region has been impressive, increasing from 9 percent in 1971 to 18 percent in 1991.

TABLE 6-14 Area Under Major Crops as Percentage of Gross Cropped Area by Region, Haryana, 1971–1991

	Cereals	Pulses	Oilseed	Cotton	Sugarcane	Total
1971						
Arid region	40.8	32.9	4.4	9.7	0.6	88.3
Semiarid region	63.7	17.8	2.9	1.5	3.4	89.3
Central tract	65.8	14.5	2.0	1.9	3.5	87.6
Southern tract	61.2	21.8	4.0	1.0	3.3	91.4
All Haryana	54.5	23.9	3.5	4.8	2.3	88.9
1981						
Arid region	39.0	30.9	4.8	10.5	0.4	85.5
Semiarid region	69.3	9.3	2.8	1.6	4.2	87.3
Central tract	71.2	7.7	1.8	1.9	4.7	87.3
Southern tract	65.3	12.8	5.1	0.9	3.2	87.3
All Haryana	55.5	19.1	3.7	5.7	2.5	86.5
1991						
Arid region	43.4	11.3	17.6	18.2	0.3	90.8
Semiarid region	68.1	3.6	8.7	2.0	4.9	87.2
Central tract	71.6	2.8	4.3	2.4	5.4	86.6
Southern tract	58.9	5.5	19.7	0.9	3.6	88.8
All Haryana	57.2	7.0	12.6	9.1	2.9	88.8

SOURCE: Prepared by the author based on district-level data obtained from Statistical Abstract of Haryana (various issues).

TABLE 6-15 Soil Degradation by Agroecological Region, Haryana

	Area (square kilometers)	(as percent of all Haryana)	Degraded Area (square kilometers)	(as percent of all Haryana)	(percent of region)
Arid region	18,937	42.83	6,410	14.50	33.85
Semiarid region	25,275	57.17	8,267	18.70	32.71
Central tract	15,999	45.57	6,101	13.80	38.14
Southern tract	9,276	11.60	2,166	4.90	23.35
All Haryana	44,212	100.00	14,678	33.20	33.20

NOTE: These figures are approximate, because the area has been computed by superimposing arid and semiarid zones of Haryana showing district boundaries.

SOURCE: Prepared by the author based on district-level data obtained from the National Bureau of Soil Survey and Land Use Planning. 1996–1997. Soil of India. NBSS Publication 44, Series 3. Indian Council of Agricultural Research, Nagpur.

Both the arid and semiarid regions suffer from soil degradation of one kind or another (Table 6-15). About one-third of both regions are categorized as degraded area. In the central tract of the semiarid region, the heart of Haryana's rice production, 39 percent of the land suffers from degradation; the water table in this region also is markedly low.

TABLE 6-16 Yield of Major Crops by Region, Haryana, 1971–1991 (kilograms per hectare)

	Cereals	Pulses	Oilseed	Cotton	Sugarcane
1971					
Arid region	1,001.9	476	547.9	351.2	4,621.8
Semiarid region	1,577.7	683	575.2	218.7	4,476.6
Central tract	1,842.5	707	585.7	209.5	4,594.3
Southern tract	1,224.8	664	568.8	240.0	4,321.3
All Haryana	1,403.9	568	561.4	326.9	4,491.7
1981					
Arid region	1,352.8	319	696.8	366.7	3,153.2
Semiarid region	1,953.8	287	692.9	280.0	4,037.3
Central tract	2,180.5	180	725.2	285.4	3,941.2
Southern tract	1,423.6	426	668.0	255.9	4,343.8
All Haryana	1,761.1	311	695.2	353.4	3,969.7
1991					
Arid region	2,479.5	660	1,102.4	471.3	5,588.2
Semiarid region	2,903.7	806	1,046.2	301.8	5,626.2
Central tract	3,115.5	912	1,233.1	316.4	5,778.7
Southern tract	2,246.9	670	941.2	207.3	5,046.7
All Haryana	2,762.4	702	1,080.7	450.7	5,624.6

SOURCE: Prepared by the author based on district-level data obtained from Statistical Abstract of Haryana (various issues).

The overall difference in productivity between the arid and semiarid regions is narrowing over time (Table 6-16). While the semiarid region has attained much higher yields of cereals and pulses than the arid region, the latter has performed better with crops that require relatively little water such as oilseed and cotton. In 1971 cereal yields in the semiarid region were 57 percent higher than in arid region. By 1991 this difference in yield had declined to 17 percent. By contrast, in 1971 the cotton yield in the arid region was greater than that in the semiarid region, and the difference had increased further by 1991.

The semiarid region has more advanced irrigation and agricultural technology than the arid region as indicated by the number of tube wells and tractors per thousand hectares of net sown area utilized by the semiarid region from 1971 to 1991. But in both regions the amount of fertilizer applied per hectare and the percentage of irrigated area increased signifi-

TABLE 6-17 Proxy for Agricultural Technology by Region, Haryana, 1971–1991

	Gross Irrigated Area as Percent of Gross Cropped Area	Cropping Intensity (percent)	Use of Agricultural Technology (per thousand hectares of net sown area)		Fertilizer Consumption (kilograms per hectare)
			Tube Wells	Tractors	
1971					
Arid region	41.5	139	10.1	3.0	7.3
Semiarid region	49.2	143	50.4	6.7	18.3
Central tract	62.1	147	64.2	7.2	26.5
Southern tract	33.1	138	34.4	6.2	8.1
All Haryana	46.1	142	33.9	5.2	13.9
1981					
Arid region	50.9	163	33.4	17.8	20.5
Semiarid region	66.3	156	100.0	38.5	55.6
Central tract	75.2	161	122.1	46.5	72.3
Southern tract	47.4	147	56.9	22.9	19.8
All Haryana	59.3	159	70.3	29.3	39.6
1991					
Arid region	70.7	159	77.4	49.5	84.6
Semiarid region	83.5	159	195.5	83.8	121.4
Central tract	90.9	169	230.6	95.8	142.0
Southern tract	64.8	138	122.4	58.6	69.0
All Haryana	77.9	159	143.6	68.7	105.3

SOURCE: Prepared by the author based on district-level data obtained from Statistical Abstract of Haryana (various issues).

cantly during this period (Table 6-17). The level of adoption of high-yielding rice varieties did not differ significantly between the two regions. While differences in the pattern of crop allocations and agricultural development between the two regions can be attributed in part to differences in their climatic and natural resource endowments, the regional differences also have been accentuated by policies that tend to favor the better-endowed regions. Although several public policies influence the pace and pattern of development, two of these policies—on infrastructure development and the pricing of crop inputs and outputs—appear to be critical.

The policies on crop input and output pricing, unlike the infrastructure policies, do not have an apparent regional bias. Most of these policies are decided at the national level and do not vary much across states. Within the state, the pricing of inputs and outputs does not differ between regions, but the pricing policies tend to favor the better-endowed regions indirectly by offering more remunerative prices for crops suitable for cultivation in such regions. Because these crops use large amounts of fertilizer, water, and electricity, input subsidies prove more beneficial to farmers in the better-endowed regions. Even research and extension activities favor the crops suitable for cultivation in such regions. Thus unintended biases emerge from the actual implementation of such policies. The better-endowed regions gain relatively more, although not at the expense of the less-well-endowed regions.

WATER RESOURCES

Paradoxically, Haryana is facing the threat of a declining water table because of the exploitation of resources in some areas and a rising water table caused by increased waterlogging and soil salinity in others. The decline in the water table is more marked in the semiarid region than in the arid region. The semiarid region, which has good groundwater quality, derives approximately 80 percent of water for irrigation and drinking purposes from subsurface sources. The arid region, by contrast, consists of desert and drought-prone areas and has poor groundwater quality. Approximately 76 percent of the water used for irrigation in the arid region is obtained from surface water canals.

Declining Water Table

Over the last two and a half decades a shift has been observed in the cropping pattern for irrigated crops in Haryana. The area devoted to wheat cultivation has increased by more than 150 percent, and the area used for the cultivation of paddy, a highly water-intensive crop, has increased threefold (Gangwar and van den Toorn, 1987; Joshi and Tyagi,

1991). After remunerative price policies for paddy rice were initiated in the late 1970s, the area devoted to rice cultivation expanded, resulting in exploitation of groundwater resources. Subsidies for the use of electricity in the rural sector and the lack of regulatory measures for the use of groundwater only exacerbated the exploitation and encouraged ineffi-cient use of groundwater. As a result, the water table declined rapidly, especially in the semiarid region.

At the state level, more groundwater could be harnessed, because only 68 percent of the resources are being utilized (M. C. Agarwal, 1995). The semiarid region, however, is experiencing an average fall in the water table of 0.3–0.6 meters annually, indicating that groundwater utilization is exceeding recharge. The districts of Yamunanagar, Karnal, Kurukshetra, and Ambala have shown signs of overextraction, and in other districts the rate of decline of the water table is alarming. In Kurukshetra the water table declined from 8.2 meters in 1974 to 17.8 meters in 1994 (Table 6-18). The phenomenon of a declining water table is not confined to the semi-arid region. In Mahendragarh, in the arid region, the water table declined from 19.7 meters in 1974 to 30.4 meters in 1994. The cost of replenishing groundwater in these locations will be enormous if the trend continues. For example, according to the Tata Energy Research Institute (TERI), the cost of replenishing groundwater in districts like Karnal and Panipat is likely to be Rs. 371 million ($8.5 million) and Rs. 169 million ($3.9 million), respectively.

The overdependence on subsurface sources of groundwater stems from low natural recharge, meager tanks and surface water reservoirs, and uncertain and low canal water supplies in good-quality groundwater zones (R. P. Agarwal, 1995; Singh, 1995; Tanwar, 1994). Researchers and

TABLE 6-18 Water Table in Selected Districts of Haryana

District	Water Table Depth in October 1974 (meters)	Water Table Depth in October 1994 (meters)	Rate of Fall of Water Table (meters/year)	Projected Water Table Depth in 2047, Assuming Past Trends (meters)
Karnal	5.27	8.47	0.16	17.00
Panipat	4.60	7.90	0.17	18.00
Rewari	11.85	15.80	0.20	26.00
Kurukshetra	8.18	17.79	0.48	41.00
Mahendragarh	19.65	30.41	0.54	57.00

NOTE: The districts of Karnal, Panipat, and Kurukshetra are in the semiarid region; the others are in the arid region (see Table 6-12).

SOURCE: The figures on water table depth in October 1974 and October 1994 were ob-tained from the State Groundwater Board, Chandigarh, Haryana.

others fear that overuse has lowered the water yield from tube wells. Lower yield may affect overall irrigation efficiency at the farm level, thereby increasing energy consumption and operating costs as farmers must pump water for longer hours to irrigate the same area. Otherwise, they must increase operating costs by purchasing high-powered electric motors. This situation often leads to conflicts and competition over the use of the resource.[5] In addition, the falling water table already has contributed toward a nutritional imbalance, deterioration in soil health and texture, and the emergence of weeds and insects (Tanwar, 1994).

The falling water table in Haryana does not result entirely from the overuse associated with paddy cultivation and maintaining the rice–wheat rotation. It also results from faulty drainage operations, leading to a diminished recharge. This situation was brought about by the increased drainage efficiency achieved by the large-scale construction of river control works and lined drains, which had the secondary effect of reducing recharge of the aquifer (Tanwar, 1994). Thus the environmental problems related to the falling water table must be addressed on two levels: at the policy level, by discouraging the rice–wheat rotation, and at the operations level, by dealing with the engineering aspects of drainage operations. The underlying problem is that profit-driven farmers are making excessive use of groundwater through tube wells. The problem of faulty drainage calls for appropriate technical solutions.[6]

Waterlogging and Salinization

In contrast to the emerging water scarcity in Haryana's semiarid region, the water table is rising elsewhere in the state, primarily in the arid region. This rise is occurring below canals underlain with brackish and highly saline water, leading to waterlogging and salinization. Estimates reveal that nearly 65 percent of the central, southern, and western parts of the state covering districts such as Sirsa, Jind, Bhiwani, and Hisar are affected by waterlogging. Heavy rainfall, compounded by high discharges from the rivers and inadequate drainage outlets to the Yamuna and Ghaggar Rivers, has contributed to a rise in the level of groundwater, increased waterlogging, and salinity. As a result, the water level in the area is rising at a rate of 0.30–1.0 meters a year (Tanwar, 1997).

---

[5]Interstate conflicts over water sharing, intrabasin conflicts between upstream and downstream users of water, and allocation of water between domestic and agriculture uses are problems in various parts of India. See Chopra and Bathla (1997) and Bhalla and Singh (1996) for descriptions of such conflicts in Punjab and the Sabarmati basin in Gujarat.

[6]Tanwar (1994) points out that drainage systems should not be overly oriented toward flood management. In fact, they should be regulated and reoriented to focus on water conservation and recharging.

Overall, an estimated 18 percent (8,000 square kilometers) of the state is waterlogged, of which 3,500 square kilometers are highly saline (Tanwar, 1997). The waterlogging will degrade some areas, and flooding could be more frequent and severe in the future. Chaudhary Charan Singh Haryana Agricultural University (1996–1997) has estimated the loss in agricultural production from waterlogging and soil salinity at Rs. 270 million ($6.2 million). The amount may increase to Rs. 860 million ($20 million) in 2000 if no remedial measures are taken to rectify the situation.

Water Table Dynamics

A study of water table dynamics in the semiarid district of Karnal has just been completed by the Agricultural Economic Research Centre at the University of Delhi (Bathla, 1998). Researchers chose this district for further analysis because it is representative of irrigated, mechanized, and agriculturally developed cropping systems and because it faces exploitation of its water resources. To examine the potential water scarcity in Karnal, they enlisted a dynamic model that simulates the interactions between water resources and agricultural demand. Researchers determined the annual water supply through observed precipitation patterns and the hydrological cycle. They then linked the hydrological cycle to demands originating from increases in cropping intensity and population growth rate in the district's rural and urban areas.

The simulation was conducted over a 30-year period, 1997–2027; it assumes no changes in cropping pattern and policy interventions in that period.[7] Model results reveal that Karnal receives an average of 210,000 hectare-meters of replenishable recharge in its annual groundwater supply, including the initial stock. The estimated base year demand, derived on the basis of crop requirements and drinking water norms, is approximately 300,000 hectare-meters for irrigation, 3,500 hectare-meters for drinking water, and 2,000 hectare-meters for industrial uses. The irrigation demand is projected to rise to 450,000 hectare-meters in 2027, based on an increase in cropping intensity of 1.3 percent a year. Of the total estimated irrigation demand, approximately 65 percent will be met by groundwater resources, the rest by surface water and rainfall.

The model indicates that when demand for drinking water is given priority, the total demand for water for irrigation purposes is constrained by the supply over the simulation period. The result, then, is an unsustainable pattern of resource use, where the extraction of the resource exceeds its supply. If the existing pattern of resource use continues and the resource is extracted to meet demand, the water table will continue to

---

[7]A statistical package, SENECA (Simulation Environment for Ecological Applications), was used to develop and implement the simulation model.

decline at the annual rate of 11 centimeters over the period 1997–2007, 9.4 centimeters over 2007–2017, and 7.9 centimeters over 2017–2027. If it is assumed that land allocation in Haryana is more responsive to the price of rice-wheat relative to the price of sugarcane, more land will be allocated to the cultivation of rice, thereby contributing to the overuse of water.

As long as farmers are able to manage the declining water table by incurring higher capital costs to pump water from greater depths, and as long as they continue to reap profits from farming, they will likely continue the existing rice–wheat cropping sequences.[8] Nevertheless, the growing shortage of water may defeat the goals of achieving higher levels of foodgrain production and productivity and endanger efforts to achieve sustainable use of the resources.

Water Resource Policies

The falling water table is a direct threat to the future of agriculture in Haryana. Policy alternatives for conserving and increasing the water supply are available, however. They include support for development of technological options; implementation of incentives for efficient water allocation and use; and pricing of crop inputs and outputs to encourage cultivation of less water-intensive crops.

Artificial recharge, efficient irrigation practices, and a watershed management approach that saves and mobilizes water resources have long been implemented in Haryana, but it is essential to continue these operations. Moreover, information should be adequately disseminated on optimum irrigation scheduling and efficient irrigation practices in the case of water-intensive crops, with the objective of conserving water without a negative impact on crop yields. Sophisticated technologies, such as drip and sprinkler irrigation, should be evaluated, but these technologies may not be feasible or easily accessible because of the high capital costs involved.

Water must be used efficiently and allocated equitably across regions. A reduction in per capita water consumption or a reduction in quantity allocated can aid in conserving existing water resources. Researchers have recommended that, on an international level, populations reduce their water consumption, meeting a basic water requirement criterion of 50 liters per capita per day in urban areas (Gleick, 1997). India's Ministry of Urban Development (1991) has recommended a quantity of 70–100 liters per capita per day, which is believed sufficient to meet urban domestic requirements. In Karnal the urban population consumes 225 liters per capita per day, which is quite high in view of the recommended consumption level.

---

[8]Lower discharge rates and the higher cost of pumping water will adversely affect small farmers, who may lack access to water.

Changes in the state-level commodity pricing policies are another avenue toward conserving resources. The output pricing of products can, at best, encourage the substitution of less water-intensive crops for wheat and paddy, but in light of the present trend toward adopting the highly profitable rice–wheat production sequence, such a substitution may not be feasible in Haryana. Farmers could increase the area used to cultivate vegetables and fruits, but, because storage facilities for these perishable commodities are not available, farmers often do not fetch higher returns for these crops.

An increase in input prices could have a substantial impact on efficient use of available resources. At present, the state government provides subsidized electricity to farmers based on a flat rate structure. The government might consider following a more rational pricing policy, based on a unit rate, that would prevent exploitation and misuse of water resources.[9] Moreover, if consumers were aware of the growing water scarcity in the region, they might find higher electricity charges more acceptable, provided the power supply is uninterrupted. In one of the studies done in the Karnal and Kurukshetra Districts of Haryana, water consumers were willing to pay one-third more than the present rate of Rs. 29 (0.67 cents) per BHP (break horsepower) per month for a dependable supply of electricity. Indeed, during kharif season, when rice is grown, they were willing to pay from Rs. 30.2 (0.70 cents) to Rs. 78.9 (2 cents) per BHP per month, or an average of Rs. 40.1 (0.9 cents) per BHP per month (Malik and Goldar, 1998).

A mix of these policy measures could be adopted to solve the emerging problem of water depletion in Haryana. Government intervention also is required to achieve a solution. India's Ministry of Water Resources has proposed a bill that would regulate and control the development of groundwater (Government of India, 1992). It proposes to set up a single, unified agency of the groundwater authority at the state level, which would operate under the jurisdiction of the Central Groundwater Authority.[10] The former would regulate and manage groundwater resources through technical planning and also take the necessary remedial measures. Moreover, it would help to create awareness of the need for judicious use of water and promote education among farmers and other users. The canal irrigation system also should be reviewed in accordance with the irrigation demands of the existing cropping pattern across districts.

---

[9]Researchers have found that farmers are overirrigating rice and wheat to safeguard the crops against electric power disruptions.

[10]Personal communication with B. S. Tanwar, director, Haryana State Minor Irrigation and Tubewell Corporation, Karnal.

SOCIOECONOMIC INDICATORS

A closer look at changes in the size and composition of income across different sectors of Haryana's economy will shed light on the dynamics of population and land use in the state over time. This section examines the nature of the economic changes and changes in household consumption taking place in Haryana.[11]

Economic Indicators

In India the primary sector consists of agriculture, forestry, logging, fishery, mining, and quarrying; the secondary sector is made up largely of manufacturing; and the tertiary sector comprises services that support other sectors and expands along with urbanization. The absolute number of workers engaged in each sector has increased substantially over time, and the distribution of workers engaged across sectors has changed significantly as well. According to the census of India, the proportion of workers engaged in the primary sector was 48 percent in 1971 and 55 percent in 1991. The proportion of these workers has gone up as the proportion of those engaged in the secondary and tertiary sectors has gone down. The share of workers in industry declined from 19 percent in 1971 to 15 percent in 1991, and the share of workers in the service sector declined from 33 percent to 30 percent over the same period.

In 1970 the per capita net state domestic product (NSDP) of Haryana was 1.2 times the national average and 1.5 times greater in 1992 (Table 6-19). Among all states, the per capita NSDP of Haryana ranks second, after Punjab. While the contribution of the primary sector to the NSDP declined substantially between 1971 and 1991, its share of workers increased over the same period. The shares of the secondary and tertiary sectors, however, declined over the corresponding period. The primary sector (mainly the agricultural sector) thus continues to absorb large numbers of the workforce despite its decline in relative importance in the NSDP.

Changes in Household Consumption

Consumption patterns changed throughout India between 1972 and 1993 (Table 6-20). In terms of total household expenditures, the overall share of food declined in rural areas from 73 percent in 1972 to 63 percent in 1993 and in urban areas from 65 percent to 55 percent. The share of cereal grains in total food expenditure declined from 63 percent in 1972 to

---

[11]The section on household consumption is largely based on surveys on "Consumer Expenditure in India," carried out in Haryana between 1972 and 1993 by the National Sample Survey Organisation (NSSO).

TABLE 6-19 Per Capita Net Domestic Product at Factor Cost, Haryana and India, 1970–1996 (rupees, at 1980–1981 prices)

	Haryana	India	
Year	(1)	(2)	(1)/(2)
1970	1,944	1,572	1.24
1980	2,370	1,625	1.46
1990	3,467	2,258	1.54
1992	3,411	2,267	1.50
1996	3,956	2,774	1.43

SOURCE: National Accounts Statistics 1998. Central Statistical Organization, Ministry of Planning, Government of India; State Domestic Product 1998, CSO (floppy).

45 percent in 1993 in rural regions and from 42 percent to 32 percent in urban regions. Conversely, the shares of other food products, especially fruits, vegetables, and livestock products, increased significantly. The substantial increase in the per capita monthly household expenditure in both rural and urban areas stemmed from large increases in prices. Expenditures on nonfood items increased more than expenditures on food. A decline in the fraction of income spent for food is customarily recognized as an indicator of improved economic well-being. It is interesting to note that this change occurred in both urban and rural areas.

In Haryana's expenditure on food from 1972 to 1993, the share of cereal grains, as expected, declined significantly in rural and urban areas, indicating a shift in consumption from cereal grains to other food products (Table 6-21). An important feature of the food consumption pattern

TABLE 6-20 Changes in Pattern of Household Expenditures, India, 1972 and 1993 (current prices)

	Rural		Urban	
	1972	1993	1972	1993
Percent share of total expenditure				
Food	72.8	63.2	64.5	54.7
Nonfood	27.2	36.8	35.5	45.3
Percent share of total food expenditure				
Foodgrains	63.1	44.8	42.1	31.7
Fruits and vegetables	6.3	12.3	9.9	14.8
Livestock products	13.4	20.3	19.5	24.1
Edible oil	4.9	7.0	7.5	8.0
Sugar	5.2	4.8	5.6	4.3
Spices and salt	3.8	4.2	3.5	3.8
Beverages and refreshments	3.3	6.6	11.8	13.2

SOURCE: Sarvekshana, Vol. 2 (January 1979) and Vol. 20 (October–December 1996), National Sample Survey Organisation.

TABLE 6-21 Monthly Average Household Consumption Expenditure on Food, Haryana, 1972 and 1993 (rupees, at current prices)

	Rural			Urban		
Product	1972	1993	Percent Change	1972	1993	Percent Change
Per capita monthly expenditure (rupees)						
Food	46.97	231.24	392	44.19	255.33	478
Foodgrains	19.80	59.10	198	14.94	61.19	309
Vegetables	1.86	16.95	811	2.80	25.25	802
Fruits	0.48	6.10	1,170	1.61	12.62	683
Milk and dairy products	16.16	98.19	507	12.56	87.08	593
Meat, fish, and eggs	0.35	1.77	405	0.62	3.43	453
Sugar	4.83	20.68	328	3.80	16.05	322
Edible oil	0.87	9.13	949	2.97	16.85	467
Beverages and refreshments	1.52	11.78	675	3.32	24.26	630
Percent share of total food expenditure (percent)						
Foodgrains	42.15	25.55	−17	33.80	23.96	−10
Vegetables	3.96	7.34	3.4	6.33	9.89	3.6
Fruits	1.02	2.64	1.6	3.64	4.94	1.3
Milk and dairy products	34.41	42.46	8.05	28.42	34.10	5.7
Meat, fish, and eggs	0.75	0.76	0.1	1.41	1.35	−0.1
Sugar	10.28	8.95	−1.3	8.60	6.28	−2.32
Edible oil	1.84	3.95	2.11	6.72	6.60	−0.12
Spices and salt	2.35	3.26	0.91	3.56	3.37	−0.19
Beverages and refreshments	3.24	5.09	1.85	7.52	9.51	1.99
Total food	100	100		100	100	

SOURCE: Sarvekshana, Vol. 2 (January 1979) and Vol. 20 (October–December 1996), National Sample Survey Organisation.

was the relatively higher expenditure on milk and dairy products. In 1972 these products accounted for 34 percent of the expenditure on food in rural areas, compared with a national rural average of 10 percent. From 1972 to 1993 the expenditure on dairy products in rural areas increased by 507 percent. As a result, the share of these products in the total expenditure on food increased from 34 to 43 percent over the same period. Dairy products have replaced cereal grains as the most important component of food expenditure in both rural and urban areas.

Trends in Livestock

The rapid growth of agriculture has significantly shifted the pattern of household food consumption in favor of livestock products, particularly milk. Other livestock products, such as meat and eggs, have exhibited marginal increases in consumption. The proportion of households reporting consumption of meat, eggs, and fish in Haryana is smaller than

138 GROWING POPULATIONS, CHANGING LANDSCAPES

the national average proportion, primarily because of the strong religious taboos on nonvegetarian food.[12]

Judging from the large increase in the consumption of livestock products observed over the last three decades, it appears likely that this consumption will continue to increase in Haryana and in India. Because Haryana fulfills a sizable portion of the demand for livestock products from Delhi and several other urban centers, increased consumption of livestock products may bring about significant changes in land use. Production of livestock products requires much more land than production of cereal grains, although currently only 2 percent of cereal grains produced in India are fed to livestock, compared with 20 percent in China, 50 percent in Japan, and 70 percent in the United States (Dunning and Brough, 1991).

Animal husbandry is an integral part of Haryana's agriculture. Several agroclimatic features, such as the dry climate, presence of lime in the soil, availability of abundant grazing land, and predominance of semi-fodder crops, have favored the rearing of quality livestock. Bovines, camels, horses, ponies, mules, donkeys, pigs, sheep, goats, and poultry made up the 1992 livestock census of Haryana. Changes in the livestock population in recent decades are attributable to several factors (Table 6-22). Intensive cultivation of wheat and rice after the spread of the Green Revolution necessitated rapid completion of tillage and sowing operations. Thus farmers invested heavily in tractors and threshers, and the number of bullocks, which constituted about 85 percent of the draft animal force for cultivation, declined by 41 percent between 1972 and 1992. All in all, the number of working animals declined by 13 percent. Their share of total livestock (in terms of standard feed units) declined from 35 percent to 23 percent during this period.

Another factor affecting changes in the livestock population is the increased demand for milk, eggs, and meat caused by the 64 percent increase in the human population and rising incomes. As a result, the number of milch animals increased by 47 percent between 1972 and 1992. Because of the strong cultural taboo against consumption of beef, nonvegetarians depend on goat, sheep, chicken, and pigs for meat. Thus the population of these animals increased substantially over 1972–1992, though it continues to constitute only a small proportion (5 percent) of the total livestock population.

Social Welfare

In spite of making considerable progress on the economic front, particularly in the agricultural sector, Haryana has not shown equally en-

---

[12]National Sample Surveys Organisation, 50th Round, 1993–1994.

TABLE 6-22 Changes in Livestock Population, Haryana, 1972–1992

| Animal | Number (thousands) | | Percent Change |
	1972	1992	1972–1992
Cattle			
Adult male	948.0	557.4	–41.20
Adult female	726.0	716.2	–0.13
Young stock	777.0	860.0	10.68
Total	2,451.0	2,133.6	–12.95
Buffalo			
Adult male	61.8	246.5	298.86
Adult female	1,283.1	2,262.5	76.33
Young stock	1,173.0	1,863.9	58.90
Total	2,517.9	4,372.9	73.67
Others			
Camels	132.8	128.3	–3.38
Horses and mules	33.3	75.2	125.82
Donkeys	72.7	73.6	1.24
Sheep and goats	937.5	1,843.2	96.61
Pigs	143.2	517.3	261.24
Poultry	963.3	8,580.2	790.71
Draft animals			
Cattle	948.0	557.4	–41.20
Buffalo	61.8	246.5	298.86
Camels	132.8	128.3	–3.38
Other (horses, mules, etc.)	106.0	148.8	40.37
Total	1,248.6	1,081.8	–13.42
Milch bovine			
Cattle	717.0	702.8	–1.99
Buffalo	1,273.0	2,219.7	74.36
Total	1,990.0	2,922.5	46.86

SOURCE: Livestock Census, 1972 and 1992.

couraging results in reducing its population growth rate, which is currently 2.5 percent. The National Family Health Survey indicates that fertility rates are lower among women in urban areas than those in rural areas and are inversely proportional to the level of education of women (Table 6-23). Furthermore, urban households have lower infant mortality rates than rural households. Infant mortality rates seem to decline with higher levels of education among women and with the availability of maternal and prenatal care.

High income standing and relatively high human development in Haryana do not appear to translate into improved welfare for all segments of society. Of the sixteen major states of India, Haryana ranks third

TABLE 6-23 Fertility and Infant Mortality Rates by Selected Background Characteristics, Haryana, 1993

Background Characteristic of Woman	Desired Fertility Rate (desired number of children per woman in the 15–45 age group) (1)	Total Fertility Rate (number of children per woman in the 15–45 age group) (2)	Infant Mortality Rate (number of infant deaths per thousand live births) (3)	Under 5 Mortality (number of deaths in the age group 0–5 per thousand children below 5 years of age) (4)
Residence				
Urban	2.16	3.14	59.20	80.60
Rural	3.05	4.32	86.20	116.40
Education				
Illiterate	3.33	4.69	86.60	121.80
Literate				
Less than middle school completed	2.58	3.52	77.20	95.50
Middle school completed	2.26	3.48	66.00	68.50
High school completed	2.06	2.75	46.30	50.80
Medical maternity care				
No prenatal or delivery care			87.00	113.70
Either prenatal or delivery care			71.00	84.40
Both prenatal and delivery care			57.07	68.70
Total	2.81	3.99	79.70	107.60

NOTE: Information in columns (1) and (2) refers to the three years preceding the survey. Information in columns (3) and (4) refers to the 10-year period preceding the survey.

SOURCE: National Family Health Survey (NFHS) 1992–1993: India, Haryana, Kerala, Tamil Nadu, Uttar Pradesh. International Institute for Population Sciences, Bombay.

in income and sixth in human development. Yet Haryana ranks ninth in terms of a gender-related health index and tenth in female literacy rate, indicating that females appear to be at a disadvantage in social status, health, and education.

CONCLUSION

Known as a Green Revolution state, Haryana has become the breadbasket of India, playing a crucial role in the food security of the nation. Because Haryana's rice and wheat production far exceeds the demand for these two crops by the local population, the state has become a net exporter of these crops to the rest of the nation. Most of the production surpluses are procured by government agencies for sale through public distribution system networks in India.

The Green Revolution also brought profound changes in land use in Haryana through a complex set of interacting biophysical and socioeconomic factors. The driving forces behind land use change in both semiarid and arid regions are increased cultivation intensity, utilization of high-yielding varieties of wheat and rice, and high inputs of fertilizer and water. Other forces are infrastructure development, private investment in irrigation sources, and a wheat/rice support policy regulated by the government of India.

Even though Haryana has benefited from its enormous agricultural achievements brought about by the Green Revolution, its success is built on a receding water resource. Intensification of agriculture has caused the groundwater table to drop in some areas and has caused waterlogging in others. The economic growth resulting from urbanization, industrialization, and the changing lifestyles of an increasing population also has led to overextraction of groundwater. Equally worrisome, excessive use of fertilizers and pesticides has led to a deterioration of land and soil quality.

To cope with falling water tables, farmers often must replace their pumps with higher-capacity ones and incur higher capital and operating costs to pump the same amount of water from a greater depth. The thousands of farmers with small operational holdings in Haryana who meet a large part of their staple food requirements from rice and wheat are unlikely to comprehend the long-term problems of resource degradation and environmental pollution and thus are likely to continue this lucrative cropping system. Such a development could deteriorate the environmental resource base and make the rice–wheat cropping sequence environmentally unsustainable. In response, researchers are trying to identify technologies that are more resource conserving and less environmentally polluting. Government policy initiatives also could be used to encourage farmers to adopt such technologies, thereby enhancing food security and environmental sustainability.

In fact, government policies are responsible for changes in land use patterns aimed at intensification of agriculture and development. These policies generally give priority to expansion of canals and groundwater irrigation through large-scale investments, the provision of subsidized electricity for tube wells, credit and marketing facilities, crop output price supports, and other institutional support. The policies related to infrastructure development and pricing of crop inputs and outputs seem to be the most crucial.

While the Green Revolution has contributed to achieving food security in Haryana as well as in the country at large, environmental constraints arising out of the shifts in cropping patterns in favor of crop rotation such as rice–wheat are beginning to surface. The development policies aimed at increasing the production of cereal grains did not take into consideration the possible effects of these policies on the environment and the use of natural resources. Some of the research results indicate that factor productivity and the input use efficiency of the system are declining and that crop yields in the system lack sustainability. Average crop yields have been increasing, yet the rate of increase in crop yields is on the decline; they have not been rising in proportion to the increased use of inputs. As a result, although the rice–wheat farming system is still financially profitable and economically viable, the profitability of the system is declining. Thus the sustainability of the Green Revolution in Haryana in economic, social, and environmental terms is now a matter of serious concern.

ACKNOWLEDGMENTS

This paper is based on Vashishtha et al. (1999), the project report prepared for the Indian National Science Academy and the National Research Council, USA. The authors are grateful to P. S. Ramakrishnan for being a constant source of encouragement to the study team at all stages of this study, to Gordon M. Wolman for steering the proceedings of the Tri-Academy meetings, and to Michael Greene for a very patient and meticulous handling of both academic and administrative problems of the project. The authors would also like thank their colleagues C. S. C. Sekhar and Narinder Singh for data management, Soma Bhattacharya for her efficient and untiring research assistance in bringing the study to the present form, Moolchand and S. P. Sharma for helping in field trips, and N. L. Sharma and Munish Sindwani for providing overall administrative and secretarial support. Thanks are due to the Indian National Science Academy, particularly to A. K. Jain, collaboration with whom made the implementation of the project possible.

REFERENCES

Agarwal, M. C. 1995. Extent and utilisation of groundwater resources in Haryana. In: Proceedings of 2nd Dr. D. P. Motiramani Memorial Lecture and Panel Discussion on Agricultural Water Management: Issues and Priorities, October 21, 1995, Chaudhary Charan Singh Haryana Agricultural University, Hisar.

Agarwal, R. P. 1995. Water management in rice–wheat cropping system in Haryana. In: Proceedings of 2nd Dr. D. P. Motiramani Memorial Lecture and Panel Discussion on Agricultural Water Management: Issues and Priorities, October 21, 1995, Chaudhary Charan Singh Haryana Agricultural University, Hisar.

Bathla, S. 1998. Sustainability of Land and Water Resources in Haryana: Some Ecology–Economy Interactions. Report submitted to Agricultural Economic Research Centre (AERC), University of Delhi, Delhi.

Bhalla, G. S., and G. Singh. 1996. Impact of GATT on Punjab Agriculture. Chandigarh: Institute for Development and Communication.

Chaudhary Charan Singh Haryana Agricultural University (CCSHAU), Hisar. 1996–1997. Indo–Dutch Operational Research Project on Hydrological Studies. Project initiated by CCSHAU, Hisar; International Institute for Land Reclamation and Improvement, The Netherlands; and DLO Win and Staring Centre for Irrigated Land, Soil and Water Research, The Netherlands.

Chopra, K., and S. Bathla. 1997. Water Use in the Punjab Region: Conflicts and Frameworks for Resolution. Paper presented at the IDPAD Seminar on Managing Water Scarcity: Experience and Prospects, Amerfoort, The Netherlands, October 1997.

Dunning, A. B., and H. B. Brough. 1991. Taking Stock: Animal Farming and the Environment. Worldwatch Paper 103, July.

Gangwar, A. C., and W. H. van den Toorn. 1987. The economics of adverse groundwater conditions in Haryana state. Indian Journal of Agricultural Economics 42(April–June).

Gleick, Peter H. 1997. Human population and water: Meeting basic needs in the 21st century. In: Population, Environment and Development, R. K. Pachauri and L. F. Quershy, eds. New Delhi: Tate Energy Research Institute.

Government of India. 1992. Model Bill to Regulate and Control the Development of Groundwater. Ministry of Water Resources, Government of India.

Grover, D., et al. 1998. Haryana: Current population scenario, problems, policies and strategic thrust areas for the future. Photocopy.

Indian Council of Agricultural Research (ICAR). 1998. Decline in Crop Productivity in Haryana and Punjab: Myth or Reality? Report of the Fact-Finding Committee, Indian Council of Agricultural Research, New Delhi.

Joshi, P. K., and N. K. Tyagi. 1991. Sustainability of existing farming system in Punjab and Haryana—Some issues in groundwater use. Indian Journal of Agricultural Economics 46(July–September).

Malik, R. P. S., and B. N. Goldar. 1998. Electricity Pricing and Sustainable Use of Groundwater: Farmers' Willingness to Pay for Electricity in Haryana. Paper presented at the Third Applied Development Economics Workshop, Centre for Development Economics, Delhi School of Economics, January 15–17, 1998.

Ministry of Urban Development, Government of India. 1991. Manual on Water Supply and Treatment. 3d ed. Prepared by the Expert Committee Constituted by Government of India, Central Public Health and Environmental Engineering Organisation, Ministry of Urban Development, New Delhi, March.

National Bureau of Soil Survey and Land Use Planning. 1992. Agro-Ecological Regions of India. Indian Council of Agricultural Research, Nagpur.

Richards, J. F. et al. 1994. Historic Land Use and Carbon Estimates for South and Southeast Asia, 1880–1980. Environmental Sciences Division Publ. No. 4174. ORNL/CDIAC-61 NDP-046, Oak Ridge National Laboratory.

Singh, P. 1995. Efficient utilisation of canal water. In: Proceedings of 2nd Dr. D. P. Motiramani Memorial Lecture and Panel Discussion on Agricultural Water Management: Issues and Priorities, October 21, 1995, Chaudhary Charan Singh Haryana Agricultural University, Hisar.

Tanwar, B. S. 1994. Environmental Impact of Groundwater Development. Paper presented at the Regional Workshop on Environmental Aspects of Groundwater Development, Kurukshetra, Haryana, October 17–19, 1994.

Tanwar, B. S. 1995. Disposal of drainage effluent options for Haryana. In: Reclamation and Management of Waterlogged Soils, K. V. G. K. Rao, ed. Reclamation and Management of Waterlogged Saline Soils, National Seminar Proceedings, April 5–8, 1994, Central Soil Salinity Research Institute, Karnal, Haryana.

Tanwar, B. S. 1997. Strategy for Water Logging and Flood Control in Canal Commands of the Semiarid Region. Paper accepted for 7th ICID International Drainage Workshop, November 17–21, 1997.

Vashishtha, P. S., R. K. Sharma, and R. P. S. Malik. 1999. Interactions between Population Growth, Consumption and Land Use Change in Haryana (India). Research Study No. 99/2, Agricultural Economics Research Centre, University of Delhi, Delhi.

7

Gender Dimensions of the Relationship Between Population and Land Use in the Indian States of Kerala and Haryana

Sumati Kulkarni
International Institute for Population Sciences,
Mumbai, India

Environmental degradation in developing countries like India, especially its manifestation in the form of soil erosion, deforestation, and desertification, is often attributed to rapid population growth. Many other factors, however, also affect the relationship between population and land. Changes in production techniques, patterns of utilization of natural and human resources, lifestyles, and consumption patterns, as well as industrialization, urbanization, and rising aspirations are just some of the macro-level factors that make the relationship between population and land use much more complex. Land reform and other policies that bring about institutional changes, especially the processes of nationalization (appropriation of natural resources by the state) and privatization (appropriation of community resources by citizens), inject more complications into this relationship.

In a country characterized by poverty and inequality, the complex interplay of these factors can have favorable or adverse effects on different regions and on different classes of society. A group's position in the class hierarchy and in the overall power structure, as well as its environmental vulnerability, are likely to determine its role in the changing patterns of labor utilization. Generally, people from the poorer strata are likely to be the greatest sufferers in this process.

In patriarchal societies, not only class but gender is an important dimension of patterns of labor utilization. Recent feminist research on the effects of development on women has clearly revealed that in many areas of the world colonial and capitalist institutions did not destroy precapitalist institutions. Rather they preserved, blended with, and built on pre-capitalist institutions in ways that often were inimical to women (Hartmann, 1976; Leacock and Safa, 1986). In India, where the population is predominantly rural, few women own land or have access to other resources, including knowledge systems. In fact, the low status of women is reflected in a variety of indicators. In the agricultural sector, for example, most women workers are either landless laborers working for wages on other people's farms or unpaid laborers working on their own family farms. In the meantime, agriculture in India is changing. As a result of the agricultural development spawned by the five-year plans since the 1950s and the Green Revolution in 1970s, India has seen significant changes in its cropping patterns and cropping intensity. As for related developments, since the 1994 UN International Conference on Population and Development in Cairo, India has been committed to a population policy that is pro-poor, pro-nature, and pro-women.

How, then, have women fared in India in the context of a growing population and changing land use? To answer this question, this study will examine the gender dimension of the relationship between population and land use in two states of India, Kerala and Haryana. More specifically, it will examine the following:

• present a suitable framework and hypotheses for examining the gender dimension of the population–land use relationship, with a focus on the Indian experience;
• review briefly the demographic change, social development, and gender gap in Kerala and Haryana for 1971–1991;
• discuss the pattern of land use changes in Kerala and Haryana for 1971–1991;
• explore evidence of gender differentials in employment trends, based on relevant census data; and
• examine the direct evidence available from micro studies of these states on the gender dimension of the population–land use relationship.

A FRAMEWORK FOR AND HYPOTHESES ABOUT THE GENDER DIMENSION OF THE POPULATION–LAND USE RELATIONSHIP IN INDIA

According to Boserup (1989), both the status of women and type of family organization are related to the agricultural system, which in turn is affected by population density and technological choices. A woman's status in a rural society, apart from her role as a mother and wife, depends on how her labor is utilized—a decision made by men. Her contribution to the required labor depends on the type of agricultural system in place, the pattern of land use, the crops grown, and the labor intensity of the methods of cultivation. Although the role of women continues to be largely subordinate to that of men, demographic and land use changes are introducing forces that may lead to new opportunities for women as well as new risks. Such forces can be categorized in the four ways described in this rest of this section.

Effects of Land Use Patterns on the Demand for Female Labor

Boserup (1989) has identified several stages of agricultural development and has described women's role under different land use patterns as follows:

- *Stage One.* In sparsely populated regions with free access to the cultivation of common land, the head of a family can combine the advantages of a large family with a negotiable work burden, with the result that all the work is done by wives and children.
- *Stage Two.* As population density increases, farmers replace long fallow production on common land with more intensive systems of agriculture using animal draft power. In this system men perform all operations involving animals; women and children, using only muscle power, contribute a smaller share of the total agricultural work.
- *Stage Three.* At this stage, growing population density and the expansion of cultivated area lead to increased cash crop production, which in turn leads to another pattern of division of labor by sex. Men produce cash crops; women produce subsistence crops and gather fuel and fodder, which is more labor intensive and is perceived as a low-status activity.
- *Stage Four.* With growing population density and increasing cash crop production, common land tenure moves gradually to private ownership of land. Because having a large family no longer confers the right to additional land, there are fewer inducements to have a large family. With privatization, men become less dependent on family labor, but women become more dependent on their husbands. With more intensive cultivation, the growing season is prolonged by means of irrigation, and women are obliged to do the jobs that involve hand operations. Many of these operations, such as weeding or transplanting rice to permit multicropping, are onerous and highly labor-intensive. The availability of unpaid female family labor promotes the labor intensification of agriculture.
- *Stage Five.* The advent of the Green Revolution in Asia entails the use of both labor-intensive and modern chemical inputs as well as new cropping systems. In this new system the application of chemicals to cash crops and the use of mechanized equipment are considered high-status occupations reserved for males. Thus in all the operations where these new chemicals and devices are used, female labor is systematically replaced by male labor. Once Green Revolution techniques are introduced in rice farming areas, women do much more hand weeding and trans-

planting. They also become assistants to the male operators of the newly introduced rice planting tractors and threshing machines. Such machines, however, do not reduce their work burden; it increases because the machines cover a much larger area. Thus, by and large the intensification of agriculture and diversification of cropping patterns usually lead to a higher demand for female labor. Demand also goes up if those crops requiring labor-intensive methods of cultivation are grown more widely.

Low yield per hectare was a major problem of Indian agriculture before the Green Revolution. Thus in India the Green Revolution has mainly consisted of new cultivation technologies—greater use of irrigation, fertilizers, insecticides, and, above all, high-yielding varieties of seeds. These technologies have been particularly successful in wheat-growing areas such as Punjab.

One result of the Green Revolution is that agriculture in India has been experiencing major changes in cropping patterns. In response, researchers have tried to analyze distinct patterns in the supply and demand for female labor generated by the ecological variations in cropping patterns (Miller, 1981; Rosenzweig and Schultz, 1982). Some have hypothesized that the rice–wheat dichotomy in Indian agriculture broadly coincides with North-South differences in female employment patterns and to some extent with the sex ratios in the population (Agarwal, 1986). Sen (1987) added another agroecologic zone, coarse grain-growing regions, to that analysis. K. Bardhan (1985) elaborated on how women's work is structured in relation to poverty and hierarchy, and Chen (1989) presented empirical evidence of the specific patterns of the work of landless and land-poor women within each zone.

According to Chen (1989), the studies just noted reveal several distinct patterns. Female labor force participation rates are consistently lower in the traditional wheat-growing belt of the northwest (Punjab, Haryana) than in the rice-growing eastern and southern states. Within the rice-growing regions, they are lower in the eastern states than in the southern states. The incidence of female labor is higher in irrigated paddy areas than in nonirrigated areas. Perhaps as a result, in paddy regions high productivity is positively associated with the proportion of female agricultural laborers. However, in wheat- or coarse grain-growing regions high productivity is negatively associated with the proportion of female agricultural laborers, except in hilly or tribal regions.

In all regions except those of rainfed paddy and irrigated wheat, women predominate as family farm labor in all agricultural operations except plowing (done by men) and harvesting (done by both men and women). Weeding, winnowing, drying, storage, and husking or milling traditionally have been left to women across regions. Although the adoption of high-yielding crop varieties generally has increased the demand for labor, the more widespread use of chemical fertilizers and herbicides often has displaced women from typically female-dominated operations such as manuring and weeding. Similarly, the increased mechanization of operations such as planting, hulling, and milling has affected female labor adversely—that is, for women working on their own family farms, use of machines means a smaller workload but also less control over production. In the poorer households, however, female labor and income still play a central role.

Technological development by itself, then, does not ensure that women will be better off. In a male-dominated society, men are likely to take over the functions associated with power and control key decisions. Thus the higher participation of women in productive work alone will not necessarily substantially improve their conditions. So long as they are not involved in decision making, they are not likely to enjoy their due share of the total gains, which increase thanks to technological development. In fact, women may, like other disadvantaged populations, be marginalized in the process, and they may move from a state of dependency to a state of exploitation. This conjecture is borne out by the available evidence. Rural labor employment reports for 1964–1965 and 1974–1975 indicate that for both periods the average number of days of employment was lower for women than for men. When their employment opportunities shrink, women often are forced to work at lower wages. Agarwal (1986) has observed, however, a heartening narrowing of the wage differentials for men and women in the southern states of India.

Effects of the Demographic Transition Process on the Female Labor Supply

Curiously, demographers have identified in India a North-South dichotomy in fertility and mortality levels as well as in the pace of the demographic transition. By and large, the southern states in India, especially Kerala and Tamil Nadu, have achieved birth and death rates significantly lower than those of some northern states such as Uttar Pradesh, Bihar, Madhya Pradesh, and Rajasthan. In addition, demographers have noted a North-South dichotomy in the status of women, and they have attributed lower fertility in the southern states to greater female autonomy associated with the different kinship structure and marriage system prevailing in the south (Dyson and Moore, 1983).

During the demographic transition, mortality usually declines earlier than fertility, and the time lag varies for different populations. Thus the North-South dichotomy can have significant implications for female labor:

• Larger birth cohorts in earlier decades result in larger cohorts of new entrants to the labor force in the current decade.

• The decline in female child mortality means that more females survive to working age.

• The decline in female mortality for working-age groups lengthens the work span of female labor.

• A decline in fertility implies a smaller burden of child-bearing and -rearing, as well as a reduced role conflict because of the smaller family size. These behavioral changes can increase women's ability to participate in economic activity.

Thus the demographic transition process is likely to increase the supply of female labor. Whether the larger supply will be reflected in the rising female participation rates will depend on the employment opportunities available to women, which, as noted earlier, are influenced by land use and cropping patterns.

The observed increase in female labor also depends on the extent to which female workers are underenumerated, a phenomenon typical to patriarchal societies. With development and modernization, however, the resulting increased recognition of women's productive work will lead to more accurate enumeration. In India, conceptual, definitional, and operational problems with the censuses and large-scale surveys such as the National Sample Surveys (NSS) generally lead to underenumeration of rural women workers. As a result, the alleged decline in female participation rates has been controversial. A slow shift away from agriculture also has been observed, and there is some evidence of the increasing casualization of the workforce. Often, men and women workers are affected differently by these processes (Unni, 1989). The interplay of the factors affecting the supply and demand for male and female labor is likely to be reflected in different sex ratios among workers in different occupational categories.

Effects of a Decline in Common Property Resources on Women's Lives

Women are likely to be adversely affected by a decline in common property resources; in India, these are community pastures, forests, wasteland, common dumping and threshing grounds, watershed drainage, village ponds, and rivers, rivulets, and their banks and beds. A decline in these resources is associated with a variety of forces such as population pressure, intensification of agriculture, and increased integration of agriculture into the monetized market economy.

Historically, common property resources have been an important source of sustenance in a rural subsistence economy, especially in dry tropical regions. In recent years, the increased marketability and profitability of the products of common property resources have led to their overexploitation, as well as to the privatization of and encroachment on common property resources in many states in India (Jodha, 1989). Jodha, who studied 82 villages located in 21 districts spread among seven states of India, confirms that common property resources have declined by as much as 50 percent in recent years. This decline probably has an adverse effect on the lives of the rural poor, especially women. Because rural women are the main gatherers of fuel, fodder, and water, it is primarily their workday (already averaging 10–12 hours) that lengthens with reduced access to forests, water, and land. In parts of Bihar, where up to a few years ago women in poor households could get wood for self-consumption or sale within a distance of 1–2 kilometers, they now have to trek 8–10 kilometers a day. In some villages of Gujarat, even a daily search of 4–5 hours no longer yields enough wood for fuel (Agarwal, 1988). Given the limited rights in private property resources, common property resources have been for rural women and children among the few independent sources of subsistence. They acquire special significance in areas where women's access to a cash economy and markets is constrained because of strong cultural norms that forbid females to own property. Whenever there is encroachment on or the privatization of common property resources, women and other weaker parts of society are likely to be marginalized in this process and deprived of their sources of subsistence.

Land Use Changes and Their Implications for Women's Health

Clearly women are less likely to be neglected and more likely to be healthy in societies that attach more economic value to their work. In the course of a demographic transition and technological development, the reproductive and productive roles of women are likely to change, and they may become exposed to new health hazards and risks.

Sex differentials in mortality are one striking feature of Indian demography. Female-to-male mortality ratios are lower in southern states than in northern states, and P. Bardhan (1974) has suggested that the higher economic value of women in paddy cultivation is a plausible reason. This hypothesis should be reexamined, however, in the context of the changing division of labor between sexes in the new land use pattern.

More broadly, poor rural women who fetch water and wash clothes near ponds and canals are more directly exposed to waterborne diseases from rivers and ponds polluted by excessive use of fertilizers and pesticides. Women engaged in paddy cultivation have to stand for long hours in paddy fields, and they are more exposed to the problems caused by waterlogging and salinity. Transplanting rice and picking cotton, the jobs typically done by women, expose them to pesticides and may cause limb and vision disabilities or gynecological infections (Mencher and Saradamoni, 1982; Mohan, 1987).

DEMOGRAPHIC PROFILES OF KERALA AND HARYANA

Lying on opposite sides of the Indian subcontinent, the states of Kerala in the south and Haryana in the north are revealing in their demographic differences (see Table 7-1 for a comparison of the two states). The death rate has declined in both Kerala and Haryana, as has the infant mortality rate, and female literacy has increased in Haryana. Nevertheless, there are significant differences in levels of well-being observed in the demographic characteristics of each state.

Kerala, a small state with 3.4 percent of India's population and 1.18 percent of its land area, is sometimes known as a "model state"' because of its impressive achievements on the demographic front even though its economic performance has been poor. Salient features of Kerala's population follow.

• Kerala has always been a high-density state (749 persons per square kilometer in 1991). Even in 1901 its density was twice the average for all India.

• In 1991 Kerala had the lowest crude birth (18 per 1,000) and death (6 per 1,000) rates and the lowest decadal growth (14 percent) of the Indian states.

• The infant mortality rate has declined dramatically in Kerala—from 58 in 1971 to 17 in 1991.

• Fertility declined rapidly in Kerala from 1971 to 1991 (the crude birth rate from 31 to 18 and the total fertility rate from 4 to 1.8), which has helped the state to reach below-replacement-level fertility. The couple protection rate (CPR, defined in Table 7-1) increased from 15 percent to 55 percent over the two decades.

• Kerala has been a net out-migrating state for more than five decades (Zachariah and Irudaya Rajan, 1997) with a predominant outflow to the Gulf countries (0.25 million men from 1971 to 1981).

• Unlike other states, Kerala always had a sex ratio favorable to women (1,036 females per 1,000 males in 1991), indicating both the high status of women and the sex-selective out-migration.

• Kerala's notable achievements in the social development area include high female literacy, higher female life expectancy, high age at marriage for girls, and an excellent health infrastructure (88 percent of infants are delivered in health institutions compared with 25 percent for all India).

• Another important feature of Kerala is its large average settlement size, which makes the provision of social sector services more economical. Nearly 90 percent of the rural population lives in settlements of 10,000 or more.

Haryana has a population size and density almost half that of Kerala, but it is growing at a much faster rate. Its social development parameters tend to be low among those of Indian states.

TABLE 7-1 Demographic Change, Kerala and Haryana, 1971–1991

Indicator		1971	1981	1991
Population (millions)	Kerala	21.3	25.4	29.1
	Haryana	10.0	12.9	16.5
Decadal increase in population	Kerala	26.3	19.2	14.3
(percent; over previous decade)	Haryana	32.2	28.7	27.4
Population density per square kilometer	Kerala	549	655	749
	Haryana	227	292	372
Urban (percent)	Kerala	16.2	18.7	26.4
	Haryana	17.7	21.9	24.6
Sex ratio (females per thousand males)	Kerala	1016	1032	1036
	Haryana	867	870	865
Ages 0–14 (percent)	Kerala	40.3	35.0	29.7
	Haryana	46.2	41.7	37.8
Ages 65 + (percent)	Kerala	4.0	4.8	5.4
	Haryana	3.2	3.7	3.8
Scheduled caste/tribe[a] (percent)	Kerala	9.6	11.0	11.0
	Haryana	18.9	19.1	19.8
Literacy Male	Kerala	66.6	75.8	93.6
(percent)	Haryana	37.3	48.2	69.1
Female	Kerala	54.3	65.7	86.2
	Haryana	14.9	22.3	40.5
Total	Kerala	60.4	70.4	89.8
	Haryana	26.9	36.1	55.8
Crude birth rate per thousand	Kerala	31.1	25.6	17.7
	Haryana	42.1	36.5	31.9
Crude death rate per thousand	Kerala	9.0	6.6	6.3
	Haryana	9.9	11.3	8.6
Exponential growth rate (percent)	Kerala	2.33	1.76	1.34
	Haryana	2.79	2.53	2.42
Total fertility rate (TFR)[b]	Kerala	4.1	2.8	1.8
	Haryana	6.7	5.0	4.0
Infant mortality rate (IMR)[c]	Kerala	58	37	17
	Haryana	72	101	75
Life expectancy[d] Male	Kerala		65.2	66.8
	Haryana		61.4	63.4
Female	Kerala		69.9	72.3
	Haryana		59.6	62.0
Couple protection rate[e]	Kerala	15.2	29.7	55.4
	Haryana	12.2	28.3	55.9

[a] "Scheduled castes/tribes" are socially disadvantaged groups that are given some concessions by law (for example, educational opportunities and jobs) for their upliftment. Haryana does not have a scheduled caste/tribe population.
[b] TFR = average number of children a woman can expect to have throughout her reproductive span according to the current age-specific fertility rates.
[c] IMR = number of deaths within first year of birth per thousand live births.
[d] Life expectancy = expected years of life at time of birth.
[e] "Couple protection rate" is the percentage of couples effectively protected by contraception in a given year. This rate is estimated from the available service statistics, which gives the number of women and men sterilized, number of women using intrauterine devices, number of condoms distributed, and number of oral pill users. It is different from contraceptive prevalence rate, which is the percentage of couples using contraception at a given point in time and is based on survey data.

SOURCES: Office of the Registrar General, Census Commission, and Ministry of Health and Family Welfare, Government of India.

- Unlike Kerala, Haryana has a sex ratio that is unfavorable to females. In fact, in 1991 Haryana had the lowest ratio of all the states in India.
- In 1991 Haryana's death rate was almost as low as that of Kerala, but its birth rate was almost double. Fertility in Haryana is higher than that of Kerala despite the almost same level of couple protection rate, indicating greater use of temporary birth control methods in Haryana. The gap revealed when refined measures are used is much wider for both fertility and infant mortality, which were almost four times higher in Haryana than in Kerala in 1991.
- The population growth rate of Haryana can be explained in part by its rapid decline in mortality unaccompanied by an equally rapid decline in fertility.
- Haryana is a net in-migrating state. Its proportion of in-migrants has been estimated at 12–14 percent and its share of out-migrants at 8–9 percent (CMIE, 1993).
- Haryana has almost the same urbanization level as Kerala, and 56 percent of its rural population is concentrated in villages of 1,000 or more. Haryana has a high and rapidly increasing urban density.
- The gender gap in life expectancy is wider in Haryana than in Kerala, and Haryana is the only state in which men have a higher life expectancy than women.
- The literacy rate is much lower for women than for men in Haryana, and levels for both are substantially lower than those in Kerala. Both states are improving, however.
- In Haryana only 17 percent of births take place in health institutions, much fewer than the 88 percent in Kerala.
- Finally, 88 percent of women in Haryana are married by age 24. The comparable figure for Kerala is only 52 percent (PRC, Kerala University, and IIPS, 1995; PRC, Punjab University, and IIPS, 1995).

Haryana is a rich state that ranked third in per capita state domestic product in 1990–1991 (Rs. 3,499 at constant prices), while Kerala (Rs. 1,886) ranked tenth among the 17 states. In terms of agricultural performance indicators such as gross cropped area per person, per hectare income, and per capita rural income, Haryana is lower than only one state in India, Punjab. It also has a rapidly growing industrial sector.

Yet despite living in a richer state, the women of Haryana are not in as advantageous position as the women of Kerala. Not only is the gender gap in Kerala narrower than in Haryana, Kerala also is known as a state where births are kept down but women are not (Jeffrey, 1993). Historically, a matrilineal system has been a distinguishing feature of Kerala. Social reforms and women's organizations also have contributed to the higher status of women in Kerala.

TABLE 7-2 Land Use Pattern, Haryana, 1971–1990

	Years					
Land Use	1971– 1972	1981– 1982	1982– 1983	1983– 1984	1984– 1985	1989– 1990
Forest	2.51	3.05	3.09	2.97	3.01	2.82
Nonagricultural use	6.66	8.06	7.48	6.82	6.76	6.53
Barren and uncultivated land	4.20	1.59	2.00	2.41	2.39	2.37
Permanent pasture	1.06	0.57	0.62	0.62	0.61	0.89
Miscellaneous tree crops	0.06	0.01	0.01	0.01	0.01	0.07
Cultivable waste	0.85	0.92	1.09	1.06	1.04	0.66
Fallow land other than current fallow	0.00	0.02				
Current fallow	3.60	2.72	3.89	4.20	3.83	3.97
Net sown area	81.05	83.09	81.82	81.92	82.35	81.68

SOURCE: Indian agricultural statistics, Directorate of Economics and Statistics, Department of Agriculture and Co-operation, Ministry of Agriculture, Government of India, New Delhi.

LAND USE TRENDS IN KERALA AND HARYANA

In both Kerala and Haryana, the area put to nonagricultural uses is well under 10 percent but increasing (see Table 7-2 for land use trends in both states). In Kerala the net area sown is about almost 60 percent and increasing, while in Haryana the figure is stable at about 80 percent. The amount of barren land and land under permanent pasture is miniscule in both states. Although the official statistics for Kerala do not indicate any change in forest area (assuming 28 percent), a study based on topographical maps (Chattopadhyay, 1985) clearly shows a strong downward trend in forest vegetation cover (from 44 percent in 1905, to 28 percent in 1965, to 17 percent in 1983).[1]

The available official statistics on cropping patterns reveal that, although the area under most crops increased up to 1975, the area under food crops, especially under rice, declined after 1975, and the area under tree crops such as rubber and coconut and export-oriented crops such as pepper, ginger, and coffee increased substantially. These changes suggest that population pressure is having little effect on the use of agricultural lands in both Kerala and Haryana. In Kerala the amount of sown land is increasing, but basic grain production is declining in favor of cash crops. In Haryana the reduction in sown areas, which cover a little over 80 percent, has been very small despite a 30 percent increase in population density.

As noted earlier, however, two important aspects of land use trends— the smaller area of common property resources and the decline in the area under labor-intensive crops such as rice—are likely to have significant

---

[1]Because all percentages in allocation of land use total 100 percent, all the official data are within 10–15 percent of actual amounts.

implications for women. In addition, in Kerala strong trade unions, land reform legislation, and inheritance laws have played a significant role in changing the agrarian system. Because the matrilineal system is an important feature of Kerala society, it is important to see how these aspects have affected the position of women there.

Punjab and Haryana, the "Wheat Bowl" of northern India, are the country's key Green Revolution areas. An analysis of land use for the last 40 years by Singh (1993) suggests that Haryana has almost reached its limit in expanding the area under cultivation (see Table 7-2). Almost 82 percent of the area is sown; about 6–7 percent is under nonagricultural uses; and another 3 percent is under forests. "Cultivable waste" and "fallow land other than current fallow" as categories have virtually disappeared. Such intensive land use for agriculture is sustainable only with the ongoing application of high doses of balanced nutrients and other inputs such as chemical fertilizers and insecticides.

The cropping pattern in Haryana has changed substantially, with wheat and rice emerging as a major crop rotation in half of the state. Among other things, gram, bajra, barley, millets, and pulses have been replaced by wheat and rice, and the area under cotton has increased substantially while the area under sugarcane has remained the same (Table 7-3). In Singh's opinion the cropping pattern of the region has become unnecessarily energy intensive and is affecting the balance of underground water resources in Haryana.

From 1966–1967 to 1982–1983 the area under irrigation in Haryana almost doubled (from 1.3 million hectares to 2.4 million hectares). Irrigation, however, is a mixed blessing. While it has helped to increase productivity, it also has raised the water table and led to waterlogging in canal-

TABLE 7-3 Crop Areas, Haryana, 1966–1967 and 1982–1983 (thousands of hectares)

Crop	1966–1967	1982–1983
Rice	190	490
Wheat	740	1,560
Cotton	180	400
Potato	4	91
Jowar	270	120
Maize	87	69
Bajra	890	850
Pulses	83	67
Gram	1,060	1,050
Barley	180	130
Sugarcane	150	150
Oilseed	210	170

SOURCE: Singh, V., and M. S. Kairon. 1987. An Agricultural View of Haryana. Delhi: B. R. Publishing Corp.

irrigated and low-lying areas of the east-central region. The problem is more acute for the saline and saline sodic water belts under Rohtak, Sonipat, Jind, Hisar, Mahendragarh, Gurgaon, and Faridabad. In those areas the water table is only 1.5 meters from the ground surface, leading to salinization of the soil (Singh and Kairon, 1987).

According to N. Singh (1993) Haryana's basic problems are related to its scarcity of freshwater on the surface and abundance of brackish to saline water underground. Indeed, brackish subsoil water, unfit for drinking and irrigation, runs under about two-thirds of the state. Because large portions of Haryana lie in a topographic depression between the Siwalik hills in the northeast and Aravali hills to the southwest, both flooding and waterlogging can occur even when water is scarce. In fact, the water table in the tube well-irrigated area in northeastern Haryana has fallen to critical levels. Other environmental problems related to land use are the deforestation of the Siwalik hills, leading to soil erosion; overgrazing on the Aravalis, causing removal of soil cover; and the spread of the Rajasthan desert toward Haryana.

All of these changes in Haryana—especially the expansion of the area under labor-intensive crops such as rice, the problems with drinking water, the falling water table in the tube well-irrigated area, waterlogging in the canal-irrigated areas, and the decline in common property resources— are gender-sensitive and are likely to have significant implications for women's work and health.

OCCUPATIONAL BREAKDOWN BY GENDER

This section, which is based on an analysis of census data in India, presents findings that demonstrate a gender gap in the relative increase in rural workers in Kerala and Haryana and the unbalanced sex ratios of workers in various occupational categories (Kulkarni, 1997). Findings from another study based on census data for Kerala indicate that the female participation rate in that state is declining (Kumar, 1994).

As defined by the census of India, main workers are those who were engaged in productive work for more than 180 days during the reference period of one year preceding the census. Marginal workers worked less than 180 days during the reference period. From 1981 to 1991 in Haryana, the number of male main workers rose from 3.38 million to 4.26 million, while the number of female main workers increased from 0.28 million to 0.46 million. In the agricultural sector the number of male cultivators (unpaid family workers) increased from 1.50 million to 1.61 million; the number of female cultivators increased from 0.14 million to 0.21 million. Meanwhile, the number of male agricultural laborers increased from 0.53 million to 0.78 million; the corresponding increase for females was from 0.06 million to 0.11 million.

In Kerala during the period 1981–1991 the number of male main work-ers increased from 5.14 million to 6.40 million and female main workers from 1.65 million to 1.90 million. In the other category, male cultivators increased from 0.80 million to 0.91 million and female cultivators from 0.08 million to 0.10 million. During the same period, male agricultural laborers saw their numbers increase from 1.20 million to 1.44 million, while females in the same category saw their numbers decrease from 0.72 million to 0.68 million.

The differences between Haryana and Kerala become even clearer in Table 7-4, which compares the percentage change in the number of male and female workers in each category and also compares the direction and magnitude of change over the period 1981–1991 with that of the earlier decade. In Kerala the percentage increase among female workers is sub-stantially lower than that among males over 1981–1991, although in the earlier decade female workers had recorded higher increases. Haryana, by contrast, saw the number of female workers grow much faster than the number of male workers in both decades. The growth, however, was less for 1981–1991 than for 1971–1981. Total marginal workers declined sub-stantially in Haryana from 1981 to 1991, but the number of female mar-ginal workers increased slightly. In Kerala the numbers of both male and female marginal workers have declined, but the decline among males is much greater. These trends reveal the increasing participation of female workers in Haryana and their declining role in Kerala. It confirms as well the process of greater marginalization of women than men in both the states. Table 7-4 also reveals that the numbers of female cultivators and agricultural laborers have grown much more than the numbers of their male counterparts. This finding suggests that a growing number of women are participating in agricultural work on their family farm as well as outside for cash. The increase is much more pronounced among culti-vators—a finding that corroborates the trends discussed earlier.

In Kerala women cultivators have increased faster than men cultiva-tors only in the decade 1981–1991. Because a large percentage of women are engaged as agricultural laborers in Kerala, of most significance is the decline in their percentage during 1981–1991 while male agricultural workers recorded substantial increases. This suggests that women are gradually being thrown out of the labor market in Kerala, perhaps be-cause of the decline in rice cultivation.

Table 7-5, which presents the sex ratios for various categories of work-ers in the two states in 1971, 1981, and 1991, reveals that women in Haryana form a smaller percentage of total workers, but, significantly, that the sex ratio of main workers in Kerala is declining slightly, while for Haryana it is gradually improving, from 4 percent to 11 percent. Striking is the large increase in the sex ratio among marginal workers in Haryana. That increase may stem from the marginalization of women workers, but

TABLE 7-4 Percent Change, Male and Female Workers in Various Categories, Haryana and Kerala, 1971–1991

	Haryana				Kerala			
	1971–1981		1981–1991		1971–1981		1981–1991	
Category	Male	Female	Male	Female	Male	Female	Male	Female
Population	28.50	29.04	27.75	27.00	18.32	20.13	14.06	14.57
Main workers	33.06	150.96	25.96	62.66	7.90	13.65	24.57	14.95
Marginal workers			−67.40	2.00			−18.31	−9.38
Nonworkers	22.00	18.21	31.38	26.78	18.56	15.80	8.49	15.62
Cultivators	18.78	234.78	7.85	53.98	−22.49	21.31	13.03	29.08
Agricultural laborers	31.69	112.71	48.01	85.14	0.25	0.87	19.79	−4.75
Other categories of main workers	54.16	94.49	37.39	60.31	24.01	26.42	29.36	30.24

SOURCE: Computed from Census of India data, 1971, 1981, and 1991.

TABLE 7-5 Female Workers per Hundred Male Workers by Category of Worker, Haryana and Kerala, 1971–1991

Category	Haryana 1971	1981	1991	Kerala 1971	1981	1991
Population	88.65	87.01	86.5	101.62	103.18	103.64
Main workers	4.4	8.34	10.77	30.47	32.09	29.61
Marginal workers		519.75	1623.38		103.01	114.26
Nonworkers	160.35	155.37	149.93	159.84	156.12	166.38
Cultivators	3.30	9.28	13.25	6.48	10.04	11.58
Agricultural laborers	7.27	11.75	14.70	59.57	59.94	47.66
Other categories of main workers	4.74	5.98	6.98	26.57	27.09	27.27

SOURCE: Computed from Census of India data, 1971, 1981, and 1991.

it also may be attributable to the trend that finds women who used to consider many productive activities as household chores now reporting them as work (though for less than 180 days).

The sex ratio among cultivators in Kerala rose slightly during the decade 1981–1991. In Haryana it occurred twice as fast, which means that more women are acting as unpaid family workers. The sex ratio among agricultural laborers doubled from 1971 to 1991 in Haryana, while in Kerala it has declined by 20 percent. In the "other worker" category, there is not much change in either state.

Out of the total increase in the rural labor force during 1981–1991, a greater proportion of females than males was absorbed in agriculture in Haryana (Table 7-6). By contrast, in Kerala, even though the number of rural male workers absorbed in agriculture increased substantially, the number of females declined. This finding suggests not only that Kerala's agriculture did not absorb any more new female workers, but also that some of those working in agriculture had to find work outside the agricultural sector.

Kumar (1994), in her work on the impact of demographic change, economic growth, and structural changes on female work activities in

TABLE 7-6 Percentage of Total Increase in Rural Main Workers Absorbed by Agricultural Sectors, by Gender, Haryana and Kerala, 1981–1991

State	Rural Total	Rural Male	Rural Female
Haryana	71.6	65.3	87.7
Kerala	26.6	41.5	–119.4

SOURCE: Kulkarni, S. 1997. Dependence on agricultural employment in rural India. In: India's Demographic Transition: A Reassessment, S. Irudaya Rajan, ed. (New Delhi: M.D. Publications).

Kerala, has pointed out that the high level of fertility prevailing in Kerala before the sixties produced a lag effect on the size of the labor force, manifested by an increase in the proportion of women in the 20–24 age group. That factor, coupled with the dramatic fall in the female mortality rate for the 20–39 age group after 1970, has had the effect of increasing the size of the female labor force.

These factors and other behavioral changes, as explained earlier, should be reflected in increasing female participation rates for Kerala. Yet the female work participation rates for Kerala hardly show any substantial improvement (Kumar, 1994). In fact, the percentage of unemployed women in Kerala has increased (from 29 percent to 31 percent in rural areas and from 25 percent to 29 percent in urban areas during the 1973–1983 National Sample Survey), while the percentage of unemployed males has been almost constant—around 24 percent in rural areas and 22 percent in urban areas (Kumar, 1994).

Evidence further shows that in Kerala female employment in the agricultural, industrial, and service sectors declined from 1961 to 1991 by 38.3, 50.0, 31.5 percent, respectively. The corresponding decline for males was much less—9.9, 20.2, and 1.7 percent, respectively (Kumar, 1994). The decline in female agricultural employment could perhaps be attributed to the rapid changes in cropping patterns and the shift from paddy cultivation to coconut. Moreover, the economic forces behind this change may well have something to do with the rising price of coconut, from Rs. 150–200 per thousand in 1950 to Rs. 543 in 1970 to Rs. 2,414 in 1986–1987 (Jeffrey, 1993; also see Chapter 5).

In most developed countries expansion of the service sector has drawn more women workers into the labor force. In Kerala the growth of the tertiary sector was not a natural concomitant of the growth of the primary and secondary sectors. Rather, it was the result of the high priority the government has given to expanding services and infrastructure development, and most of the employment generated was in the public sector. In summary, changes in the economic structure in Kerala appear to have led in general to a reduced demand for females in the labor force.

FACTORS INFLUENCING THE GENDER-LINKED SOCIAL STRUCTURE

In her study of the Palghat district in Kerala, Saradamoni (1982) examined how the progressive breakdown of landlordism in Palghat, changing agrarian relationships, and the accompanying sociocultural changes affected women belonging to different strata in an agricultural community. The author observed that the traditional structure of the agricultural society in Malabar was based on feudalism, reaching hierarchically down to the lowest strata. The *jenmi* (landlord), *kanakaran* (protector), and the peasant shared the produce equally. While the customary laws kept the land intact and prevented division and alienation, the system was reinforced by the laws of inheritance and marriage practices. Most of the cultivation communities, like the Nayars throughout Kerala state, practiced *marumakkathayam*—a matrilineal system under which inheritance and succession passed through nieces and nephews on the female side. Under that system, women enjoyed a pivotal role and the right to maintain the *tharawad* or the family property. They did not depend on husbands for support; rather, they entered into *sambandham*, a kind of informal alliance with men of their caste or above. Also under this system, there was no private right to property ownership—that is, it was controlled corporately by the members of the family. Although the eldest male member of the household was its manager (*karanavar*), his sisters had significant influence and had to be consulted on all matters related to property. All the members had the right to see the property was not wasted by the Karanawan.

As just noted, in the state of Kerala the *sambandham* consisted of an informal union between Nayar women and Nayar, Namboothiri, Brahmin, or Kshatriya men. Under this arrangement, the male presented the female with a cloth, *pudava*, and then began to visit her regularly at her house. The children of such unions were the responsibility of the maternal house, where they lived with their aunts, uncles, cousins, nieces, and nephews. Children had little to do with their fathers, and, because women had unions with more than one man (polyandry), the children bore their mother's name. A woman was thus known as belonging to a particular *tharawad*, not as the daughter or wife of a particular man. The oldest woman in the *tharawad* headed the matriarchal family.

The original Nayars were soldiers who held lands and served as a militia. Some members of the present-day Nayar caste, however, have taken up other occupations. In the early days, the Nayars were forbidden by their law to marry, so that no one had an acknowledged son or father and all children belonged to the mother. Because three or four men often cohabited under mutual agreement with a woman, the Nayars never looked on any of their children as belonging to them. All the inheritances among the Nayars went to their brothers or the sons of their sisters, and all relationships were connected only by female consanguinity and descent. Although polyandry is now said to be dead, children are still known by their mothers and *tharawad*.

Agrarian struggles and a series of land reform legislation in the second half of the twentieth century brought about changes by which a fair deal could not be denied to the less advantaged. Jeffrey (1993) describes these changes as a movement from "inherited to achieved status." Women achieved some gains with these changes, but, in Saradamoni's opinion (1982), the societal contradictions they produced also pushed women to a

position of subordination. Although the motivating ideas behind the social reforms were freedom, fairness, and equity, inequalities of various
kinds prevented the benefits of fairness and justice from reaching all
groups. Women were the greatest victims of these contradictions, because
they were less equipped to get the new jobs.

One study by Mencher and Saradamoni (1982), based on detailed
data on the role of women in the production and processing of paddy in
six villages in three states (two villages in Kerala), points out the significance of female employment lost when rice mills were introduced to replace the hand pounding of rice by women. Gopinathan and Sundaresan
(1990) also found that wetland conversion in two districts, Thiruvananthapuram and Mallapuram, adversely affected female labor. Parasuraman
et al. (1995) examined the relationship between population pressure and
environment and its effect on institutional conditions and gender and
class positions. The authors based their study on a survey of three villages
in Kerala (in the Alappuzha, Kollam, and Waynad Districts) and four
villages in West Bengal. According to this study, population pressure and
land reforms have led to the fragmentation of land and a decline in per
capita land ownership, which in turn has reduced the capacity of land to
support households. Moreover, the shrinking land base apparently has
made cultivation of the traditional labor-intensive crops uneconomic. This
finding is reflected in the shift from cultivation of rice to coconut or from
coconut to tapioca or rubber. Overall, several factors have affected the
participation of Kerala women in economic activity: the decline in wage
labor opportunities in the agricultural sector because of changes in the
cropping pattern, the boom in construction-related employment, rising
wages, improved access to a university education, the possibilities of out-
migration to Gulf countries, and a drastic decline in fertility which has
made more women available for jobs. Furthermore, a higher level of unemployment and underemployment among men has forced them to move
into activities that once were considered women's domain. As a result,
women gained little from these changes. They were even forced out of
activities meant exclusively for them. For example, landed households
normally hired women workers from landless and marginally land-
owning households, but, because of the high level of unemployment, jobs
were redirected toward men.

The study by Parasuraman et al. demonstrated the combined gender–
class effect by showing the gender gap in utilization of labor by the size of
landholding. Table 7-7 reveals that in the "own labor" category (family
labor), woman-hours are nearly one-third of man-hours. Indeed, in all
landholding categories except 10+ acres, women work one-third to one-
half as much as men. The results for big farmers (10+ acres) reveal no
gender gap in the utilization of labor nor do the overall results for hired
labor. Small farmers (less than one acre), however, use more man-hours

TABLE 7-7 Gender Gap in Labor-Hours per Household per Month in Kerala Villages by Landholding Size, 1994

Landholding	Own Labor		Hired Labor		Total
Size (acres)	Men	Women	Men	Women	Households
Landless	3.22	1.25	7.25	5.56	36
0.01–0.50	45.18	22.13	13.68	7.74	205
0.51–1.00	106.30	23.29	89.19	60.45	73
1.01–1.50	120.76	69.69	130.45	205.10	42
1.51–2.00	226.07	88.37	232.15	208.67	54
2.01–5.00	331.51	98.26	427.77	407.63	43
5.01–10.0	361.65	52.60	713.70	751.00	20
10+	233.83	256.83	261.50	345.50	6
Average	119.64	43.42	129.08	126.73	479

SOURCE: S. Parasuraman et al. 1995. Class and Gender Aspects of the Interface between Population Pressure, Institutional Conditions and Environment, A Study for ICSSR Indo-Dutch Programme on Alternatives in Development. Bombay: Tata Institute of Social Sciences.

of hired labor. For middle-level farmers, the gender gap is not consistent, while big farmers (with 10+ acres) use more woman-hours of hired labor. Because the observations about big farmers are based on small numbers, not too much should be read into the reversal of the gender gap from own labor to hired labor.

According to Table 7-8, the gender gap in the utilization of own labor is unfavorable to women for all crops. It is strikingly wide for rubber, tapioca, coconut, coffee; for rice and ginger it is much less. For hired labor, the gender gap is favorable to women for rice, ginger, and coffee and markedly unfavorable for rubber and coconut. Because more and more land is being devoted to rubber and coconut, the implications of that shift are not good for women.

The labor utilization trends in the three Kerala villages become clearer when related to the predominant crops in those villages. In Patazhi rubber is a major crop, followed by coconut and banana. In Noolpuzha it is coffee, followed by paddy and pepper. In Edathuva paddy is the dominant crop (83 percent). According to Parasuraman et al. (1995), changes in cropping patterns have affected women in the rural labor market in these villages. In Patazhi the demand for women laborers has declined. In Noolpuzha women are affected adversely because the amount of rice and ginger cultivated has fallen due to lack of irrigation. In Edathuva the intensification of cultivation has generated employment, but women have not benefited in this process. And, overall, except in Patazhi, women's contribution to family income has declined—in many cases by 50 percent—with the greatest impact on poor and scheduled caste women.

Finally, Parasuraman et al. found that the strong trade unions in Kerala and frequent wage revisions in recent years were perceived by

TABLE 7-8 Labor-Hours per Month in Kerala Villages by Crop and Gender, 1994

Landholding Size (acres)	Own Labor		Hired Labor		Total Households
	Men	Women	Men	Women	
Rubber	129.43	7.22	139.52	18.69	113
Tapioca	36.26	4.82	20.27	6.66	89
Rice	118.97	72.24	167.6	278.40	179
Coconut	14.17	3.67	17.7	0.59	184
Pepper	73.54	22.92	27.1	1.0	100
Bananas	9.49	0.42	5.3	1.23	97
Ginger	75.21	52.48	77.7	85.58	52
Coffee	54.48	13.04	56.9	64.38	48
Other	17.09	5.91	22.5	6.73	44

SOURCE: S. Parasuraman et al. 1995. Class and Gender Aspects of the Interface between Population Pressure, Institutional Conditions and Environment, A Study for ICSSR Indo-Dutch Programme on Alternatives in Development. Bombay: Tata Institute of Social Sciences.

many respondents to be the causes of lower employment. These developments have affected women more adversely than men.

For Haryana, many studies have described the environmental problems caused by land use changes (Ansari, 1991; N. Singh, 1993; R. B. Singh, 1993), but micro studies by Chowdhary (1993) and Bhalla (1989) provide more insight into the gender dimension of these problems. Chowdhary has observed that in Haryana the dominant cultural norms did not hinder women's participation in manual work outside their own fields. But when women were working for others it was considered a status problem. Women's participation is lower in the richest regions than in poor regions or drought-prone areas. The larger the size of the holding, the greater are women's labor-hours in the field. Chowdhary illustrated his finding with some of the aphorisms used by women in Haryana:

Kheti, pali, bandgi aur ghode ka tang, charon aap hi kijiye, chahe lakho log ho sang
(Even if you have thousands of attendants, you should do four things yourself: farming, letter-writing, worship, and harnessing a horse. . . . A nineteenth-century proverb.)

Jeore se nara ghisna hai
(Women as cattle bound, working and enduring all.)

The studies by Chowdhary and Bhalla reveal some very interesting trends for Haryana. The Green Revolution increased the demand for all kinds of labor. Thus with the increasing demand and the escalating labor costs, family women must continue to work. The extensive use of female labor in Haryana has cut across all caste and class divisions. Even so, when women engage in manual work on others' farms, they lower their family's prestige. Women from well-to-do families also contribute to all agricultural tasks but only on their family farm. Yet in some rich districts like Karnal (Table 7-9) women are slowly withdrawing from agricultural work in all size categories of landholding and shifting their efforts from the fields to the courtyard, where women may supervise food preparation for the hired workers who replaced them in the field because of the tremendous increase in agricultural processing work. Haryana's pattern of utilization of female labor is closer to that of the state of Rajasthan than that of the states of Punjab, Madhya Pradesh, and Maharashtra, where employment of female labor is related negatively to size of holding and adoption of new technology.

In any work related to animal husbandry carried out by women, the class and caste barriers are clearly evident. Not only is Haryana a rice bowl, but in the wake of the "White Revolution" in 1970–1971, it became a milk bowl as well. As a result, the work of family members has increased substantially, and women and children contribute nearly 82 percent of the total work (regardless of caste and class). Here again, because of the decline in common property resources, women from economically weaker households in both the dry and the Green Revolution areas find life harder. Free fodder is hard to find, forcing women to roam wider in their search. Among the animal-related tasks—preparing feed mix for cattle, bathing them, making dung cakes—men have taken over the tasks now aided by electricity; the labor-intensive tasks are left to women. Yet women remain invisible in the statistics since their work is not reported.

Another phenomenon that has sustained women's involvement in agricultural work is the migration of men outside the state to work. In short, even after Green and White Revolutions women have continued to

TABLE 7-9 Unpaid Woman-Days as Percentage of Unpaid Family Person-Days, Haryana

Operated Land Area (acres)	All Haryana	Richest Region
0–2.5	13.9	0.0
2.5–5	27.9	26.7
5–10	21.5	12.5
10–15	16.5	14.4
15 or more	23.7	18.7
All average	21.9	16.2

SOURCE: Bhalla, S. 1989. Technological change and women workers: Evidence from the expansionary phase in Haryana agriculture. Economic and Political Weekly 24(October 28): WS69. Of the 153 surveyed villages, the richest regions are those where a large area is under high-yielding varieties (Green Revolution) or where dairy farming is predominant (White Revolution).

TABLE 7-10 Percentage of Casual and Permanent Laborers among Male and Female Agricultural Laborers in High-, Moderate-, and Low-Technology Regions, Haryana, 1972–1973

Agricultural Laborers	Region A (High Technology)			Region B (Moderate Technology)			Region C (Low Technology)		
	Total	Casual	Permanent	Total	Casual	Permanent	Total	Casual	Permanent
Total men	126,975 (100%)	43.1	56.9	125,873 (100%)	70.0	30.0	54,683 (100%)	91.2	8.8
Men from landless households	77,396 (61%)	17.7	43.3	65,595 (52%)	32.0	20.1	20,204 (37%)	28.1	8.8
Total women	22,599 (100%)	93.6	6.4	23,251 (100%)	100.0		5,084 (100%)	100.0	
Women from landless households	11,700 (52%)	45.3	6.4	7,554 (33%)	32.5		4,132 (81%)	81.3	

NOTES: Region A: Karnal District and adjacent highly irrigated areas—the region to which the Green Revolution came first and was consolidated more effectively.
Region B: Most of the Hisar and Rohtak Districts (west to east-central belt) where new technology has been less widely accepted.
Region C: Semidesert area where the impact of the Green Revolution is negligible.

SOURCE: Based on Table 1 in: Bhalla, S. 1976. New relations of production in Haryana agriculture. Economic and Political Weekly (March 27):A25.

work on the family farm or with the family cattle, but the evaluation of their work has not changed. Female wage earners are hard hit because they are increasingly marginalized. Indeed, there are strong gender differentials in both work and wages (see Tables 7-10 and 7-11). A woman is considered inferior and handicapped in acquiring new skills. Thus, despite the enormous rise in productivity in Haryana, women, especially women wage earners, have remained adversely affected. More specifically, in the moderate- and low-technology regions of Haryana there are essentially no permanent female agricultural laborers, while in the high-technology areas there are some permanent female laborers, but their percentage is only about one-ninth of the corresponding percentage for men (Table 7-10). With better technology, then, the employment position of women improves, but that improvement does not imply that poorer households gain in this process. In low-technology areas, as many as 81 percent of female casual agricultural laborers come from landless households, but in moderate- and high-technology regions, the percentage of such women is much smaller. All the female laborers from landless laborer households are casual laborers in low- and moderate-technology areas, whereas in high-technology areas about 12 percent are permanent. As Table 7-11 demonstrates, although female wages continue to remain lower than male wages, generally the gap has narrowed.

TABLE 7-11 Agricultural Laborer Wage Rates, Haryana, 1970–1985

Year	Daily Wage (rupees) Male (1)	Female (2)	Female Wages as Percentage of Male Wages (3)	Consumer Price Index (1970–1971) (4)	Real Wages Male (5)	Real Wages Female (6)
1970–1971	6.44	3.96	61.5	100.00	6.44	3.96
1971–1972	6.84	4.17	70.0	105.67	6.47	3.94
1973–1974	7.40	4.26	57.6	140.72	5.25	3.02
1974–1975	8.58	5.02	58.5	173.71	4.93	2.88
1975–1976	8.55	5.22	61.1	158.76	5.38	3.28
1976–1977	8.75	6.32	72.2	157.21	5.56	4.02
1977–1978	10.44	6.68	64.0	171.13	6.10	3.90
1978–1979	11.17	6.61	59.2	173.19	6.44	3.81
1979–1980	11.89	8.35	70.2	192.78	6.16	4.33
1980–1981	12.41	9.62	77.5	225.25	5.50	4.27
1982–1983	16.14	13.81	85.6	247.42	6.52	5.58
1983–1984	18.15	14.40	79.3	264.94	6.85	5.43
1984–1985	19.35	14.99	77.5	291.23	6.00	5.14

SOURCES: (1)–(3) Jose, A. V. 1988. Agricultural Weekly 23(June 25):A48–A49; (4) calculated from Ministry of Labour, Labour Bureau, Indian Labour Journal, Chandigarh (various issues); (5) = (1)/(4) × 100; (6) = (2)/(4) × 100.

CONCLUSION

The evidence available from the micro studies and census data reveals that in Kerala and Haryana—states representing two different types
of population—the population–land use relationships have different implications for women's work and life. In Kerala, where the area under rice
is declining, the women have seen their position in rural markets gradually weakened and marginalized. In Haryana, where productivity has
increased tremendously and where rice is emerging as a cash crop, women
have a greater role in productive work. Yet their position continues to
remain subordinate to men, who do the more mechanized jobs. Women's
work continues to be less valued and wage differentials persist. Technological development and the consequent changes in patterns of land use
alone do not ensure that women will get their due share unless these
changes are accompanied by efforts to empower women.

ACKNOWLEDGMENTS

Thanks are extended to B. N. N. Chowdary and K. Neelakantan for
assistance in research and to Dandapani Lokanathan for computer work.

REFERENCES

Agarwal, B. 1986. Women, poverty and agricultural growth in India. Journal of Peasant
    Studies 13 (July):167–220.
Agarwal, B. 1988. Neither Sustenance nor Sustainability: Agricultural Strategies, Ecological
    Degradation and Indian Women in Poverty. New Delhi: Indian Association for
    Women's Studies.
Ansari, S. H. 1991. Agricultural resources development and environment at district level in
    Haryana. In: Essays on Environment and Resources: Some Regional Issues, P. Nag, ed.
    New Delhi: Deep and Deep Publications.
Bardhan, K. 1985. Women's work, welfare and status: Forces of tradition and change in
    India. Economic and Political Weekly 20(December).
Bardhan, P. 1974. On life and death questions. Economic and Political Weekly 11:1293–1304.
Bhalla, S. 1989. Technological change and women workers: Evidence from the expansion-
    ary phase in Haryana agriculture. Economic and Political Weekly 24(October 28):
    WS67–WS89.
Boserup, E. 1989. Population: The status of women and rural development. In: Population
    and Development Review. Vol. 15: Rural Development and Population: Institutions
    and Policy, G. McNicoll and M. Cain, eds. Based on the Expert Consultation on Popu-
    lation and Agricultural and Rural Development convened by FAO. Rome and New
    York: Population Council.
Centre for Monitoring Indian Economy (CMIE). 1993. Basic Statistics Relating to the Indian
    Economy (States). Bombay: CMIE, Table 1.10.
Chattopadhyay, S. 1985. Deforestation in parts of Western Ghats region (Kerala), India.
    International Journal of Environmental Management 20:219–230.
Chen, M. A. 1989. Women's work in Indian agriculture by agro-ecologic zones: Meeting
    needs of landless and land-poor women. Economic and Political Weekly 24(October
    28):WS79–WS89.

Chowdhary, P. 1993. High participation, low evaluation, women and work in rural Haryana. Economic and Political Weekly (December 25):A135–A148.

Dyson, T., and M. Moore. 1983. Kinship structure, female autonomy, and demographic behaviour in India. Population and Development Review 9(March):35–60.

Gopinathan, C., and C. S. Sundaresan. 1990. Cropping Pattern Changes and Employment Effects in Selected Districts of Kerala. Thiruvananthapuram: Centre for Management Development.

Hartmann, H. 1976. Capitalism, patriarchy and job segregation by sex. Pp. 137–169 in Women and the Work Place: The Implications of Occupational Segregation, M. Blaxal and B. Reagan, eds. Chicago: University of Chicago Press.

Jeffrey, R. 1993. Politics, Women and Well Being: How Kerala Became "A Model." New Delhi: Oxford University Press.

Jodha, N. S. 1989. Depletion of common property resources in India: Micro level evidence. In: Population and Development Review. Vol. 15: Rural Development and Population: Institutions and Policy, G. McNicoll and M. Cain, eds. Based on the Expert Consultation on Population and Agricultural and Rural Development convened by FAO. Rome and New York: Population Council.

Kulkarni, S. 1997. Dependence on agricultural employment in rural India. In: India's Demographic Transition: A Reassessment, S. Irudaya Rajan, ed. New Delhi: M.D. Publications.

Kumar, R. 1994. Development and women's work in Kerala. Economic and Political Weekly 29(51-52):3249–3254.

Leacock, E., and H. I. Safa, eds. 1986. Women's Work: Development and Division of Labor by Gender. South Hadley, Mass.: Bergin and Garvey.

Mencher, J., and K. Saradamoni. 1982. Muddy feet, dirty hands: Rice production and female agricultural labor. Economic and Political Weekly 17(52):A149–A167.

Miller, B. 1981. The Endangered Sex: Neglect of Female Children in Rural North India. Ithaca: Cornell University Press.

Mohan, D. 1987. Food vs. limbs: Pesticides and physical disabilities in India. Economic and Political Weekly 22(March 28):A23–A29.

Parasuraman, S., C. Sengupta, and S. Thiruvenkitasamy. 1995. Class and Gender Aspects of the Interface between Population Pressure, Institutional Conditions and Environment, A Study for ICSSR Indo-Dutch Programme on Alternatives in Development. Bombay: Tata Institute of Social Sciences.

Population Research Centre (PRC), Kerala University, and International Institute for Population Sciences (IIPS). 1995. National Family Health Survey, Kerala, 1992–93. Bombay: PRC-Kerala, Thiruvananthapuram and IIPS.

Population Research Centre (PRC), Punjab University, and International Institute for Population Sciences (IIPS). 1995. National Family Health Survey, Haryana, 1992–93. Bombay: PRC-Haryana, Chandigarh and IIPS.

Rosenzweig, M. R., and T. P. Schultz. 1982. Market Opportunities, Genetic Endowment and Intrafamily Resource Contribution: Child Survival in Rural India, Center Paper No. 323. New Haven: Economic Growth Center, Yale University.

Saradamoni, K. 1982. Women's status in changing agrarian relations: A Kerala experience. Economic and Political Weekly 17(5):155–162.

Sen, G. 1987. Women agricultural laborers: Regional variations in incidence and employment. Paper presented at the National Workshop on Women in Agriculture, New Delhi, September 23–24, 1987.

Singh, N. 1993. Economic development: A case study of Haryana. Pp. 129–139 in Environment and Development: Views for the East and the West, A. Mukherjee and V. K. Agnihotri, eds. New Delhi: Concept Publications.

Singh, R. B. 1993. Land use change, agro-forestry and sustainable development in North-West India. Pp. 129–139 in Environment and Development: Views for the East and the West, A. Mukherjee and V. K. Agnihotri, eds. New Delhi: Concept Publications.

Singh, V., and M. S. Kairon. 1987. An Agricultural View of Haryana. Delhi: B. R. Publishing Corp.

Unni, J. 1989. Changes in women's employment in rural areas, 1961–83. Economic and Political Weekly (April 29):WS 23–WS31.

Zachariah, K. C., and S. Irudaya Rajan. 1997. Kerala's Demographic Transition: Determinants and Consequences. New Delhi: Sage Publications.

PART III

China

Chinese Case Studies: An Introduction

Zhao Shidong
Institute of Geographic Science and Natural Resources,
Chinese Academy of Sciences

With the rapid development of China's economy over the last decades, its land use patterns have changed significantly, especially since the central government's adoption of socioeconomic reform policies, beginning in the late 1970s. Across China, the speed and scale of land use change have varied because of the country's diverse natural and socioeconomic conditions. In order to understand the process and the mechanism of land use change, and then provide a solid basis for the future sustainable planning of land use in China's many different regions, the Chinese research team chose the Jitai Basin, a typical rural area, and the Pearl River Delta, characterized by rapid urbanization, as its study sites (see map, p. 178).

JITAI BASIN

The Jitai Basin, located in Jiangxi Province in south-central China, is made up of four counties that contain two cities. At the end of 1995, the Jitai Basin was home to 2.47 million people; its population density was 198 persons per square kilometer.

Historically, the Jitai Basin was a relatively developed area for agricultural production and handcraft industries such as shipbuilding and textiles, because the Ganjiang (Gan River) served as a main transportation artery between north and south. But with the development of modern industry and communications, the opening of foreign trade ports (Guangzhou, Shanghai, Fuzhou, Xiamen, and Ningbo) in the late nineteenth century, and the building of the Guangzhou–Wuhan and Wuhan–Beijing railways, the direction of the flow of goods changed rapidly, weakening the transportation function of the Ganjiang River. From then on, China saw its economy grow rapidly in coastal areas, and the Jitai Basin gradually lost its dominant position in communications and the economy and slipped into a declining state.

After the founding of the People's Republic of China in 1949, the central government began to promote the development of the more rural regions of the country. As a result, in the 1950s and 1960s the Jitai Basin was the beneficiary of significant investment in an industrial program, technological assistance, and an influx of trained migrants from the more developed regions. Development of the country as a whole, however, was at a very low level, and cultural, political, and economic restrictions hampered the assistance efforts. In the end, then, no significant socioeconomic development occurred in the Jitai Basin from 1949 to 1978, and, indeed, population pressure and extreme economic policies resulted in serious damage to the region's natural resources. For example, overcutting of forests to provide fuel for steel smelters caused deforestation and soil erosion. And the expansion of agriculture to marginal hilly and mountainous areas in order to meet the subsistence demands of the rapidly growing population for food and fuel further accentuated the serious problems of environmental degradation.

Since the introduction of government reforms in 1978, the Jitai Basin has achieved relatively remarkable economic development in absolute terms. With implementation of the "household responsibility" system in 1982, agricultural productivity increased and the transition from cereal production to cash crop production (such as fruits and vegetables) accelerated. Meanwhile, the local government, aware of the damage to the ecosystem generated by deforestation and soil erosion, successfully implemented a series of policies to reforest the hills and mountains. Despite these achievements, the Jitai Basin still lags behind the coastal regions in economic development and urbanization. In fact, the gap between its socioeconomic development and that of developed regions (for example, the Pearl River Delta) is widening. One important reason is that the central government's economic development strategy tends to favor coastal areas. Other reasons are the Jitai Basin's location in China's hinterlands and its limited access to investment, technology, and the markets in metropolitan areas. In addition, because the region had a surplus of agricultural laborers stemming from the significant lack of development of the nonagricultural sectors, the massive out-migration of young laborers from the Jitai Basin to developed regions such as the Pearl River Delta increased. This development relieved the pressure on local employment, but also weakened agricultural production.

PEARL RIVER DELTA

Formed by the alluvium delivered by the West, North, and East Rivers, the Pearl River Delta is located in southern China's Guangdong Province. The study region, which lies in the central part of Pearl River Delta, consists of 13 counties or cities, which belong to six municipalities and are distributed on either side of the Pearl River estuary. The Pearl River Delta is one of the most heavily populated regions of China. In 1995 its permanent population density was 743 persons per square kilometer, compared with 378 for all of Guangdong Province and 126 for China as a whole.

Historically, the Pearl River Delta was known nationally for its production of grain, sugar, silk, freshwater fish, and fruits. Indeed, the region was referred to as the "Fish and Rice County." The Delta also was one of the places in China where modern industry first appeared. However, from 1866, when industry first arrived, to 1949, when the new China was founded, the region's economy developed very slowly, and many residents of the Delta left to earn a living abroad. One factor in its slow growth was its location; because the Delta is situated at the frontier of the national defense, very few of the important industries were allowed to set up operations in the region.

After implementation of socioeconomic reforms in 1978, the Delta quickened its pace of development and now is one of the richest areas in China. But rapid industrialization and urbanization also have produced dramatic changes in the Pearl River Delta's landscape, as well as environmental pollution. Overall, within less than 20 years the Delta area was transformed from a rural agricultural area into a highly developed region through rapid industrialization and urbanization. Within this process, the interactions between population growth, land use change, and the relevant economic and environmental problems are complex and unique.

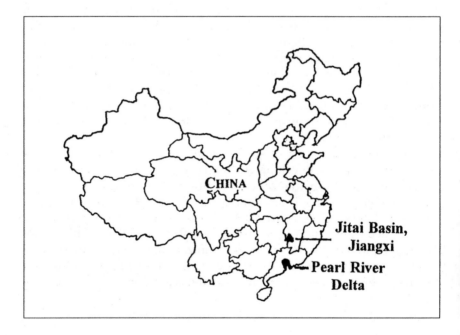

Chinese Study Regions

8

Population, Consumption, and Land Use in the Jitai Basin Region, Jiangxi Province

Zhao Shidong, Chinese Academy of Sciences; Lu Jiehua, Peking University; Zhang Hongqi, Chinese Academy of Sciences; Zeng Yi, Peking University; Qi Wenhu, Chinese Academy of Sciences; Liang Zhiwu, Peking University; Zhang Taolin, Chinese Academy of Sciences; Liu Guiping, Peking University; Qin Mingzhou, Henan University; Jiang Leiwen, Peking University

This chapter examines the relationship among population change, consumption patterns, and land use in the Jitai Basin region of China from the early 1950s to the mid-1990s. It begins by describing the physical, economic, and social conditions of the region. Then, based on a sequence of four research findings, it looks more closely at how population, consumption, and land use are related.

THE JITAI BASIN: A DESCRIPTION

Physical Conditions

The Jitai Basin is located in the midwestern part of Jiangxi Province in southeastern China. The basin covers 12,468 square kilometers. Its two major urban centers are Ji'an City, located in the plains area of Ji'an County, and Jinggangshan City, which is in the mountains (Figure 8-1).

The basin region is made up largely of mountains, undulating hills, and a small proportion of plains. The altitude in the area ranges from 1,779 meters in the mountains that surround it to less than 30 meters in the valleys of the Ganjiang (Gan) River, which runs through the basin. Many sub-basins dot the larger Jitai Basin.

The mountainous region, mainly distributed along the edges of the basin, occupies 29 percent of the region's total area. The high mountains rising above 1,000 meters are characterized by deep valleys and steep slopes. The low mountains, which range in altitude from 500 to 1,000

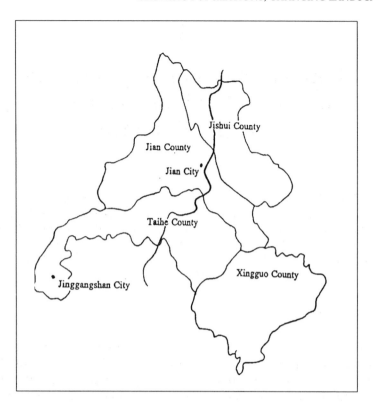

FIGURE 8-1 Jitai Basin, Jiangxi Province.

meters, have soils that are deep, fertile, and suitable for many kinds of forests.

The hills, characterized by an undulating landscape and a branch-like water system, dominate the topography of the region; they account for 52 percent of the total area. The severest soil erosion, caused by human activity and strong weathering, is found in the hills with steep slopes (Xi Chengfan et al., 1989). Grasses such as *Setose arundinella* dominate the vegetation; sparse areas of Masson pine are evident as well. Some areas with gentle slopes, water sources, and fertile soil have been planted with fruit trees or other crops.

The plains that cover 20 percent of the region's total area are located in the alluvial fans derived from the Ganjiang River and its major tributaries. Characterized by ideal water and heat conditions, fertile soil, and a high multiple crop index, the plains are the main agricultural region of the Jitai Basin.

The Jitai Basin region lies in a typical subtropical climate zone with its rich sunlight, heat, and monsoon rains. From 1949 to 1987 the annual general solar radiation was 425–452 joules per square centimeter, which decreases from south to north and from the alluvial plains along the Ganjiang River to the surrounding hills and mountains. The annual total period of sunlight is 1,720–1,815 hours. Daily temperatures vary between –7°C and 40°C throughout the year, with a mean annual daily temperature of about 17.8°C. Average annual rainfall is 1,500 millimeters, and the number of rainy days is about 165. Sixty percent of the total rainfall occurs between March and June. Jinggangshan City is in a special situation because of its mountain location. Its average daily temperature is 14.2°C, and its average annual rainfall is 1,856 millimeters. The dry season in the Jitai Basin is from July to September when crops need a lot of water. This situation easily gives rise to reduced cereal yields.

The native undisturbed vegetation of the Jitai Basin is a mix of subtropical evergreen broadleaf forest and needle forest. A large proportion of the original forest cover was destroyed by human activities. It has been replaced by secondary wood and shrub over the past 50 years. The Jitai Basin has a relatively high diversity of species (Ji'an Planning Council and Ji'an Agricultural Division Council, 1993).

The vegetation of the Jitai Basin varies according to elevation. The mixed broadleaf and needle forest is found mainly in the mountainous regions more than 800 meters above sea level. Broadleaf forests are dominated by *Lauraceae, Fagaceae, Theaceae, Aquifoliaceae, Rosaceae, Caprifoliaceae,* and *Ericaceae*; needle forests are dominated by Huanshan mountain pine and Masson pine. The evergreen broadleaf forests (less than 800 meters above sea level) are dominated by *Lauraceae, Magnoliaceae, Fagaceae, Theacea, Aquifoliaceae,* and *Elaeocarpaceae*. The shrubs under the forest are mainly *Loropetalum, Daphniphyllum oldhamii, Styrax japonica,* and *Maesa japonica*. The evergreen broadleaf forest in the Jitai Basin traditionally has served as an important catchment reserve that regulates surface runoff, prevents soil erosion, and ensures an adequate and consistent supply of clean water for human consumption. But much of this forest has been destroyed and converted to other land uses, with serious environmental consequences.

Soils in the Jitai Basin region can be divided into 15 types according to location and texture (Land Administrative Bureau and Soil Survey Office of Jiangxi Province, 1991).[1] Just over half of the area is covered by red soil (udic ferralisols), a third by paddy soil (stagnic anthrosols), and less than 10 percent by other types (Table 8-1). Paddy soil accounts for 90 percent of all cropland. Seventy percent of all the cropland (anthrosols) has medium

---

[1]Soils are classified according to the Chinese soil survey of 1981, a kind of genetic classification system. In parentheses are the suborders from the Chinese Soil Taxonomy (revised proposal) of 1995, which utilizes names homologous to the international common names. The suborders are included here because this new system is not used widely.

TABLE 8-1 Soil Types, Jitai Basin

Group Name	Percent
Red soil (udic ferralisols)	56.63
Submergenic paddy soil (stagnic anthrosols)	17.29
Hydragic paddy soil (stagnic anthrosols)	16.70
Others	9.38

SOURCE: Soil Survey Office of Ji'an Prefecture. 1983. Soil in Ji'an; Soil Survey Office of Xingguo County. 1983. Soil in Xingguo County.

or low productivity because of the medium and low soil fertility. The forest soils (udic ferralisols) are not as nutrient-deficient as the cropland soils, but the deficiency of phosphorus and potassium is still a serious problem (Qin Mingzhou, 1997).

Population and Demographics

The Jitai Basin had a population of 2.47 million in 1995, with a density of 198 persons per square kilometer. From 1951 to 1995 the population increased by 1.455 million, or 143 percent. Over the last 45 years the population has increased continually, except for very brief and small downturns in the early 1950s and 1960s (Figure 8-2). From 1951 to 1990 the net increase in population was 1.38 million, or an average 35,000 persons a year. From 1990 to 1995 the population grew more slowly, with a net increase of 55,000, or an average of only 9,000 persons a year.

Land Use Change

From 1950 to 1994 the Jitai Basin experienced relatively complicated land use changes, including deforestation and reforestation (Figure 8-3).

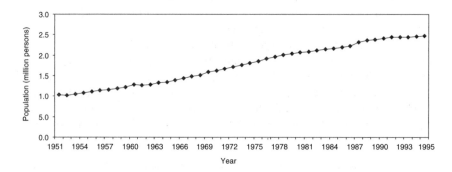

FIGURE 8-2 Total population, Jitai Basin, 1951–1995. SOURCE: Population statistics, Statistical Bureau of Jiangxi Province, 1951–1995.

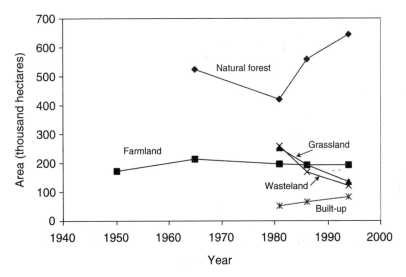

FIGURE 8-3 Land use, Jitai Basin, 1950–1994. SOURCES: Collection of agricultural statistics, 1949–1987, Bureau for Agriculture, Animal Husbandry and Fishery Production in Ji'an Prefecture, Ji'an, Jiangxi Province, pp. 107, 122, 138, 963–964; investigations of the forest situation in the Ji'an Basin, 1965, 1981, 1986, 1994, Forest Bureau of Ji'an Prefecture; Economic Statistical Yearbooks of Ji'an City, Jinggangshan City, and Ji'an, Jishui, Taihe, Xingguo Counties. 1994. Statistical Bureaus of Ji'an City, Jinggangshan City, and Ji'an, Jishui, Taihe, Xingguo Counties.

The area devoted to grassland and wasteland decreased after 1981. Meanwhile, built-up areas (including industrial districts, residential areas, and traffic zones) were on the rise.

Farmland in the Jitai Basin increased significantly between 1950 and 1957—from 174,000 hectares to 227,000 hectares, a historic peak (Figure 8-4). During that period, population pressure, together with the government's land reform policy aimed at distributing land from the landlords to individual households, led to large-scale land reclamation in the region.

In 1958, however, the central government initiated the Great Leap Forward, a policy aimed at matching China's steel output with that of the United Kingdom and the United States in a short time. When large numbers of rural laborers were shifted to setting up furnaces and smelting steel, the result was a serious labor shortage in agricultural production. Farmland located in marginal areas with lower yields or lying greater distances from villages was abandoned, leading to a decline in total farmland—from 227,000 hectares in 1958 to 212,000 hectares in 1959. In 1966 the Cultural Revolution led to another decline in farmland—from 214,000

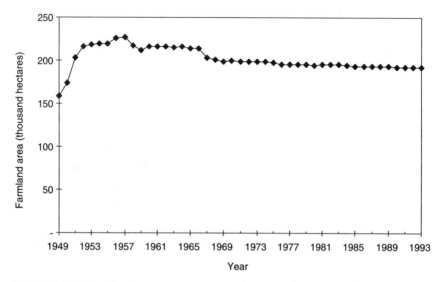

FIGURE 8-4 Farmland, Jitai Basin, 1949–1993. SOURCES: Collection of agricultural statistics, 1949–1987, Bureau for Agriculture, Animal Husbandry and Fishery Production in Ji'an Prefecture, Ji'an, Jiangxi Province, pp. 107, 122, 138, 963–964; Economic Statistical Yearbooks of Ji'an City, Jinggangshan City, and Ji'an, Jishui, Taihe, Xingguo counties. 1994. Statistical Bureaus of Ji'an City, Jinggangshan City, and Ji'an, Jishui, Taihe, Xingguo counties.

hectares in 1966 to 199,000 hectares in 1969—largely the result of people's abandonment of farming for a deep involvement in politics.

From the 1970s onward, farmland in the Jitai Basin decreased slowly. Further reclamation was impossible because the land available for cultivation had become more difficult to access or was very marginal. Meanwhile, the population had been increasing since 1950. The result was a significant reduction in the amount of farmland per capita.

Some central government policies, such as those calling for steel production (1958), "putting grain first" (1966–1976), and the "household responsibility system for forest production" (1982), have resulted in periods of deforestation in the Jitai Basin. In 1958 wide swaths of forest were cut down for fuel to support government-mandated steel smelting. From 1966 to 1976 some forestland was converted to farmland in response to government calls for increased grain production. In 1982 control of forestland shifted from the government level to the individual (family) level but for tenures as short as three years, and farmers, suddenly aware of the short-term profits to be made and the little hope for long-term benefits, cut down vast areas of forest. Logging for house construction and fuelwood only intensified the loss of forestland. It decreased from 523,000 hectares in 1965 to 420,000 hectares in 1981 (Figure 8-3). Since the 1980s the central government has actively promoted reforestation and passed a series of laws and regulations to prohibit excessive logging and to encourage local farmers to plant trees. The conversion of farmland with low yield into forestland also has helped to increase total forest area. The total forestland in the Jitai Basin increased from 420,000 hectares in 1981 to 559,000 hectares in 1986 and to 645,000 hectares in 1994 (Figure 8-3).

Patterns of deforestation and reforestation in the Jitai Basin have been documented in forest surveys conducted by the Taihe County Forest Bureau (Table 8-2 and Figure 8-5). In Taihe County, forestland decreased 25 percent from 1957 to 1975 and then increased 1 percent from 1975 to 1989 and 54 percent from 1989 to 1994 (Table 8-2). The total forest stock, however, declined from 5.11 million cubic meters in 1961 to 3.15 million cubic meters in 1994 (see Figure 8-5), indicating that forests were significantly harvested. Indeed, from just 1982 to 1989 the total forest stock decreased 28 percent. Thus implementation of the household responsibility system for forest production in 1982 led to a large decline in forest stock over a short period. In this instance, a switch to private management did little to correct earlier excesses.

Yet a 10-year effort and the implementation of a reforestation policy showed results in Taihe County between 1989 and 1994. Both forestland and total forest stock increased, 54 percent and 19 percent, respectively (Table 8-2 and Figure 8-5). The middle forest stock climbed from 1.48 million cubic meters in 1989 to 1.71 million cubic meters in 1994, which suggests that restoration of the forest ecosystem had begun.

Although forestland has increased in recent years, problems remain, caused by large-scale logging to meet policy demands and population pressure. The stock of mature forest declined from 1.48 million cubic meters in 1975 to 530,000 cubic meters in 1994, indicating that mature forest was seriously harvested and could not be easily restored in a short time—see Figure 8-5. The figure also reveals that the young and middle forest stock were disproportionately large. With the shortage of mature forest, more

TABLE 8-2 Natural Land Areas, Taihe County, 1957–1994 (thousand hectares)

	1957	1975	1989	1994
Forestland	109.98	82.37	83.40	128.69
Shrubland		21.55	20.78	1.49
Waste mountainous land		51.99	42.12	4.15

NOTE: Waste mountainous land is land suitable for forest growth.

SOURCE: Taihe County Forest Bureau.

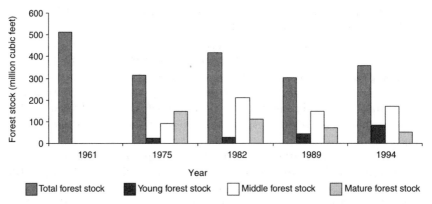

FIGURE 8-5   Forest stock change, Taihe County, 1961–1994. SOURCE: Taihe County Forest Bureau.

and more middle forest was harvested; in fact, the stock of middle forest decreased 29 percent in only seven years (1982–1989), a sign of a crisis in forest resources (Figure 8-5). Although the government adopted measures in 1989 to control the situation, it is certain that the demand for forest production will increase with further population growth and economic development.

Horticultural land is planted with cash trees such as tea, mulberry, and fruits. In the Jitai Basin the two dominant cash trees are tea and citrus. Before the central government launched a reform policy and opened China to the world in 1978, horticultural land increased slowly because of the government policy of putting grain first. In the Jitai Basin only 108 hectares were devoted to tea in 1965; 314 hectares were planted in citrus (Figure 8-6). After 1978 some farmers undertook major efforts to develop cash trees such as citrus and tea by reclaiming available wasteland on hills with gentle slopes (that is, with a gradient of less than 10°) or by converting marginal farmland to orchard. They achieved remarkable economic benefits. By 1987 the total areas planted in tea and citrus had increased to 1,362 hectares and 4,012 hectares, respectively. By 1994 the citrus areas in the Jitai Basin had reached nearly 10,000 hectares (Figure 8-6).

The grassland left in the Jitai Basin after deforestation consisted of degraded sparse shrub vegetation with a high diversity of herb plants. Most grassland is located in mountainous and hilly regions. This grassland is used mainly as pasture for draft animals and as a source of fuel for farmers' cooking and heating. Because of the poor quality of herbage, the carrying capacity for animals is low, which easily results in overgrazing. The total grassland area decreased from 251,000 hectares in 1981 to 192,000 in 1986, and then to 135,000 hectares in 1994. Most overgrazed areas are communal lands. Farmers overgraze these areas believing that the cost of

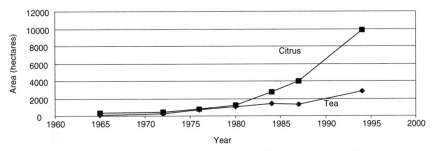

FIGURE 8-6 Areas planted in tea and citrus, Jitai Basin, 1965–1994. SOURCES: Collection of agricultural statistics, 1949–1987, Bureau for Agriculture, Animal Husbandry and Fishery Production in Ji'an Prefecture, Ji'an, Jiangxi Province, pp. 107, 122, 138, 963–964; Economic Statistical Yearbooks of Ji'an City, Jinggangshan City, and Ji'an, Jishui, Taihe, Xingguo counties. 1994. Statistical Bureaus of Ji'an City, Jinggangshan City, and Ji'an, Jishui, Taihe, Xingguo counties.

land degradation is borne by the entire community or village. Thus this grassland has become marginal; its production potential is very low, and frequently its steeper slopes are heavily eroded.

Given its isolated location and undeveloped economy, the Jitai Basin had a slow rate of urbanization until 1978, when development of the economy and the construction of industrial zones, highways, and other infrastructure began to accelerate the transition from rural area to urban area. The highway system expanded from 1,800 kilometers in 1986 to 2,800 kilometers in 1993, and the urban area increased from 5 percent to 6 percent during the same period. In addition, new township enterprises sprang up. Currently, about 6 percent of land in the Jitai Basin is urban or built-up, compared with 16 percent of the Pearl River Delta (see Chapter 9). Accordingly, the proportion of the population that can be classified as urban is lower in the Jitai Basin than in the Pearl River Delta and even lower than the average for China as a whole (Figure 8-7).

Land Quality

Land quality refers to the condition or health of land. The major indicators of land quality are types of land use, inputs of material and energy, landform, climate, soil properties (such as soil organic matter content and total nitrogen), and soil pollution.

From the 1950s to the 1980s land quality in the Jitai Basin worsened, reaching high levels of degradation by the end of the 1980s. In 1988, 28 percent of the land area of the Jitai Basin was suffering from soil erosion, up 256,000 hectares from the 1984 level. But efforts to restore land quality are under way as a result of the reforestation and other policies launched in the 1990s.

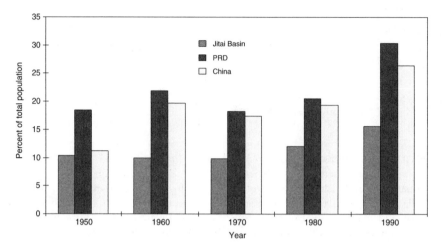

FIGURE 8-7   Urban population as a percentage of total population, Jitai Basin, Pearl River Delta, and China, 1950–1990. SOURCES: Statistical Yearbooks of Guangdong Province. 1950–1990. Beijing: Chinese Statistical Press; Economic Statistical Yearbooks of Ji'an City, Jinggangshan City, and Ji'an, Jishui, Taihe, Xingguo counties. 1994. Statistical Bureaus of Ji'an City, Jinggangshan City, and Ji'an, Jishui, Taihe, Xingguo counties; China Statistical Yearbook, 1991. Beijing: Chinese Statistical Press.

Economic Development

The economic development of Jiangxi Province is below the national average. In 1995 the gross domestic product (GDP) per capita of Jiangxi Province was 3,124 yuan, compared with 3,755 yuan for China as whole. In both 1990 and 1996 the Jitai Basin had a much lower GDP per capita than Guangdong Province, which includes the Pearl River Delta (see Table 8-3). In 1978 the GDP per capita for Guangdong Province was 1.34 times that of Jiangxi Province; by 1996 it was 2.56 times as much. Thus the gap between the two provinces was growing. Because the Jitai Basin is a less-developed region within Jiangxi Province, even in 1996 the GDP per capita for the Jitai Basin was more than 1,000 yuan lower than the average for Jiangxi Province as a whole.

Consumption Levels

Consumption is defined here as personal spending to meet one's daily life needs and wants, such as for food, clothing, housing, recreation, education, health, transportation, and communication. Consumption pattern refers to the array of expenditures made on different items. From 1978 to

TABLE 8-3 Gross Domestic Product per Capita, Guangdong Province, Jiangxi Province, and Jitai Basin, 1978–1996 (yuan)

Year	Guangdong Province	Jiangxi Province	Jitai Basin
1978	367	273.3	
1980	477.6	341.0	
1990	2,496	1,125	887
1996	9,452	3,696	2,668

NOTE: Figures for the Jitai Basin are weighted averages of the corresponding jurisdictions. Data are not adjusted for inflation. The most rapid increases may well be related to inflation.

SOURCES: Statistical Yearbook of Jiangxi Province. 1997. Beijing: Chinese Statistical Press; Statistical Yearbook of Guangdong Province. 1997. Beijing: Chinese Statistical Press.

1984 the consumption level in Jiangxi Province was similar to that of Guangdong Province. After 1984, however, the gap grew to the point that the annual average living expense in Guangdong was 4,200 yuan, while in Jiangxi it was only 1,900 yuan. Yet per capita consumption levels in Jiangxi Province are increasing (Figure 8-8). The price index for retail goods indicates that the gap in consumption levels between Jiangxi and Guangdong Provinces is in fact a real gap and not a reflection of a disparity in retail prices (see Figure 8-9).

DATA AND METHODOLOGY

Several findings of this study are based on an investigation of the historic records of land use change in the Jitai Basin and an analysis of the

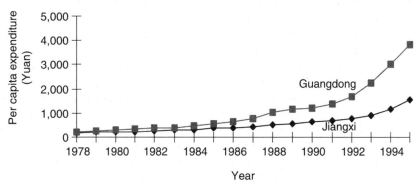

FIGURE 8-8 Average annual per capita expenditure, Jiangxi Province and Guangdong Province, 1978–1995. SOURCES: Statistical Yearbook of Jiangxi Province. 1994. Beijing: Chinese Statistical Press, p. 162; Statistical Yearbook of Guangdong Province. 1997. Beijing: Chinese Statistical Press, p. 102.

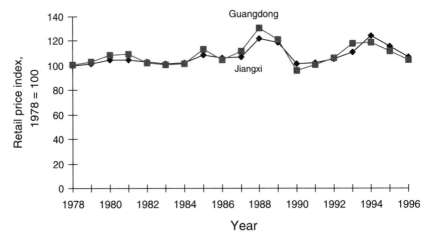

FIGURE 8-9 Retail price index, Guangdong Province and Jiangxi Province, 1978–1996. SOURCES: Statistical Yearbook of Jiangxi Province. 1997. Beijing: Chinese Statistical Press, p. 143; Statistical Yearbook of Guangdong Province. 1997. Beijing: Chinese Statistical Press, p. 203.

factors driving these changes. Data were drawn from: a geographic information system (GIS) and additional statistics to evaluate land use change; multiple time-series data for the years 1950–1995; and official data collected from the statistical bureaus of provincial and local governments. Major land use categories were: farmland, water, forestland, grassland, garden, built-up, roads and railways, and unused land at the county and regional levels. Demographic data were collected on total population, literacy (by sex), and social and economic factors such as per capita GDP, farmer income, and total consumption expenses. Data were collected at the county level on common biophysical variables such as latitude, longitude, annual temperature, and rainfall.

Some types of data on land use and population have not been recorded periodically. For example, the national population census was conducted in 1982 and again in 1990. Detailed demographic data for each county and for some townships were extracted from censuses carried out at these levels. These censuses reported on urban and rural population, family size, fertility rate, infant mortality, life expectancy, rural-to-urban migration, and literacy. Data on land use were drawn from land use investigations at the county level where two detailed surveys of the Jitai Basin were conducted in 1986 and 1992. These data are more detailed than the statistics collected regularly on a larger scale.

Some special field surveys on land quality have been conducted since the 1960s. From 1960 to 1980, 18 major soil types in the Jitai Basin were monitored continuously. The National Soil Survey of China, carried out from 1981 to 1983, and the latest field survey, conducted in 1996 by the authors of this chapter, provide detailed information on land quality at scales of 1:10,000 and 1:400,000.

Topographic maps drawn to a scale of 1:1000,000 were available for the whole study region, within the administrative boundaries of six counties. Roads, railways, and urban areas were digitized to construct base maps for a spatial database. Also incorporated into this database were 1:50,000 scale maps of land use types at the township level for some counties. Various statistical methods were then applied to examine the interactions among the forces driving land use change.

AN INTEGRATED ANALYSIS OF LAND USE CHANGE

Land use change is a complex and dynamic phenomenon. Its causes are often referred to as "drivers," which are described as either proximate or underlying (Adger and Brown, 1994). Proximate drivers are associated with activities that directly interact with and modify the physical environment (Turner and Meyer, 1994). Underlying drivers, or root causes, influence how individuals or groups interact with and change the land.

Of the main forces driving land use change in the Jitai Basin, the proximate driving forces are easier to identify and recognize. They consist of a direct causal agent, action, or process such as deforestation, reforestation, subsistence agriculture, or cash crop/tree agriculture (Table 8-4). The underlying driving forces, which are far more complex and difficult to identify, arise from sources both external and internal to the region. External sources are mainly responses to the policies of the central government, population pressure, rapid economic development in coastal areas, and an increasing emphasis in some regions on environmental protection. Internal drivers of change are a growing local population, local government policy, and changes in local economic development and consumption patterns, which have been themselves influenced by myriad factors arising from the interactions among society, environment, and development.

Since 1950 the Jitai Basin has experienced a variety of land use changes such as deforestation, reforestation, agriculture expansion, and urbanization (although at a slow rate). These changes are in various ways associated with central government policies, as well as population growth and economic development. Because of China's centralized administrative structure, the policies of the central government play a crucial role in influencing land use change, population growth, and economic development. In the area of land use, for example, both the Great Leap Forward in 1958 and the "household responsibility system for forest production" policy in 1982 triggered deforestation. Since 1982, however, a reforesta-

TABLE 8-4 Summary of Forces Driving Land Use Change in the Jitai Basin, 1950–1995

Land Use Changes	Proximate Driving Forces	Underlying Driving Forces
Deforestation	Overexploitation of forest to seek fuel for steel production, timber, and fuelwood Conversion of forestland to grain agriculture	Policy failures
Expansion of forestland	Regulation of forests	Effective policies Increasing environmental awareness at all levels of government
Changes in farmland area	Subsistence agriculture Encroachment by urbanization and expansion of industrial districts, traffic roads, and rural settlements Conversion of farmland to horticulture land and forestland	Population increase Government policies Economic development inside or outside of the Jitai Basin Changes in consumption patterns Environmental protection
Increase in cash crop and horticulture land	Cash tree/crop agriculture	Policy High financial benefits Changes in consumption patterns

tion campaign has successfully increased forestland. In the area of population growth, the national pronatalist policy that sustained a high birth rate from 1955 through the late sixties was followed by a one-child policy, launched in the early 1980s, that led to a decline in birth rates nationwide.

Population growth is an important driving force in land use change in the Jitai Basin. During 1950–1957, population pressure, combined with the land reform policies of the central government, led to agricultural expansion. In contrast, the encroachment of farmland was in part a response to increased demands for living space for the additional population.

Under its policy of "reform and open to the world" (1978), China has been gradually converting its central planning economy to a market economy system. This system has brought about dramatic changes, particularly in consumption patterns. Changes in economic development and consumption influence both migration and land use. In the 1990s economic development fostered the migration of surplus rural labor from the Jitai Basin to more developed areas. At the same time, changes in consumption patterns led to a conversion of grain crops to cash crops/trees. The next section examines in detail several research findings about changes in land use.

RESEARCH FINDINGS

Finding 1: Under certain circumstances, particularly in a planned economy, the policies of the central government have a great influence on land use change, population growth, and economic development.

Although population is often cited as the major underlying force driving land use changes in developing countries, that is not always the case. Population growth is, of course, likely to be an important factor driving land use change, but it has not been the determining one in the Jitai Basin, especially during 1950–1982, the period the planned economy system was in effect in China.

Since the founding of the People's Republic of China in 1949, the administrative structure of the country, based on the principle of centralization, has consisted of a national central government that sits atop descending provincial, district, county, township, and village governments. The relationship between the center and the periphery can be described as patron–client, whereby the patron, in return for obedience and loyalty, provides the client with the necessary economic conditions and services. Under this top–down approach, regional development activities have been strongly associated with national development policies and programs. The major policies of the central government that have had the most profound effect on the Jitai Basin are listed in Table 8-5.

After 1949 the Chinese government announced a series of policies to stimulate agricultural development. Under the land reform policy, large areas of land were redistributed from a small number of landlords to numerous small farmers. From 1949 to 1957, this policy played an important role in encouraging farmers to reclaim wasteland. In the Jitai Basin, cultivated land increased from 174,000 hectares in 1950 to 227,000 hectares in 1957.

In 1957 the central government established agricultural producers' cooperatives in rural areas of the Jitai Basin. Land ownership shifted from the individual farmer to the collective, and land use decisions became a key element of national policy. The next year the government implemented its Great Leap Forward policy by setting up furnaces for steel smelting throughout the cities and rural areas of the Jitai Basin. Workers then proceeded to cut down large areas of nearby forest to supply the fuelwood needed to make steel. The resulting deforestation led to serious soil erosion.

From 1955 through the late sixties the Chinese government encouraged farmers to have more children, especially boys, in order to provide the farmers and soldiers needed to develop the agriculture and military

TABLE 8-5 Main Government Policies Affecting the Jitai Basin, 1950–1993

Period	Policy	Description	Results
1950–1957	Land reform	Ownership of land distributed to the individual farmers, thereby stimulating land reclamation	Increase in cultivated land
1958	Great Leap Forward	Policy promoting steel production	Sharply decreased forestland, causing soil erosion
1955–1976	Pronatalist policy	Policy encouraging child-bearing aimed at providing enough people for production activities and to serve as soldiers	Collection of fuelwood results in deforestation. Need for living space for additional population leads to loss of farmland.
1966–1976	Grain production first Cultural Revolution	Dedication of farmland to grain production and the upheavals of the Cultural Revolution	Agriculture limited to one-crop farming
1978–present	Economic reform and opening to the world	Rapid economic growth External investment	Turning point of planned economy to market economy Acceleration of economic development Speeding up of urbanization Diversification of agriculture Increase in cash crops/trees
1982	Household responsibility system for agricultural production	Established a system of contracts between the farmers and local government in which the farmer could use the land for a certain period	Deforestation, a result of the government giving rights to a long-term asset for short-term gain
1980–1993	Family planning	Policy in urban and some rural areas calling for one child per couple	Lower birth rate, which reduced the population pressure on the land

SOURCES: Statistical Bureau of Shenzhen City. 1991, 1993, 1994. Economic Statistical Yearbook of Shenzhen City; Statistical Bureau of Xingguo County. 1991, 1993, 1994. Economic Statistical Yearbook of Xingguo County.

sectors. But larger families require more living space. In the Jitai Basin villages expanded into the surrounding farmland. Forestland was then cleared to provide more timber for both house construction and fuelwood and to make room for the new farmland needed to meet the subsistence needs of the additional population. But then, in a turnabout, the Chinese government began in the early 1980s to discourage population growth by adhering to a policy calling for one child per couple. In the Jitai Basin this policy has led to a decline in the rate of population increase and reduced some pressures caused by population growth.

From 1966 to 1976 the central government implemented a policy of "putting grain first" in order to meet increased demands for food. In the Jitai Basin large portions of forest and grassland were converted to cultivated grain.

Since 1978 China has followed a basic policy of economic reform. This policy is a turning point in the conversion of a planned economy to a market economy. At the beginning of the 1980s the policy of a "household responsibility system for agricultural production" was implemented in rural areas, making farmers once again landholders and the decision-makers on land use. In recent years, market factors have become more important in influencing decisions on land use, with the result that cash crop and fruit trees with higher economic value are now being planted in the Jitai Basin. The agricultural system has changed from one based on subsistence farming to one based on multiculture.

The policy of a "household responsibility system for agricultural production" has been declared a great success by many observers. But the "household responsibility system for forest production" (1982) has brought about a disaster in the forests. Originally, policymakers had expected farmers to enthusiastically develop and protect forests, just as they had embraced agricultural production. However, farmers' eagerness for short-term benefits and their lack of understanding of sustainable forestry practices and of the need for environmental protection resulted in another round of large-scale deforestation. The government eventually discontinued implementation of this system.

In essence, then, national policies, from land reform, to the Great Leap Forward, to "reform and open to the world," to the "household responsibility system," to family planning, have been the central factors driving land use change in the Jitai Basin. In other words, land use change in the Jitai Basin can be explained more by policies issued by the central government than by the oft-cited factor of population pressure.

Finding 2: Population growth in the Jitai Basin correlates only marginally with farmland development.

From 1950 to 1990 the population of the Jitai Basin grew rapidly (Figure 8-2). Because economic development in the region was limited, tradi-

tional agriculture occupied a very important position in the local economy. For farmers, larger families (and more workers) translated into larger
incomes. But after 1979 and implementation of the national economic
reform policy, the economy developed more rapidly. More jobs were
available, and family size was no longer the main determinant of income.
The government's family planning policy was implemented more strictly
in the 1970s, and contraceptives were provided to persons of childbearing
age. By 1993 the annual rate of population increase in the Jitai Basin was
only 0.036 percent.

Like many other parts of China, the Jitai Basin experienced several
peaks and valleys in its rate of population change from 1950 to 1994
(Figure 8-10). In 1952 the government relocated large groups of citizens
(cadres) in the border districts in south and west China, many from the
Jitai Basin, accounting for a trough in the population growth rate. In 1960,
after the initiation of the Great Leap Forward, the government began to

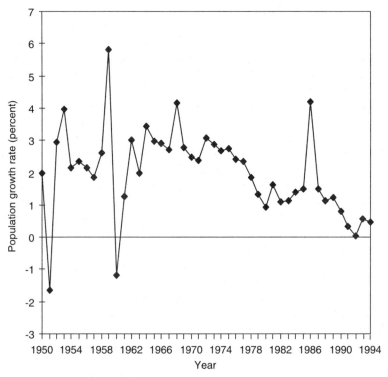

FIGURE 8-10 Population growth rate, Jitai Basin, 1950–1994. SOURCE: Population statistics, Statistical Bureau of Ji'an Prefecture, 1950–1994. NOTE: Peak in
1987 is due to the "open a small hole" temporary relaxation of the one-child
policy.

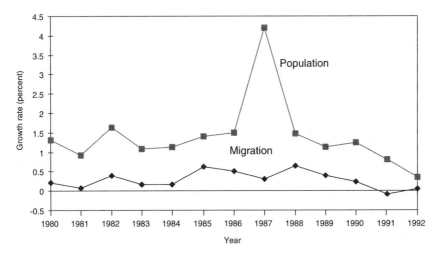

FIGURE 8-11 Population growth rate and net migration rate, Jitai Basin, 1980–1992. SOURCE: Population statistics, Statistical Bureau of Ji'an Prefecture, 1980–1992.

officially encourage childbearing. At the same time the death rate fell with the establishment of a national public health services system. The Great Leap Forward was followed in 1961, however, by famine and a massive death toll. Because Jiangxi Province is one of the grain bases of China, the government shipped grain from the Jitai Basin to meet demand elsewhere and left very little for the local population. Population growth spiked again in 1969. In the Cultural Revolution period many school graduates moved to the countryside, including Jiangxi Province, in response to a government appeal. This political movement climaxed in 1969. In 1986, when the government relaxed the family planning policy, another major population increase occurred. Finally, in the early 1990s the population born in the 1970s became of childbearing age. Because this was a small population cohort arising from the strict family planning policy of the 1970s, the population growth rate again declined.

Net migration has contributed relatively little to population growth in the Jitai Basin (Figure 8-11). In 1987 the rate of increase of the population was 4.19 percent, but the net migration rate was only about 0.5 percent. Most of the increase in population came from natural population growth.

Population pressure, external demand, and government policy encouraging farmers to plant grain resulted in expansion of farmland in the Jitai Basin prior to 1958. After 1958 changes in farmland were driven mainly by government policies mandating other activities for the rural population. In 1958–1959, during the Great Leap Forward, most peasants

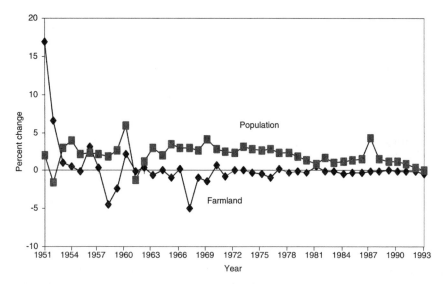

FIGURE 8-12 Rates of change in farmland and population, Jitai Basin, 1951–1993. SOURCES: Population statistics, Statistical Bureau of Ji'an Prefecture, 1950–1993; Collection of agricultural statistics, 1949–1987, Bureau for Agriculture, Animal Husbandry and Fishery Production in Ji'an Prefecture, Ji'an, Jiangxi Province; Economic Statistical Yearbooks of Ji'an City, Jinggangshan City, and Ji'an, Jishui, Taihe, Xingguo counties. 1988–1993. Statistical Bureaus of Ji'an City, Jinggangshan City, and Ji'an, Jishui, Taihe, Xingguo counties.

participated in government-mandated steel making, and much of the farmland was abandoned (see Figure 8-12). It decreased from 227,000 hectares in 1956 to 212,000 hectares in 1958, a drop of 15,000 hectares in only two years. Farmland decreased again in 1967—by –4.9 percent; farmers were now busy with the Cultural Revolution.

Finding 3: Consumption patterns in the Jitai Basin have changed. This change may be associated with decreased grain production and increased cash crop production in the region.
 Consumption patterns are closely related to the social and economic development of a society. In a less-developed economy, basic existence is the primary concern, and food is the main consumption item.
 Because of the lack of complete data sets on the Jitai Basin, subsites were selected for analysis. Ji'an Prefecture, containing five of the six study sites in the Jitai Basin, is examined here in more detail. One county also was selected, because a complete data series exists for it.
 The rest of this section discusses the evolution of consumption patterns in terms of stages in the economic development of the region. These stages are based on changes in natural conditions and government politi-

cal and economic policies and demonstrate graphically the effects of these conditions and policies on the Jitai Basin region.

• *Stage One: Struggle for Existence.* Before the mid–1970s the struggle for existence was the primary concern of residents of the Jitai Basin. During three years of natural disasters (1959–1961) and again during the Cultural Revolution (1966–1976), the supply of food fell well short of demand and many people died of starvation. For example, according to the records of Xingguo County, on June 10, 1959, heavy rains led to flooding of more than 28,700 hectares of arable land. Then from June 18 to June 21, 203.2 millimeters of rain fell, flooding 57,000 hectares. That year, 15,000 hectares did not produce any grain. Several years later, in 1961, 281.3 millimeters of rain fell from June 10 to June 12, covering 51,000 hectares of cultivated land.

The effects of these disasters and other events were worsened by the rapid natural growth of population. But by the 1980s an upward trend was evident in food production (see Figure 8-13, which shows grain, pork, egg, and fish production for the Ji'an Prefecture—Ji'an City, Ji'an County,

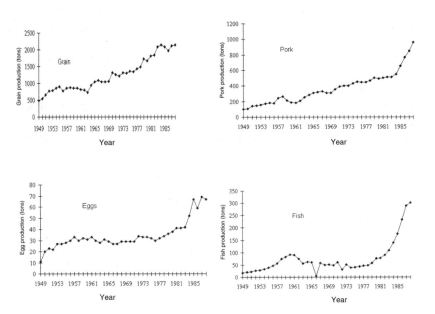

FIGURE 8-13 Production of grain, pork, eggs, and fish, Ji'an Prefecture, 1949–1988. SOURCE: The Progress in Forty Years—The Social and Economic Statistical Materials of Ji'an Prefecture, 1949–1988. 1994. Statistical Bureau of Ji'an Prefecture, Ji'an, Jiangxi Province. NOTE: Ji'an Prefecture comprises Ji'an City, Ji'an County, Jishui County, Taihe County, and Jinggangshan City.

Jishui County, Taihe County, and Jinggangshan City—from 1949 to 1988). Per capita production increased slowly prior to the early 1980s because of rapid population growth, even though total production showed an overall rise.

• *Stage Two: Diversification of Agricultural Production.* With implementation of the national economic reform policy and the "household responsibility system," the production of grain, pork, eggs, and fish increased in the 1980s (Figure 8-13). Three factors led to these increases. First, an increase in grain production provided a basis for production of other forms of food. Second, with the market economy developing rapidly, agricultural products could be sold on the free market, and farmers sought additional sources of income from, for example, selling eggs or pork. Third, people's standard of living increased, and the demand for food became more diversified. From 1989 to 1996 the production of grain increased by 6.7 percent, eggs by 30 percent, meat by 95 percent, and fish by 127 percent. It was significant that the increase in the production of fish and meat products and eggs is much higher than that of grain.

The value of food exports from the region rose from 1978 to 1988. For example, in the late 1980s the value of cereal and food oil exports abroad was nearly five times what it had been in 1978; the value of exports of particular local goods and livestock increased at the same rate. Value fell in both categories in 1984 largely because of fluctuations in the international market. After 1984 the export values of cereal and food oil rose at a higher rate.

• *Stage Three: Changing Patterns of Expenditure and Diversification of Food.* In the Jitai Basin consumption patterns in both urban and rural areas have changed in recent years. Consumption of housing, clothing, and fuel has increased in urban areas, while relative spending on food has decreased. By contrast, in the rural areas of Jiangxi Province relative consumption of food has remained stable, while the proportion of purchases of clothing, housing, and fuels has decreased.

According to the per capita purchasing patterns in the urban and rural areas of Jiangxi Province in 1989 and 1996, both grain and vegetable consumption decreased, while the consumption of food oil, meat (pork, beef, mutton, and poultry), eggs, fish, and wine increased. As for fuel consumption, coal is being replaced by natural gas in urban areas.

In rural areas consumption patterns show some similar trends, but with a smaller change from 1989 to 1996. In 1996 people consumed more food oil, meat, eggs, fish, and wine than in 1989. Also significant, residents consumed 4.8 times more fruit in 1996 than in 1989.

Changes in consumption were paralleled by changes in crop production. In Taihe County, where data were available, the land devoted to

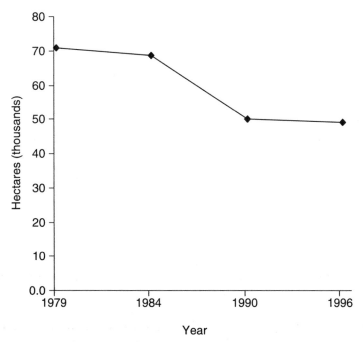

Year

FIGURE 8-14 Land devoted to grain production, Taihe County, 1979–1996. SOURCES: The Progress in Forty Years—The Social and Economic Statistical Materials of Ji'an Prefecture, 1949–1988. 1994. Statistical Bureau of Ji'an Prefecture, Ji'an, Jiangxi Province; Statistical Yearbook of Jiangxi Province. 1997. Beijing: Chinese Statistical Press.

grain production decreased from 1979 to 1996 (Figure 8-14); grain crops accounted for 73 percent of the total area sown in 1989 and 66 percent in 1996. By contrast, the land planted in cash crops increased throughout the 1980s, except in 1988 when the government launched the campaign to restore grain production (Figure 8-15). Cash crops accounted for 27 percent of total area sown in 1989 and 34 percent in 1996.

Finding 4: An increase in the floating population is promoting local private economic development.

Recent reform policy has brought major changes to the Jitai Basin. One of these changes is the growth of the "floating population."

Everyone in China has a registered permanent residence that is assigned at birth; usually it is the permanent residence of one of a citizen's parents. A person may live in that location legally. Citizens who move to a location where they do not have a local registered permanent residence may not remain in that place unless they obtain a license from the police every half-year. This is known as the household registry system. Migrants,

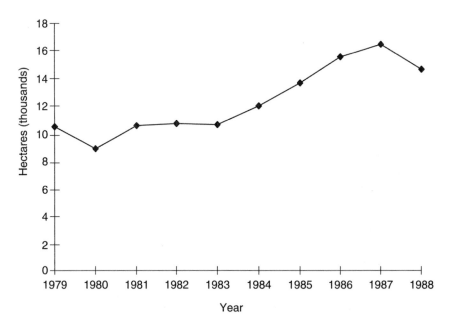

FIGURE 8-15 Land devoted to cash crop production, Taihe County, 1979–1988. SOURCE: The Progress in Forty Years—The Social and Economic Statistical Materials of Ji'an Prefecture, 1949–1988. 1994. Statistical Bureau of Ji'an Prefecture, Ji'an, Jiangxi Province.

in the Chinese context, are people who have changed domiciles by registering with the local police station in a new location. Floating population refers to people who move from one place to another, usually staying less than a half-year with no official change in their registered permanent residence. Members of the floating population are required to get a license from the local government every half-year; otherwise, they are considered illegal residents. In the Jitai Basin the floating population mainly refers to the labor force that leaves the region temporarily to find work.

Before 1978, laborers were forbidden to "float" by the strict household registry system, and there was almost no floating population during the Cultural Revolution. Even in 1984 the floating population in the Jitai Basin consisted of fewer than a thousand persons. After 1984, however, the government invested in massive urban construction projects outside the area that required labor. Thus the surplus of rural labor moved to the big cities to seek the new jobs. Many of these rural laborers found construction jobs either in the big cities or in the coastal areas in east or south China. The Jitai Basin at that time was isolated and relatively undeveloped and among the poorest regions in China. Jobs in the cities offered much higher income potential.

As noted, at the beginning of the economic reform period only a few laborers left the region to seek work. After 1990, however, the floating population became a larger group; population growth and the decrease in arable land had created a larger surplus rural labor force. Nevertheless, both the high population density of the big cities and coastal areas in east and south China and the household registry residence system served to limit the formal migration of the population. The result has been a very special phenomenon: a large movement of the floating population twice a year, before and after the Spring Festival in China. Because the floating labor force cannot officially migrate to the place where they work, floaters have to move between their working place and their household registry residence twice a year.

From Xingguo County in Jiangxi Province, most of the floating-out labor force goes to Shenzhen City on the South China Sea or Shanghai on the East China Sea to work temporarily (see Table 8-6, which compares the average income of the labor forces in Xingguo County with that of the floating labor forces in Shenzhen City from 1991 to 1994). The income of the floating labor force in Shenzhen is representative of the income of the floating labor force from Xingguo. In 1991 the proportion of the floating labor forces to total labor forces in Xingguo was 1.2 percent. That proportion rose to 9 percent in 1993 and 15 percent in 1994. The large differences in income levels between the local labor force and floating labor force have fostered this movement of people.

The growth of the floating labor force has spurred the growth of the local economy. Most members of that labor force are young and educated. When they return home, which they must do under the household registry system, they bring with them money, technology, and knowledge. Some workers attempt to start their own careers in their hometown. Some invest in agriculture, but most invest in industry, establishing private enterprises. In 1991 the GDP from private enterprises was 83.5 million yuan, increasing to 615 million in 1994. Most private enterprises are supported financially by members of the floating labor force and by technical

TABLE 8-6 Average per Capita Income of Floating Labor Force in Shenzhen City and Local Labor Force in Xingguo County, 1991–1994 (yuan)

Year	Shenzhen City	Xingguo County
1991	5,146	768
1993	9,530	1,079
1994	12,972	1,533

SOURCES: Statistical Bureau of Shenzhen City. 1991, 1993, 1994. Economic Statistical Yearbook of Shenzhen City; Statistical Bureau of Xingguo County. 1991, 1993, 1994. Economic Statistical Yearbook of Xingguo County.

workers who once were floaters. Former floating workers also have set up several industrial and agricultural technology schools to train the local population, thereby improving the technical level of the local labor force.

CONCLUSION

Land use changes in the Jitai Basin have essentially stemmed from a combination of government policy, population growth, and economic development. This finding implies that relevant, acceptable policies aimed at achieving sustainable development in the Jitai Basin will rest on an understanding of the dynamics of population, land use, and socioeconomics.

One factor that has influenced the impact of government land use policy on the Jitai Basin has been its isolation. The Jitai Basin is a remote, somewhat inaccessible region of China. The north–south railway that connects Ji'an with the larger city of Nanchang and the south was only recently constructed, and Jinggangshan still has no rail connection. The same isolation that was the reason for the region's success as a remote communist base area later caused it to develop only slowly, and the reform policies pursued by the central government after 1978 resulted in its relative stagnation when compared with the vibrant development of coastal areas, like the Pearl River Delta, where foreign capital flowed in and fueled the rapid construction of new factories, transport lines, and residential areas.

The forces driving land use change vary. While some forces act slowly over decades, others trigger events quickly and visibly. In the Jitai Basin, government policies not only affected land use gradually over the long term, but also dramatically over the short term. For example, the policy of "putting grain first" caused between 1966 and 1976 the gradual conversion of forestland to grain crops and an overall lack of change in the land devoted to cash crops. But the implementation of policies such as the Great Leap Forward calling for increased steel production (1958) and the "household responsibility system for forest production" (1982) triggered dramatic deforestation in only one or two years. The success of some policies such as reforestation suggests that environmental degradation can be brought under control, at least to some degree, in spite of the tremendous population pressure and the limitations of low economic development in rural areas. In a country with a centralized administrative structure, government policy has more of an effect on land use change than does population growth, particularly during periods of a directly planned economy.

The total population of the Jitai Basin increased from 1951 to 1995, mainly through natural growth. The family planning policy in effect since the early 1980s has played an important role in controlling further population growth, and the average growth rate of the population is declining. The floating population did not emerge in large numbers until 1990. Because the Jitai Basin is a relatively undeveloped region, its consumption patterns have changed slowly. The market economy stimulated farmers to produce more profitable products and so more land was converted from grain crops to cash crops. Urbanization, however, can lead to increased encroachment into agricultural areas, especially farmland adjacent to cities. Currently, about 5.9 percent of land in the region is urban or developed. In the long run, urban-based pressures may exacerbate the deterioration of natural resources if these resources are not managed appropriately.

REFERENCES

Adger, N., and K. Brown. 1994. Land Use and the Causes of Global Warming. Chichester: John Wiley.

Ji'an Planning Council and Ji'an Agricultural Division Council. 1993. Agriculture Nature Resources Development and Division of District in Ji'an District. Nanchang: Science and Technology Press of Jiangxi Province.

Land Administrative Bureau and Soil Survey Office of Jiangxi Province. 1991. Soil in Jiangxi. Beijing: Agriculture Science and Technology Press of China.

Qin Mingzhou. 1997. Amount and quality changes in the process of red soil resource development in South China. Postdoctoral report, Institute of Soil Science, Chinese Academy of Sciences, pp. 5–30.

Turner, B. L., and W. B. Meyer. 1994. Global land use and land-cover change: An overview. In: Changes in Land Use and Land Cover: A Global Perspective, W. B. Meyer and B. L. Turner, eds. Cambridge: Cambridge University Press.

Xi Chengfan, et al. 1989. The Development and Management of the Red Soil Hilly Area, An Experimental Study of the Qianyanzhou Station. Beijing: Science Press.

9

Population, Consumption, and Land Use in the Pearl River Delta, Guangdong Province

Zhao Shidong, Chinese Academy of Sciences; Zeng Yi, Peking University; Bai Wanqi, Chinese Academy of Sciences; Lu Jiehua, Peking University; Qi Wenhu, Chinese Academy of Sciences; Liu Guiping, Peking University; Zhang Taolin, Chinese Academy of Sciences; Qin Mingzhou, Henan University; Jiang Leiwen, Peking University

A densely populated region in southeastern China, the Pearl River Delta has undergone dramatic changes in its population, land use, and environmental quality, stemming from its rapid economic development and urbanization. This chapter begins by describing the physical conditions, demography, land use, and environmental quality of the region, as well as the methodology used to evaluate the interactions among them. A set of research findings on the nature of these interactions, corroborated by the use of extensive empirical data, follows.

THE PEARL RIVER DELTA: A DESCRIPTION

Physical Conditions

The Pearl River Delta, situated in southern China's Guangdong Province, is formed by alluvium delivered from the West, North, and East Rivers. Located in the subtropical monsoon zone, the region has an annual average temperature of 22°C, annual precipitation of 1,714 millimeters, and annual sunshine of 1,990-2,300 hours. Various landforms are found in the Delta: wetland, estuary, lowland, plain, dryland, and upland hills. The specific region examined in this chapter is in the central part of the Pearl River Delta, which covers 17,219 square kilometers. The region is made up of 13 counties and cities distributed among six municipalities that lie on either side of the Pearl River estuary (see Figure 9-1 and Table 9-1).

This study covers the period before Hong Kong was reunited with the rest of China, and thus Hong Kong is not explicitly studied here.

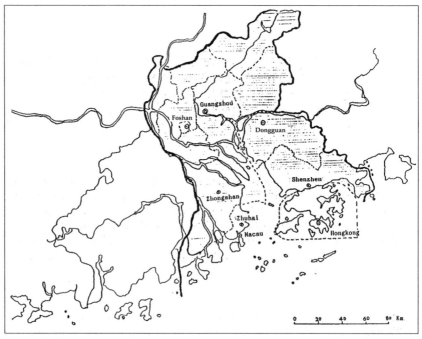

FIGURE 9-1 Pearl River Delta, Guangdong Province.

Nevertheless, Hong Kong has always been a key part of the ecological region of the Pearl River Delta and frequently a destination for out-migrants from the region. With the socioeconomic reforms beginning in 1978, Hong Kong's investments in and influence on the study area increased dramatically.

Demographics

The Pearl River Delta is one of the most populated areas of China. In 1995 its permanent population density was 743 persons per square kilo-

TABLE 9-1 Municipalities, Counties, and Cities in the Pearl River Delta Study Region

Municipality	County/City
Dongguan	Dongguan City
Foshan	Foshan City, Nanhai City, Shunde City
Guangzhou	Conghua City, Guangzhou City, Huadu City, Panyu City, Zengcheng City
Shenzhen	Shenzhen City
Zhongshan	Zhongshan City
Zhuhai	Zhuhai City, Doumen County

TABLE 9-2 Percent Increase in Permanent Population, Pearl River
Delta, Guangdong Province, and China, 1960–1990

	1960–1970	1970–1980	1980–1990
Pearl River Delta	19.70	17.10	35.20
Guangdong Province	26.25	19.28	21.41
China	29.41	15.81	15.83

SOURCES: Selected Statistical Yearbooks for subregions, Guangdong Province, and China,
1960–1991.

meter, as compared with 378 for all of Guangdong Province and 126 for
China as a whole. The total permanent population of the Delta region has
grown at a substantially faster rate than populations elsewhere in China
(Table 9-2). From 1960 to 1970 all three areas shown in Table 9-2 experienced high population growth. Smaller increases in the permanent population were evident during 1970–1980, until a one-child policy, launched
in the early 1980s, led to a decline in birth rates nationwide.

Overall, the population of the Pearl River Delta has grown considerably over the last two decades (Figure 9-2), but this growth cannot be
attributed to natural increase because the crude birth rate in the Delta
area is below those at the provincial and national levels (Figure 9-3). The
natural growth rate (the difference between the crude birth rate and crude
death rate) of the Delta area also is lower than those for Guangdong
Province and China as a whole, and a declining population growth rate
might have been expected because of implementation of the one-child
policy.

The Delta region owes its rapid population growth mainly to massive
in-migration (see the net migration rates for 1980–1994 in Figure 9-4). Of
the Chinese provinces, Guangdong has one of the highest net in-migration
rates, and this rate is considerably higher in the Delta region than in the
province as a whole. Within the region, the more industrialized subregions attract the most migrants. For example, the cities of Zhuhai and
Shenzhen, two of the special economic zones[1] located in the Delta, have
the greatest relative gain in in-migration, more than 10 times the average

---

[1]The towns of Shenzhen and Zhuhai were redefined as cities in 1979 and a year later
were established among China's first special economic zones (SEZ) by Chinese leader Deng
Xiaoping. The special economic zones were implemented by the Communist government
as a virtual laboratory for experimentation with a free market economy. These zones, which
operate under an entirely different economic premise than that of the mainland, emphasize
exports and are intended to serve as an attractive environment for foreign direct investment
through favorable tax incentives. When the special economic zones were first established,
the majority of the new businesses that settled in Shenzhen and Zhuhai were Hong Kong-
and Macao-based enterprises drawn to the zones to take advantage of, among many other
things, the abundance of low-wage labor and the customs-free industrial environment.

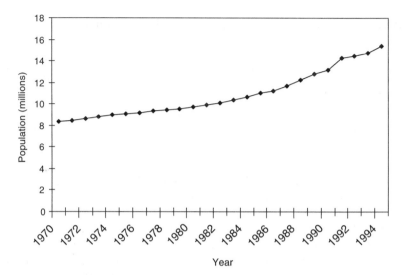

FIGURE 9-2 Total population, Pearl River Delta, 1970–1994. SOURCES: Selected Statistical Yearbooks for subregions of Pearl River Delta, 1970–1995. NOTE: Total population includes only persons registered in the Pearl River Delta and excludes the floating population registered in other places.

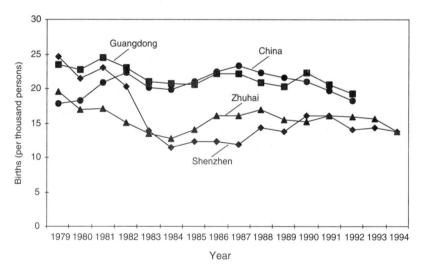

FIGURE 9-3 Crude birth rate, China, Guangdong Province, Shenzhen City, and Zhuhai City, 1979–1994. SOURCES: Yao Xinwu and Yinhua. 1994. Basic Data of China's Population. Beijing: China Population Press; Statistical Yearbooks for Shenzhen and Zhuhai.

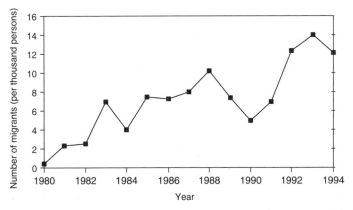

FIGURE 9-4 Net migration rate, Pearl River Delta, 1980–1994. SOURCES: Selected Yearbooks for subregions of Pearl River Delta, 1980–1995.

level of Guangdong. By contrast, Guangzhou, Foshan, and Zhongshan have experienced a medium gain in in-migration, more than five times the average level of Guangdong, and Dongguan has experienced the smallest gain, similar to that for Guangdong.

Population growth statistics are calculated on the basis of numbers of permanent residents, but China also has a "floating" population living away from their permanent residence (this phenomenon is described more fully later in this chapter and in Chapter 8). In the Delta area the floating population has been increasing because of the rapidly growing job market there. In 1995, for example, the floating population of the Delta made up more than half of the floating population of Guangdong Province (Table 9-3). Thus if this massive temporary population is taken into account, the population growth in the Delta area has been dramatic indeed—a 74.3 percent increase from 1986 to 1995. In 1995 the population density of the Delta area was 1,173 persons per square kilometer, compared with 439 persons per square kilometer in Guangdong Province as a whole.

TABLE 9-3 Ratio of Floating Population to Permanent Population, Selected Subregions, 1995

Subregion	Ratio of Floating to Permanent Population (percent)
Guangdong Province	10.7
Guangzhou City	33.1
Shenzhen City	108.4
Zhuhai City	30.8
Foshan City	23.2
Dongguan City	39.4
Zhongshan City	6.0

SOURCE: 1% Sampling Census of 1995 in Guangdong. 1997. Beijing: China Statistical Press.

Urbanization also is occurring at a rapid pace, but in China it is difficult to measure because of the ambiguous definition of the term and frequent changes in the stated boundaries of urban areas (Ma Xia, 1988; Zeng Yi and Vaupel, 1989). Three indicators of urbanization are used here to describe the process in the Pearl River Delta. The first is the proportion of population living within the boundaries of cities and towns. By this measure, which is the official definition used by the Chinese statistical system, the urban population of the Delta area more than doubled from 1982 to 1990, rising from 32 percent to 70 percent of the total permanent population. A considerable portion of this tremendous increase, however, resulted from the redrawing of administrative boundaries. Thus some suburban residents who were actually engaged in agricultural activities were counted as belonging to the urban population.

The second indicator is the nonagricultural workforce. It increased from about 45 percent of the total workforce in 1982 to about 80 percent in 1995. This indicator also overestimates the true level of urbanization, however, because some people who engaged in nonagricultural work lived in rural areas where there has been rapid growth in rural enterprises.

The third indicator is the proportion of persons who are officially registered as members of nonagricultural households. Among the total permanent residents of the Delta area, this proportion increased from about 36 percent in 1980 to about 52 percent in 1995. Because the government strictly controls nonagricultural household registration, some people who have lived in urban areas for many years and have worked in nonagricultural activities still have not been given nonagricultural household registration status. Thus this indicator can be said to underestimate the true level of urbanization in the Delta.

Land Use Change

Historically the Pearl River Delta was an important grain-growing region of China, and farming played a dominant role in basic land use patterns until the 1980s. In the decades that followed, however, economic reform policies greatly changed the region's social and economic conditions and, in turn, its land use patterns (see Table 9-4).

In 1973 the proportion of farmland to total area was 33.1 percent, dropping to 31.6 percent in 1982, only a slight decline. Farming thus still played a dominant role. Over the next 13 years, however, the proportion of farmland dropped, to 17.6 percent of total land area in 1995. In the meantime, the proportion of urban/built-up land increased from 2.4 percent in 1973 to 15.7 percent in 1995. Because most of the farmland and urban areas are situated in the flatlands of the region, it is logical to conclude that most of the expansion of urban areas has taken place at the expense of farmland. Increases in land devoted to gardens and forests are

TABLE 9-4 Land Use Patterns, Pearl River Delta, 1973–1995 (percent of total area)

Land Use	1973	1982	1995
Farmland	33.1	31.6	17.6
Garden	4.9	3.0	16.1
Forestland	29.6	32.3	37.0
Grassland	12.3	3.03	0.2
Urban/built-up	2.4	7.5	15.7
Water	12.6	16.8	12.8
Unused land	5.0	5.80	0.7

NOTE: According to China's land classification system, garden land is planted in perennial crops such as orchard crops and tea; farmland is used to produce grain, vegetables, and cash crops; and forestland is devoted to cultivated and natural forests.

SOURCES: The data for 1973 are from Landsat MMS and for 1995 from TM images; the 1982 data are from a field survey.

tied to declines in grassland, because most of the grassland, gardens, and forests are located on mountain slopes and hillsides.

Urban and built-up land now makes up a significant proportion of the Delta region, thanks largely to the ongoing industrial development and infrastructure construction in the area (Figure 9-5). The unique location of the Pearl River Delta, with its proximity to neighboring Hong Kong and Macao, have made it a major area for foreign investment, particularly in industry.

From 1950 to 1995, farmland in the Delta region dropped from 550,000 hectares to 310,000 hectares. The change in farmland can be divided into two periods: the period before 1980 when farmland decreased relatively slowly, and the period after 1980 and particularly after 1990, when the rate of decline was more significant (Figure 9-5).

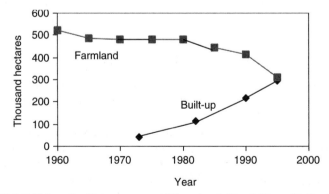

FIGURE 9-5 Urban/built-up areas and farmland, Pearl River Delta, 1960–1995. SOURCES: Urban/built-up: data for 1973 and 1995 are from Landsat images; data for 1982 and 1990 are from field surveys. Farmland data from Statistical Yearbooks from every city.

As for urban growth, the urban area of the special economic zone of Shenzhen, for example, increased from only 2.9 square kilometers in 1979 to 84 square kilometers in 1994. As the Delta area entered the 1980s, the pace increased for all kinds of nonagricultural construction (communications, housing, factories, and recreation). The highway system also expanded—by 82 percent from 1980 to 1994, reaching 0.6 kilometers per square kilometer. These changes were mostly at the expense of farmland.

Environmental Quality

Since the late 1970s, when China began to implement socioeconomic reforms and its Open Door Policy, rapid growth in the Delta area has served to raise the standard of living. This growth, however, has been accompanied by environmental pollution.

The total amount of wastewater discharged in the Delta area more than doubled from 1986 to 1995. Nonindustrial consumers generated 41.7 percent of total wastewater in 1986, rising to 66.4 percent in 1994. The capacity for processing wastewater has lagged far behind the increased output (Tang Yonglun, 1995). The proportion of wastewater processed up to industrial discharge standards decreased from 30 percent in 1986 to 21 percent in 1994.

The volume of automobile and factory emissions in the Delta area more than tripled from 1986 to 1995, and the volume of sulfur dioxide released into the atmosphere is estimated to be about 24 times higher than the average for China as a whole. In response to these problems, the government has stepped up its efforts to limit the discharge of air pollution emissions. Thus the proportion of treated industrial emissions increased from 50 percent in 1986 to 87.2 percent in 1995 in Guangdong Province as a whole, and from 47 percent to about 93.1 percent in the Delta area over the same period. Nevertheless, air pollution in the Delta worsened because of the large increase in the total quantity of emissions.

DATA AND METHODOLOGY

This study of a portion of the Pearl River Delta is based on an investigation of the historic record of land use change and an analysis of the factors driving such change (for more on these "driving factors," see Chapter 8). From this investigation and analysis, several research findings were developed. Data generated by a geographic information system (GIS) were used to test these findings. Additional research findings on the process of land use change emerged from an examination of historical records and physical background information. Statistical data were used to test and validate these findings.

This study used multiple time-series data for the years 1950–1995 at the regional (entire study area) and subregional levels. The data used fell into two categories: official statistics and independent survey data. The statistical bureaus of the provincial and local governments provided official data for 1950–1995 on major land use categories such as farmland, water, and forestland. They also provided demographic data on literacy (by sex) and social and economic factors such as gross domestic product (GDP), per capita GDP, farmer income, and total consumption expenses.

Very detailed demographic data on each municipality and some townships were provided by the national population censuses conducted in 1982 and 1990. The censuses included many categories of population variables, such as urban population, rural population, family size, fertility rate, infant mortality, life expectancy, rural to urban migration, and literacy. In addition, two detailed surveys of land use in the Pearl River Delta dating from 1982 and 1990 were available. The major land use types, based on the Chinese land use classification, were: farmland, forestland, garden, grassland, built-up, roads and railroads, water bodies, and unused land. These survey data were more detailed than the official statistical data. Finally, several special field surveys on land quality have been conducted since the 1960s. Sixteen major soil types were observed continually in the Delta region from 1960 to 1980. The National Soil Survey of China, carried out during 1981–1983, and the field survey of 1996 provided detailed information on land quality at scales of 1:10,000 and 1:400,000.

AN ANALYSIS OF LAND USE CHANGE

Finding 1: Population growth, in particular migration and increases in the floating population, is at once a cause and a consequence of land use change in the Pearl River Delta.

The new economic policy put in place for the Pearl River Delta and the corresponding loosening of the regulations for migration provided opportunities that attracted a large floating population. Farmland was cleared to provide space for industry and for housing for the migrants. Thus population growth and land use change were both responses to the new economic model, and neither would have been possible without the other. Industries were built in response to market demands. The demand for labor exceeded local supply, and the new migrants required further and more extensive conversion of land for housing.

As a result, in the Delta total farmland has dropped as total population has increased (Figure 9-6). Overall, as net migration rates rose in the Delta between 1980 and 1994, farmland decreased (see Figure 9-7), despite the increasing local consumption of farm products.

Since economic reform was implemented in China in 1978 (see Chapter 8), the country has had a "floating" population—that is, laborers who leave their registered permanent residence for less than half a year to

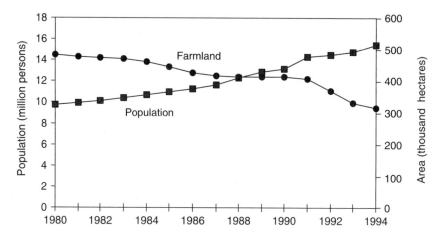

FIGURE 9-6   Farmland and total population, Pearl River Delta, 1980–1994.
SOURCES: Selected Statistical Yearbooks for subregions of Pearl River Delta,
1980–1995.

work elsewhere in China.[2] In the 1990s this population was estimated to
be 100 million a year. Most moved temporarily into coastal regions such
as the Pearl River Delta. The growing floating population in the Delta has
been accompanied by an ever-greater demand for land. The temporary
population needs space for housing which in turn requires expansion of
the urban infrastructure into the surrounding farmland.

Intensified land use has been a significant consequence of changes in
land use in the Pearl River Delta. In urban areas intensification has taken
the form of significant increases in population density since 1980 (Table 9-5)
and production. Indeed, the economic output per unit of land has increased dramatically; the gross domestic product of Delta cities increased
from 6.7 billion yuan in 1980 to 233.3 billion yuan in 1995.

Intensified land use also is evident in agriculture, where more farmland must be converted to nonagricultural uses to make room for urbanization. To compensate for the loss of farmland, farmers must increase
yields per unit of farmland, which in turn requires higher inputs of technology, capital, and labor. For example, since 1980 agricultural intensification in Shenzhen and Dongguan has generally increased grain yields
per unit of farmland (Figure 9-8). An important indicator of technological
input is the gross power consumption of the machinery used in agricultural production such as tractors and pumps. This indicator increased by

---

[2]This phenomenon is explained more fully in Chapter 8. The difference between a member of the floating population and a migrant is that the member of the floating population
does not change his or her household registration and the migrant does.

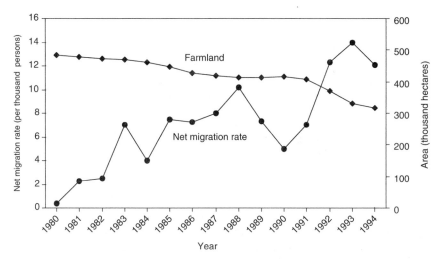

Year

FIGURE 9-7 Farmland and net migration rate, Pearl River Delta, 1980–1994. SOURCES: Selected Statistical Yearbooks for subregions of Pearl River Delta, 1980–1995.

a factor greater than four from 1980 to 1995 in much of the Delta area (Figure 9-9).

Finding 2: In the Pearl River Delta changes in consumption levels caused by the economic growth have led to changes in land use in cities and changes in crop production in rural areas.

At the early stages of economic development beginning in 1978, the local production of goods and services served mainly to supply local demand. Later, when production surpassed local demand and the economy became fully open, local products were not only consumed within the region, but also exported through interregional, interprovincial, and international trade.

TABLE 9-5 Population Density, Pearl River Delta, 1980–1995 (number of persons per square kilometer)

Municipality	1980	1985	1990	1995
Dongguan	457	490	535	587
Foshan	921	988	1,089	1,219
Guangzhou	675	733	799	870
Shenzhen	165	436	1,000	1,709
Zhongshan	600	630	683	744
Zhuhai	231	260	318	400

SOURCES: Statistical Yearbooks of Dongguan, Foshan, Guangzhou, Shenzhen, Zhongshan, and Zhuhai.

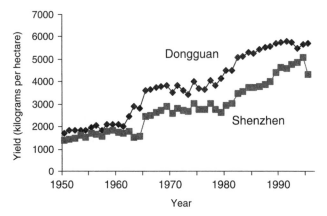

FIGURE 9-8 Unit area grain yield, Dongguan and Shenzhen, 1949–1996.
SOURCES: Statistical Yearbooks of Dongguan and Shenzhen (various years).
NOTE: Grain yield per unit farmland is a weighted average of various grains. In
the Delta area it mainly reflects rice production.

This trade set in motion a process of dramatic shifts in consumption
in the region. Among them, the increased population growth and wealth
resulting from rising production and trade caused a significant change in
the regional housing structure. For example, the per capita floor space in
Guangzhou City remained constant from 1965 to 1980, at only 3–4 square
meters. But by 1995 per capita floor space was about three times that of
the 1960s and 1970s (Figure 9-10), even though the population continued
to grow. This development stemmed in part from rising incomes and in

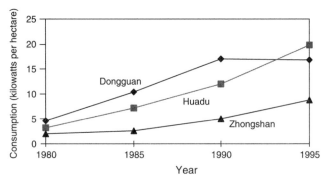

FIGURE 9-9 Gross power consumption of agricultural machinery per hectare of
farmland, Dongguan, Huadu, and Zhongshan, 1980–1995. SOURCES: Statistical
Yearbooks of Dongguan, Huadu, and Zhongshan (various years).

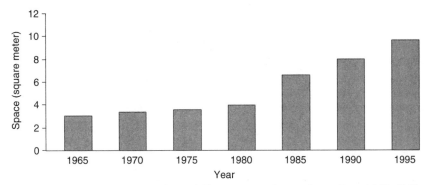

FIGURE 9-10   Per capita residential floor space, Guangzhou City, 1965–1995.
SOURCE: Statistical Yearbook of Guangdong, 1996.

part from government reform of the distribution system and encouragement of a free housing market.

Indeed, the government implemented special policies to foster housing development. One government housing reform policy allowed diversification of housing construction. As a result, not only governments and state-owned enterprises but also private real estate companies can now invest in housing development.

The expansion of green space in urban areas is another example of the changes in land use brought by economic development. In Guangzhou, known as the "dragon head" of economic development in Pearl River Delta and the whole of China as well, the municipal government allocates a portion of its large fiscal budget to the development and maintenance of green space—lawns, parks, artificial lakes, and squares (Figure 9-11). In

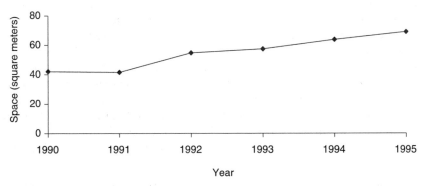

FIGURE 9-11   Per capita open space and parkland, Guangzhou City, 1990–1995.
SOURCE: Statistical Yearbook of Guangdong, 1996.

TABLE 9-6 Average Annual Food Consumption per Capita, Urban Areas of Guangdong Province, 1978–1995

Food Product (kilograms)	Average Annual Consumption per Capita				
	1978	1980	1985	1990	1995
Grain	176.4	153.53	118.7	116.48	87.94
Vegetables	147.36	136.54	95.05	100.7	102.71
Food oil	3.36	3.88	4.09	4.45	6.98
Meat	21.96	26	23.57	24.8	22.89
Poultry	3.96	4.51	6.72	8.41	14.38
Fish	11.2	14.48	16.41	17.38	20.31
Wine	1.44	1.91	3.17	3.2	3.21

SOURCE: Statistical Yearbook of Guangdong Province, 1997, p. 228.

fact, the citizens of Guangzhou pressure government urban planners to develop such areas.

Changes in diet and crop production offer additional evidence of shifts in consumption. Residents of urban areas now consume less grain than in previous years. In 1978 per capita grain consumption in urban areas of Ghangdong Province was 176 kilograms, falling to 88 kilograms by 1995 (see Table 9-6). Likewise, per capita vegetable consumption decreased over the same period—from 147 kilograms in 1978 to 103 kilograms in 1995. This decreased consumption of vegetables and grains was offset by higher consumption of oil, meat, poultry, and fish. Meanwhile, the portion of farmland devoted to grain crops in four counties of Guangdong Province fell from 1978 to 1988 (Figure 9-12), while the portion of farmland devoted to vegetable crops increased, despite falling consumption (Figure 9-13).

The changing patterns of local food consumption mask two key factors associated with the shifts in crop production. First, grains and vegetables were being increasingly fed to animals to produce meat and other animal-related products such as milk. For example, in the urban areas of Guangzhou City per capita consumption of vegetables decreased, but the amount of farmland devoted to vegetable crops increased substantially in the suburbs because large portions of the crops were used to feed pigs, ducks, chickens, milk goats, milk cows, and many other animals. The second factor is that farmers were increasingly able to export their products outside the region. Thus a large proportion of vegetable production was not consumed by local people, but rather sold to other areas. Illustrating this trend, from 1978 to 1988 in the counties of Huadu, Conghua, Zengcheng, and Panyu,[3] land devoted to grain crops decreased (Figure

---

[3]Because of a lack of data, it is hard to show the complete picture of changes in cropping patterns in the Delta region. Huadu, Conghua, Zengcheng, and Panyu, all counties in the municipality of Gangzhou, were selected to illustrate patterns of farmland use.

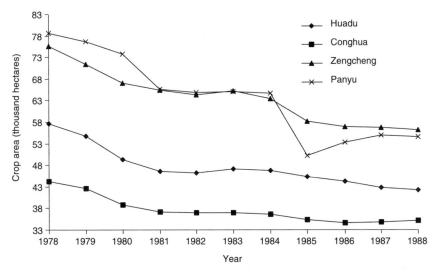

FIGURE 9-12 Grain crop areas, Huadu, Conghua, Zengcheng, and Panyu counties, 1978–1988. SOURCE: The Forty Years of Ji'an Prefecture, Ji'an Prefecture Statistics, 1988.

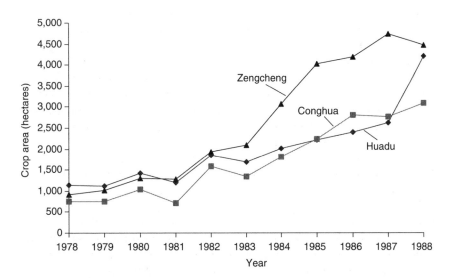

FIGURE 9-13 Vegetable land, Huadu, Conghua, and Zengcheng counties, 1978–1988. SOURCES: Guangdong Statistical Bureau. 1988. The Forty Years of Guangdong. Beijing: China Statistical Press.

9-12), while more and more farmland was shifted to production of cash crops and vegetables (see Figure 9-13).

Finding 3: The economic reform policies introduced in 1978 and known as the Open Door Policy greatly influenced the patterns of land use in the Pearl River Delta, although their impacts on land use differed over time.
Beginning in the 1980s, the Chinese central government decided to implement a variety of policies that would build Shenzhen and Zhuhai into an exporting industry base. Before the economic reforms, Shenzhen and Zhuhai were relatively small agricultural and fishing villages; after the reforms they became large metropolitan areas with millions of residents. As further evidence of its growth, Shenzhen had a built-up area of 58,507 hectares in 1990 compared with only 10,814 hectares in 1982.
The reform policies included: (1) very low or even no taxation on investments in the Delta, particularly when the industry benefiting from the investment was essential for advanced technology; (2) very low rental prices on farmland used for business site construction; and (3) extension of the right to enterprises to recruit and dismiss employees. These policies had large impacts on land use in Pearl River Delta—among them, a reduction in agricultural land.
The Open Door Policy greatly stimulated productivity in the Pearl River Delta. Living standards in the area improved substantially, leading to a rise in overall consumption levels and changes in consumption patterns. With the transition in market patterns, land use in cities continued to change, and in agricultural areas land was shifted from grain to cash crops.
The flexible spatial mobility policy allowed people to seek the economic opportunities available in the Pearl River Delta region. As a result, Shenzhen saw its floating population grow from 10,000 in 1980 to 600,000 in 1989. With the rapid increase of this population, housing construction was accelerated and grew from 0.17 million square meters in 1980 to 1.69 million square meters in 1989.
In the 1990s the pressure of population growth on the land, particularly that produced by the in-migrant and floating populations, began to attract more attention from governments at all levels. The result was development of a special policy for the floating population. In Shenzhen City, for example, the local government began to control the size of the floating population by requiring special registration forms. By the mid-1990s this measure had stabilized the growth of the floating population, although some undocumented migrants remained in the city.

Finding 4: Soil quality in the Pearl River Delta improved during periods of sustainable land use, but it has been degraded in some areas by improper land use.

Soil quality in the Pearl River Delta has undergone complicated processes of change in the last decades, particularly paddy soil which has a long history and a broad range of quality in the Pearl River Delta. The soils in the case study area can be divided into 16 groups according to their location and texture. Half of the area is covered with lateritic red soil (udic andisols) and 38.55 percent with paddy soil (stagnic anthrosols) (Lu Faxi, 1988; Guangdong Institute of Soil Science, 1988).

Many of the factors that have influenced soil quality in the region over the past two decades are associated with the changing population and consumption patterns. For example, soil quality improved from 1981 to 1996 in most areas as farmers began to shift cropland to orchards and other garden lands in order to maximize economic benefits and attain more sustainable land use. Generally, soil quality was improved because the garden land received higher inputs of farmyard manure and more intensive management than the cropland.

Prior to 1978, farmers applied few chemical fertilizers to the land. Soils with a cultivation history of over 100 years, however, tended to receive higher inputs of organic matter and more management than did soils with a shorter cultivation history. The "older" soils thus were better protected from degradation. Between 1978 and 1980 chemical fertilizer applications in general soared as the economic reform and Open Door policies were implemented. After 1981, shifts in land use pattern were associated with the development of two kinds of fertilizer regimes revolving around chemical fertilizers and farmyard manure (Table 9-7). Under the chemical fertilizer regime, the lack of soil organic matter in the soil prohibited the restoration of soil fertility and soil quality generally degraded. Under the farmyard manure regime fertility and soil quality improved. Increased inputs of farmyard manure in order to raise levels of organic matter and total nitrogen accompanied the shift of cropland, including paddy field and uplands, to garden land or vegetable land. Organic matter values also rose when paddy fields were converted to orchard or fallow land, because organic matter decomposes more readily in orchard land than in the paddy field (Qin Mingzhou, 1997).

Soil acidification in the Pearl River Delta declined after a peak in 1980. The many new township enterprises that had emerged in the region had been emitting large quantities of sulfur dioxide and nitrogen oxide into the air, acidifying the soil. But the introduction of stringent regulations led to a decline in the emissions from these enterprises after 1980 and in turn to a decline in soil acidification (Figure 9-14).

Finding 5: The urbanization policy adopted in the Pearl River Delta alleviated to some extent the population pressures on urban areas by encouraging the rapid development of small towns so they could absorb many of the surplus rural laborers who otherwise would have settled in the larger urban centers.

TABLE 9-7 Comparison of Fertilizer Regimes by Land Use Types, Pearl River Delta, 1989–1994 (fertilizer value: yuan per hectare)

Year	Paddy		Upland		Orchard/Garden		Vegetable Land	
	Farmyard Manure	Chemical Fertilizer	Farmyard Manure	Chemical Fertilizer	Farmyard Manure	Chemical Fertilizer	Farmyard Manure	Chemical Fertilizer
1989	226.50	1,111.05	169.05	4,151.40	2,038.35	3,434.40	1,525.05	2,787.45
1992	160.05	1,243.95	19.50	3,388.50	1,171.35	3,345.30	2,147.10	3,930.00
1994	82.50	1,757.85	6.45	3,940.80	545.70	4,659.60	5,422.50	7,200.00

SOURCE: Cost investigation of agricultural products in Guangzhou, 1989–1995, Guangzhou Price Bureau (systematized by Qin Mingzhou).

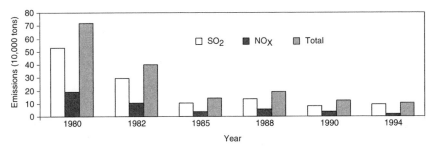

FIGURE 9-14 Sulfur dioxide (SO$_2$) and nitrogen oxide (NO$_X$) emissions, Pearl River Delta, 1980–1994. SOURCE: Environment Bulletin of Guangdong Province, 1990 and 1995. Calculations by Qin Mingzhou.

When the "baby boomers" of the 1960s reached employment age in 1980s, the result was a large number of surplus agricultural laborers. The amount of arable land had not increased, but agricultural productivity had gone up in response to reforms and intensification, so that a smaller number of laborers was required to produce the same agricultural output (Table 9-8).

During the early stages of this agricultural labor transition, surplus agricultural laborers moved to the big cities to find jobs. Job opportunities were available for some, but those with low education and skill levels in a time of rapid economic development found it difficult to find work. At the same time, cities faced the problem of providing in-migrants with

TABLE 9-8 Agricultural Output per Agricultural Laborer, Guangzhou, 1950–1988

Year	Agricultural Production (kilograms)					
	Grain	Peanuts	Sugarcane	Vegetables	Fruits	Fish
1950	858	7	126	304	76	10
1952	937	9	314	338	76	11
1957	926	11	978	554	99	14
1965	1,234	24	1,139	497	76	21
1978	953	29	1,152	478	44	27
1980	1,126	39	1,274	429	61	29
1985	1,197	53	2,536	810	182	66
1987	1,247	46	1,842	1,066	371	78
1988	1,191	46	1,839	1,291	360	83
1990	1,250	40	2,160	1,340	330	90
1995	1,090	30	840	2,400	350	90

SOURCE: The Forty Years of Guangzhou (1949–1988). 1989. Beijing: China Statistical Press, p. 311.

adequate public transportation, housing, medical care, education, and living environments. How to provide surplus agricultural laborers with employment opportunities thus became an important issue.

In response to this problem, China adopted the strategy of limiting the expansion of large cities by developing medium and small cities, as well as small towns. Governments at various levels encouraged surplus agricultural laborers to stay in small towns and set up factories and small firms and gave favorable treatment to both domestic and foreign investments aimed at creating employment in small towns for surplus agricultural laborers. Stimulated by those favorable policies, township enterprises developed rapidly in the Pearl River Delta, and today they account for a large percentage of the total economic growth (Table 9-9). In 1996 township industries absorbed 1.1 million working people.

Overall, the result of the urbanization policy in the Pearl River Delta has been a rapid population growth rate for small towns, whereas the populations of big cities such as Guangzhou have increased much less rapidly. The township population in Guangdong Province grew from 6.88 million in 1985 to 40.80 million in 1990, almost a sixfold increase. By contrast, the population of Guangzhou municipality increased by less than twofold, from 3.9 million to 6.3 million.

Finding 6: Since the early 1980s, environmental quality has deteriorated in many parts of the Pearl River Delta, particularly in some townships. Yet the case of Zhuhai City suggests that rapid economic growth accompanied by massive in-migration does not necessarily result in severe environmental degradation.

Rapid economic and population growth have led to serious environmental problems in the Delta region—among other things, high levels of air pollution and large quantities of wastewater and industrial waste residue. Some industries—particularly iron ore, pig iron, raw coal, calcium sulfate ore, phosphate fertilizer, cement, and calcium sulfate—produce considerable quantities of solid and liquid waste. In addition, paper manufacturing poses one of the greatest pollution threats, and wooden furniture manufacturing results in significant loss of local forests. Many industries, however, are reluctant to allocate financial resources toward improving the environment.

TABLE 9-9 Township Enterprises and Employees, Guangdong Province, 1980–1996 (thousands)

	1980	1985	1990	1995	1996
Enterprises	97	687	1,197	1,447	1,450
Employees	2,049	4,015	6,583	10,721	11,186

SOURCE: Statistical Yearbook of Guangdong Province, 1997, p. 273.

Does rapid economic growth unavoidably result in severe environmental pollution? The answer is "not necessarily" based on a comparative analysis of Zhuhai and the other five municipalities that, with Zhuhai, make up the Pearl River Delta. Zhuhai was an underdeveloped rural county before 1979, when, administratively, it became a municipality. As one of the first four special economic zones designated by the central government, Zhuhai has since August 1980 enjoyed special policies for stimulating economic growth.

Table 9-10 compares economic, population, farmland, and environmental pollution indicators for Zhuhai with those for the other five municipalities in the Delta area. According to the table, the economic growth rate of Zhuhai has been higher than the average for the other five municipalities. Zhuhai greatly benefits from being a special economic zone, whereas of the other municipalities, only Shenzhen benefits from that special status. The permanent population of Zhuhai is only 600,000; the other municipalities range in population from more than 1 million to several million. Zhuhai, however, is one of the fastest-growing municipalities, and its floating population is rising rapidly. Also important, compared with cities in the other municipalities, Zhuhai City has a comparatively higher proportion of light industry to heavy industry, which generally leads to lower levels of pollution.

On all indices measuring environmental pollution, the Zhuhai municipality performed better than the other five municipalities taken together. For example, during 1990–1995 in Zhuhai the average wastewater, air pollution emissions, and waste residue per capita were about 16.4, 15.3, and 53.4 percent lower, respectively, than the corresponding averages for the other five municipalities. The overall air pollution index in Zhuhai was 44.3 percent lower. Field observations suggest that Zhuhai's better performance in environmental protection was the result of several policy commitments.

First, the government of Zhuhai municipality has strongly emphasized the strategic importance of protecting the environment, and all city planning, construction, and economic development programs are expected to conform to high environmental standards.

Second, the government has established and implemented laws aimed at protecting the environment. For example, the policy "Eight Decrees of Environmental Protection" announced by the People's Congress and the municipal government forbids the establishment of any factory that does not have an effective facility for keeping the level of pollution below the required standard; prohibits noise levels in residential areas that exceed 45 decibels; and sets limits on automobile exhaust emissions. This legislation not only strictly defines what is forbidden in order to prevent pollution, but also explicitly states what must be done to protect the environment—for example, the standards that must be met for drinking water

TABLE 9-10 Comparison of Economic Growth, Population Growth, Farmland per Capita, and Indices of Environmental Pollution, Zhuhai and Other Five Municipalities

	Zhuhai	Other Five Municipalities
1. Economic growth per capita (yuan)		
GDP, average 1990–1995	11,690	8,080
Total growth rate (percent)	256.3	190.3
Industrial + agricultural prodn., average 1990–1995	18,980	15,370
Total growth rate (percent)	305.7	226.4
Government revenue, average 1990–1995	1,075	789
Total growth rate (percent)	143.5	112.2
Residents' bank balances, average 1990–1995	6,360	5,590
Total growth rate (percent)	375.9	261.3
2. Population growth		
Annual growth rate of permanent residents, 1980–1995 (percent)	3.64	1.78
Annual growth rate of total population, 1986–1995 (percent)	7.88	4.88
3. Farmland		
Decrease in farmland per capita, 1986–1995 (percent)	–63.89	–59.95
4. Indices of environmental pollution		
Wastewater per capita, average 1990–1994 (tonnes)	70.35	84.14
Air emissions per capita, average 1990–1994 (cubic meters)	10,074.7	15,564.1
Waste residue per capita, average 1990–1994 (tonnes)	70.139	0.298
Air pollution index, average 1991–1995		
Sulfur dioxide	0.27	0.658
Nitrogen oxide	0.56	0.736
Floating materials in the air	0.42	0.798
Ash fall	0.59	1.114
Total	1.84	3.306
Index of seawater pollution at junction of river and sea, average 1991–1995	1.48	1.75
Noise index, average 1991–1995		
Road	71.32	73.348
Residential community	58.66	60.528

NOTES: (1) Total growth rate (percent) is computed as the difference of the indices between 1995 and 1990 divided by the index in 1990 and multiplied by 100; (2) total population includes floating population and permanent residents; (3) index of seawater pollution at the junction of river and sea for five other municipalities includes only Guangzhou and Shenzhen.

and the discharge of waste materials. Also under this policy, each enterprise must deposit a certain sum of money in a fund managed by the Environmental Protection Bureau. If the enterprise then passes the environmental protection examination at the end of the year, the sum is returned along with an additional financial reward. If not, the money is not returned and a fine is imposed.

Third, the government has invested substantially in increasing the capacity of the Zhuhai municipality to process wastewater, air pollution, and solid waste, and it has established a sophisticated environmental protection network and environmental protection offices at various administrative levels, right down to the townships and neighborhood committees. One or two environmental managers are appointed in every village and enterprise.

Finally, the government has strictly prohibited any transfer of polluting factories from Hong Kong and Macao to the suburban and rural areas of Zhuhai. More than 90 applications for the transfer of such factories have been rejected.

All these steps have been effective at curbing pollution in the Zhuhai municipality. But an indirect result has been a sharp increase in population, attracted by a growing economy and protected environment. Clearly, the impact might be different if neighboring jurisdictions were to adopt similar regulations; the air quality might improve, but economic effects might be negative if polluting industries were prohibited throughout the region. Nevertheless, the example of Zhuhai shows that under certain conditions population, development, and environment can be positively related.

CONCLUSION

This analysis has revealed that policy shifts by the Chinese government have been the primary factors driving changes in population, land use, and consumption patterns in the Pearl River Delta. Various economic reform policies since 1978—including the establishment of special economic zones, a favorable investment environment, and favorable regulations—have fostered the emergence and growth of the region's manufacturing base and export-oriented economy. This transformation in turn has attracted millions of migrants and members of the floating workforce to the region. In the 1980s, increases in agricultural productivity, accompanied by the coming of age of the population surge of the 1960s, resulted in an influx of larger numbers of young surplus agricultural laborers into the Pearl River Delta. In response, the government adopted urbanization policies to encourage the growth of small towns in remote areas and satellite towns around the big cities to absorb most of the surplus labor.

This rapid population growth and the government policies for development of the region that inspired them have served as key forces driving changes in land use in the region. These changes have been characterized by the conversion of agricultural land into nonagricultural land and a trend toward more intensified use of land in both rural and urban areas. Rapid economic development accompanied by dramatic population growth and changes in land use have had a great impact on the environment of the Pearl River Delta. Before 1978, environmental quality in the Delta area was fairly good because of the relatively small size of the population and low industrialization levels. But since the mid-1980s, in-migration, accelerating industrialization, and land use change have led to obvious environmental degradation. Nevertheless, rapid economic growth does not necessarily result in massive degradation of the environment. As this study found in the municipality of Zhuhai, government policies can significantly ameliorate pollution levels.

REFERENCES

Guangdong Institute of Soil Science. 1988. Assessment and District Division of Soil Resource Utilization of Agriculture in Pearl River Delta. Guangzhou Branch of Popular Science Press of China.

Lu Faxi. ed. 1988. Soil in Pearl River Delta. Beijing: Environment Science and Technology Press of China.

Qin Mingzhou. 1997. Amount and quality changes in the process of red soil resource development in South China. Postdoctoral report, Institute of Soil Science, Chinese Academy of Sciences, pp. 5–30.

Ma Xia. 1988. Criterion for urban-rural classification and the level of urban development. Population and Economics (in Chinese) 6:29–33.

Tang Yonglun. 1995. Approach on macro distribution of ecological environment of Pearl River Delta Economic Zone. Guangdong Development Herald, No. 4.

Zeng Yi, and J. Vaupel. 1989. Impact of urbanization and delayed childbearing on population growth and aging in China. Population and Development Review 15:425–445.

PART IV

United States

U.S. Case Studies: An Introduction

M. Gordon Wolman
Department of Geography and Environmental Engineering,
Johns Hopkins University

Although in very different settings, the U.S. study sites—South Florida in the southeastern United States and Chicago in the American Midwest—demonstrate the dynamic changes in population that have taken place over short periods of time in their histories and the massive alterations of the landscape that have accompanied changes in population, economy, technology, and policy (see map, p. 236).

SOUTH FLORIDA

Perhaps no single place in the United States illustrates the complex relation between population and land use more vividly than South Florida. South Florida lies in southernmost North America in the humid subtropical climatic zone. The region's mild winter climate and warm summer climate lend themselves to an extended growing season. Most years the area has no freezing temperatures and enjoys a growing season of more than 320 days. Crops could be grown throughout the year, but the stresses of the summer heat and humidity on most agricultural plants reduce yields.

The natural hydrologic system in South Florida before the government began drainage projects was extensive. A hydrologic conduit connected central Florida, just south of present-day Orlando, to the mangrove reaches of Florida Bay, gateway to the tropical Florida Keys. Water flowing through the Kissimmee River was impounded by Lake Okeechobee until breaching its low banks. From there it continued south through stretches of saw grass and deepwater sloughs until it reached the high-saline waters of Florida Bay. The geographic area of slowly moving water is known as the Everglades, although the term is also often used to refer more generally to the region's natural systems.

In 1845 the population of the entire state of Florida was less than 80,000; from 1950 to 1990 it rose from 760,000 to 4.65 million and the landscape was transformed physically in heroic ways. In recent decades in South Florida, the natural wetland has given way to agriculture and to urbanization along the Atlantic and Gulf coasts. In this state known for its vast numbers of tourists and elaborate land development schemes, including some financial disasters in the latter half of the twentieth century, population growth has been driven by retirees from the north, joined by Latin American immigrants. Population concentrated on the state's eastern coast has produced a sharp contrast to the agricultural and natural landscape to the west.

To mitigate flood damage and provide drainage for potential agricultural land, the federal government and others have reengineered South Florida's wetland water systems. The immense infrastructure for water management includes levees, canals, pumping systems, and diversion structures. As a result, over the years the marshland of the Everglades has been reduced by half, and its wildlife populations of birds and mammals have been decimated. Even as the landscape has been transformed from one dominated by natural areas to one dominated by human activities, the efforts under way to return the engineered straight channel of the Kissimmee River to its "natural" meandering pattern reflect the changing values of society in the current era. In contrast, the city of Miami continues to grow and represents a major international metropolitan region, a dominant center of commercial activities between the United States and Latin America.

In summary, transformation of the landscape of South Florida has been driven by agriculture, real estate ventures to satisfy the demands for permanent housing and tourism, and commercial development. It also has been nurtured by government policies and facilitated by the provision of an engineered infrastructure on a grand scale.

CHICAGO REGION

The dynamism of the transformation of the Chicago region from the mid-nineteenth century to the present rivals that of South Florida, but in an entirely different landscape and over a somewhat different period of time. Overall, the region can be characterized as a flat plain that was, in earlier days, covered primarily with natural prairie grass; some forested areas were found in the northeastern reaches of the region. As the agricultural frontier moved west, however, the landscape was quickly transformed, and the natural grasses were eventually replaced with domestic crops such as wheat, corn, and oats.

The region's average annual temperatures range from 24°C to 26°C in the summer months and from –4°C to 0°C in the winter months. The average annual precipitation is somewhat less than 1,000 millimeters. With its combination of moderate temperatures and precipitation and fertile soils, the region is ideal for high agricultural productivity.

Land use in the Chicago region has changed dramatically since the early 1800s when it was still primarily unsettled, except for scattered indigenous encampments. This natural environment quickly gave way to agricultural production, and by 1900 more than 90 percent of the region was under cultivation. Although agriculture has dominated land use in the region even up to the present day, the urban influence has expanded.

Chicago, a small city of 5,000 in 1840, began expanding rapidly after the U.S. Civil War, growing 10.4 percent a year from 1840 to 1900. It owes its establishment to the presence of Lake Michigan and the opportunity for water transportation in a region of flat land with great potential for crop and cattle production adjacent to regions supporting vast timber- lands. Grassland, timber, and livestock provided successive commercial bases for development, including the evolution from handling live ani- mals to operating slaughterhouses to shipping refrigerated carcasses, and grain, to the East Coast. Remarkable improvements in agricultural tech- nology have enhanced agricultural productivity in the region, although the land area devoted to farming has declined.

In Chicago's earliest days, the slaughterhouses and timber handling posed severe pollution problems. Today, despite the presence of dense traffic, the favorable climate and federal regulation of automobile exhaust have limited the level of air pollution in the region.

The population of the city of Chicago peaked in 1950, but the metro- politan region continues to grow. Much of Chicago's early population growth was fed by the arrival of European immigrants from the East Coast. Chicago's economy continues to evolve—from agriculture to trans- portation, then to industry and commerce, and ultimately to finance—as employment in the modern era shifts from the secondary to the tertiary sector. Testament to the region's economic health is the thriving business district that lies adjacent to the expansive waterfront park on Lake Michi- gan and the new business centers and suburban housing developments that reflect the changing land use.

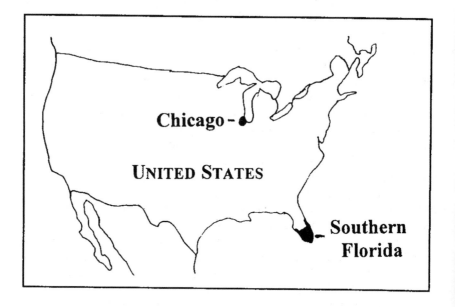

U.S. Study Regions

10

Transformation of the South Florida Landscape

William D. Solecki
Montclair State University
Robert T. Walker
Michigan State University

This chapter describes the relationship between expansion of the human system and changes in land use in the South Florida region of the United States. The actual study area comprises the seven southernmost counties in Florida: Broward, Collier, Dade, Hendry, Lee, Monroe, and Palm Beach (see Figure 10-1).

Human interventions in South Florida's natural systems have been dramatic, with notable effects on the quality of life. Since 1900, 11,027 square kilometers of natural land in the study region have been shifted to agricultural and urban uses in connection with federal, state, and private efforts to provide drainage and flood control. This land represents about 41 percent of the total study area, which covers some 27,000 square kilometers.

The shifts in land use occurred in stages, beginning in the late nineteenth century. Historically, this chapter looks at five distinct periods: pre-1900, 1900–1930, 1930–1950, 1950–1970, and 1970 to the present. Each period is characterized by a different set of human–environment interactions, along with differing relationships among population growth, consumption, and land use change.

The interactions among these elements are examined in several ways. First, we look closely at the nature of the human–environment interactions within each period and the social and physical drivers effecting transformations in them (see Merchant, 1990—the general discussion of ecological transformations—and Solecki et al., 2000). Second, we illustrate how each time period set the stage for the next phase of development by presenting certain constraints and possibilities. Finally, empirical evidence

237

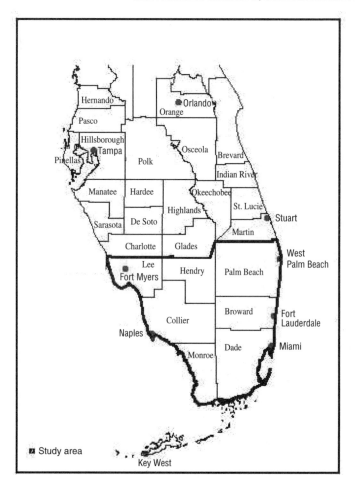

FIGURE 10-1 Counties and major cities, South and Central Florida.

of these changes and transformations are derived from an examination of the amount and rate of land use change throughout the century.

The discussion in this chapter is based generally on the concept of land use coupling, presented as a functional relationship between an agricultural hinterland and the urban markets for foodstuffs (Walker, 1998). When an agricultural region supplies only markets in nearby urban settlements—that is, the region constitutes a closed market for agricultural production—the regional land use system, including both agricultural and urban activities, is said to be coupled. Alternatively, when the agricultural sector produces for markets outside the region, the system is said to be decoupled. As decoupling took place in South Florida, the pattern of population demands on the land and land use transformation changed. This switch is fundamental to understanding the interactions between population and land use in the region. The chapter begins with a physical description of the study region, followed by a description of the evolution of land use in South Florida over the twentieth century. In doing so, it notes the ecological implications of changes in land use and, because drainage and flood control levees have been instrumental in enabling changes in land cover, describes the state's drainage activities, as well as the initial stages of federal intervention in flood control. This historical exposition is followed by a section on the empirical evidence of the changes in land use in South Florida. Specifically, it examines the impacts of the changing regional economy and certain infrastructure on land use. The chapter concludes with a discussion of the role of institutions and markets in land use.

SOUTH FLORIDA: A PHYSICAL DESCRIPTION

The South Florida study area is located on a low-relief limestone peninsula that lies largely at the southern extremity of North America in the humid subtropical climatic zone. The region has a mild winter climate, with January temperatures ranging from 11° to 23°C (mean 18°C), and a warm summer climate, with August temperatures ranging from 22° to 33°C (mean 28°C). Rainfall averages 1,400 millimeters a year. During the dry season from November to April, the average rainfall is less than 60 millimeters a month; during the rainy season from June to September, the rainfall averages over 200 millimeters a month. The study area is subject to frequent episodic events—tropical and winter storms (including hurricanes), droughts, flooding, and hard freezes (Duever et al., 1994).

The South Florida region has an extended growing season. Most years the area has no freezing temperatures and enjoys a growing season of more than 320 days. Although crops could be grown throughout the year, the summer heat and humidity are very stressful to most agricultural plants and reduce yields. In addition, plant diseases and weed control are far more serious in the summer than in the winter (Snyder and Davidson, 1994).

The Everglades

The natural hydrologic system before the initiation of government-sponsored drainage projects was extensive. A hydrologic conduit connected central Florida, just south of present-day Orlando, to the mangrove reaches of Florida Bay, gateway to the tropical Florida Keys (see Figure 10-2). Water flowing through the Kissimmee River was impounded by Lake Okeechobee until breaching its low banks, from where it contin-

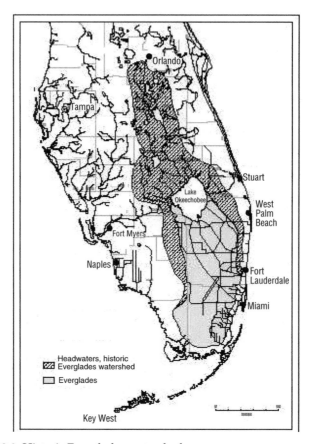

FIGURE 10-2 Historic Everglades watershed.

ued south through interminable reaches of saw grass and deepwater sloughs, freshening the high-saline waters of Florida Bay upon discharge to the tidewater.

The terrain of the South Florida hydrologic system is barely more than a few meters above sea level and has virtually no perceptible local relief. It slopes very gently south from Lake Okeechobee—that is, only 3–6 centimeters per kilometer over the 145 kilometers to Florida Bay at the tip of the peninsula. The lake regularly overflowed its southern banks, resulting in a slow "sheetflow" of water roughly 50 kilometers wide. It passed to the west of the Atlantic coastal "ridge" (less than 10 meters in elevation) in a north–south direction through Palm Beach, Broward, and Dade Counties. This area of slowly moving water is known as the Everglades, although the term is also often used as a catchall to refer to the region's natural systems. The Everglades is composed of limestone bedrock covered with calcitic mud and (in the north of the system) by peat and muck several meters thick. The freshwater that flows in rivers and streams and as a shallow sheet across the gently sloping landscape is the unifying force and sustaining element of the system. Approximately three-fourths of the study site lies within the Everglades watershed. The rest lies to the east of the Atlantic coastal ridge and in the west drain to the Gulf of Mexico (see Craig, 1991; Davis and Odgen, 1994; Lodge, 1994).

Changes in Land Use

Land use in South Florida has changed significantly since 1900. At the turn of the century almost all land in the region was in a natural or near-natural state. However, Native Americans and nineteenth-century Anglo-American hunting and grazing did modify the ecosystem in a few areas and eliminated certain species such as birds with extensive plumage (Figure 10-3). By 1953 more than 80 percent of the land remained in a relatively pristine condition (Figure 10-4), but by 1973 land use in the region

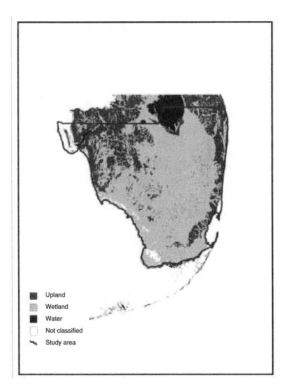

FIGURE 10-3 Land cover, South Florida, 1900. SOURCE: Center for Wetlands, University of Florida.

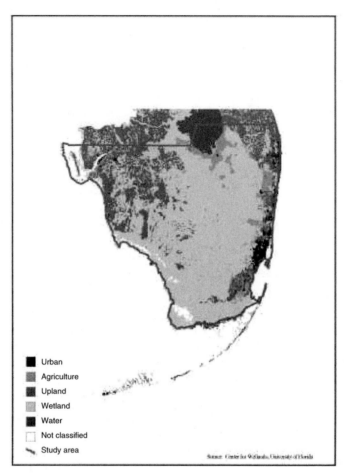

FIGURE 10-4 Land cover, South Florida, 1953. SOURCE: Center for Wetlands, University of Florida.

had changed markedly (Figure 10-5). In 1988, urban land made up 13.8 percent of the land area; agricultural land (plantations and cropland) made up 21.4 percent (Figure 10-6). Over the past several decades, the proportion of agricultural land in the region has remained steady, but that devoted to urban land uses, such as residential, industrial, and commercial, has increased substantially.

The ecological impacts of this massive change in land use have been significant. The extensive Everglades marsh, built through peat depositions over the past 5,000 years (Gleason and Stone, 1994) and once covering about 12,000 square kilometers, was reduced by 50 percent in the twentieth century, to its present territory of 6,000 square kilometers. The

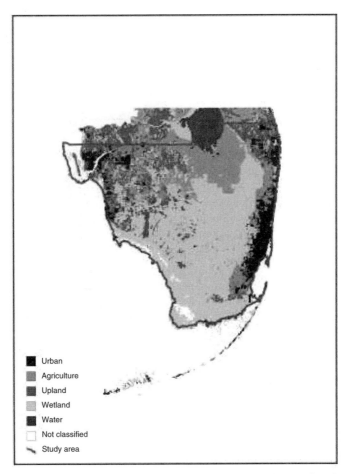

FIGURE 10-5 Land cover, South Florida, 1973. SOURCE: Center for Wetlands, University of Florida.

Everglades wetland, which makes up the noncoastal regions of the study counties, originally comprised seven physiographic landscapes; they have been reduced to four. The original landscapes were: the swamp forest (600 square kilometers), the saw grass plains (2,380 square kilometers), the slough/tree island/saw grass mosaic (3,110 square kilometers), the saw grass-dominated mosaic (1,790 square kilometers), the peripheral wet prairies (1,170 square kilometers), the coastal cypress strand (120 square kilometers), and the southern marl-forming marshes (2,490 square kilometers)—see Davis et al. (1994) and Myers and Ewel (1991). The 600 square kilometers of swamp forest once found just south of Lake Okeechobee in northwestern Palm Beach County vanished early with

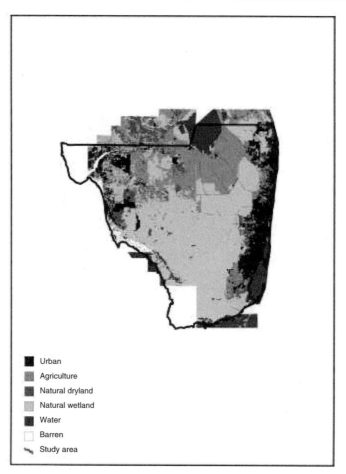

Urban

Agriculture

Natural dryland

Natural wetland

Water

Barren

Study area

FIGURE 10-6 Land cover, South Florida, 1988. SOURCE: Center for Wetlands, University of Florida.

agricultural development. Since then, the peripheral wet prairies and the coastal cypress strand have disappeared or have been reduced to scattered remnants because of urban expansion from the eastern coastal ridge. The monospecific saw grass plains once found just south of the swamp forest (mostly in western Palm Beach and Broward counties) have given way to sugarcane and are now a mere 25 percent of their former size. The remaining landscapes (marl-forming marshes and two types of saw grass mosaic) largely retained their original size, but they have felt the effects of changed hydroperiod and eutrophication. Finally, the pine forest that once covered the eastern coastal ridge has largely disappeared; only one patch remains, preserved within the boundaries of Everglades National Park.

In the Everglades several factors have seriously reduced the nesting populations of wading birds, long an aesthetic symbol of the Everglades wetland and a good indicator of environmental conditions (Ogden, 1994; Robertson and Frederick, 1994). These factors are: reduced water flow, a shortened hydroperiod in high-elevation marshes, a diminished discharge to coastal estuaries, and a loss of permanent standing water in the deeper central sloughs. It was originally thought that nesting birds in the southern Everglades maintained populations on the order of 1 million into the 1930s. Ogden (1994), however, estimated that the peak population for that period was between 180,000 and 245,000 birds (in 1933–1934). He also estimated a maximum of 50,000 for 1976, after drainage, indicating an overall decline of between 75 and 80 percent for aggregate populations of the great egret, tri-colored heron, snowy egret, white ibis, and wood stork.

Environmental changes have not been limited to obvious and marked reductions in animal populations. Of particular current concern is the worsening water quality; phosphorus concentrations in waters flowing directly from agricultural areas to the central and northern Everglades have increased by an order of magnitude. Predrainage concentrations of phosphorus in surface waters were at the limit of detection, on the order of 0.01 milligram per liter. Today, eutrophication has brought phosphorus amounts to between 0.15 and 0.20 milligrams per liter in the agricultural surface waters discharging to the water conservation areas (Davis, 1994). As a result, cattail marshes have spread extensively, replacing saw grass. This environmental impact opened the door to the federal suit filed against the state of Florida in 1988, charging that the state had failed to properly enforce federal water quality protection laws (DeWitt, 1994).

HUMAN INTERVENTION AND ECOLOGICAL CHANGE IN SOUTH FLORIDA

The history of South Florida reveals how the region has developed and become increasingly linked with nonlocal institutions and markets. Particularly important has been the rapid and complete integration of the region's emerging economy with external interests—for example, U.S. northern winter food markets, tourism, and now increasingly trade and financial services. Indeed, since the onset of regional development at the turn of the century, land use decoupling has increased in South Florida (Walker and Solecki, 2000).

Key Drivers of Changes in Land Use

Rapid population growth has been a major component of the decoupling process. The population of South Florida grew from just a few thousand in 1900 to more than 4.6 million in 1990 (see Table 10-1). But

TABLE 10-1 Population Growth, Density, Number of Households, and Percent Urban, South Florida, 1930–1990

	1930	1940	1950	1960	1970	1980	1990
Population (thousands)							
Region	49.8	429	760	1,620	2,440	3,600	4,650
Florida	1,470	1,900	2,770	4,950	6,790	9,750	12,900
Population density (persons per hectare)							
Region	0.09	0.16	0.28	0.60	0.90	1.33	1.71
Florida	0.10	0.14	0.20	0.35	0.48	0.69	0.92
United States	0.16	0.17	0.19	0.19	0.22	0.24	0.32
Number of households (thousands)							
Region	69	NA	237	531	844	1,410	1,830
Percent urban[a]							
Region	77.7	76.3	86.5	91.0	94.9	96.1	95.8
Florida	51.7	55.1	65.5	73.9	80.5	82.6	84.8
United States	56.2	56.5	64.0	69.9	73.5	74.0	75.2

[a] "Urban" encompasses territory, persons, and housing units in: (1) places of 2,500 or more persons incorporated as cities, villages, boroughs, and towns but excluding the rural portions of "extended cities"; (2) census-designated places of 2,500 or more persons; (3) other territory, incorporated or unincorporated, including areas designated as urban.

SOURCE: Census of Population, U.S. Census Bureau.

population growth did not occur evenly throughout the region. Rapid, large-scale population growth first took place in the southeastern counties—Dade, Broward, and Palm Beach—and only more recently accelerated in the other counties.

During the early decades of the twentieth century, the southeastern counties grew at rates of more than 100 percent per decade, reflecting the growth of local tourism and agriculture-related industries. The rural population grew as well, but the most significant growth came in the urban sector, particularly around Miami, Fort Lauderdale, and the Palm Beaches. After a slowdown during the Great Depression of the 1930s and World War II, rapid population growth continued in the late 1940s, driven increasingly by the tourism industry, the influx of retirees, and the development of urban-based industries more generally. During that period, population growth accelerated in the western coastal areas, including Lee and Collier counties. Meanwhile, the growth rates of the interior sections of these counties and the east coast counties, as well as of landlocked Hendry County, remained extremely low. This condition created a significant population density gradient: coastal sites had densities of well over 1,500 persons per square kilometer, while interior sites had densities of only one to five persons per square kilometer. Population growth, although at a slower rate, continued to the end of the century, stemming almost entirely from in-migration to the region, especially from the Midwest and Northeast of the United States and, internationally, from the Caribbean Basin (Table 10-2).

While factors of regional development, such as population growth, are an important factor driving changes in land use in South Florida, other forces that drive the rate of change at particular sites within the region are influential as well. In this context, sets of other institutional and societal factors become significant (see Solecki, 1997; Walker et al., 1997). These factors include land ownership issues such as public versus private; natural hazards such as hurricanes, droughts, and winter freezes;

TABLE 10-2 In-migration, South Florida, 1960–1990 (thousands)

	1960	1970	1980	1990
In-migration within Florida	69	110	172	232
In-migration other states	416	437	647	676
In-migration international	41	123	146	221
In-migration total[a]	526	670	965	1129
In-migration total as percent of population	32.4	27.4	26.8	24.3

NOTE: Figures based on residence at previous mid-decade. Migration parameters changed several times during the study period. Data are not an estimate of net migration.

[a] Total includes domestic (within Florida and other states) and international in-migration.

SOURCE: Census of Population, U.S. Census Bureau.

urban social problems such as crime, poverty, and racism; development
coalitions such as northern U.S. investors with governments such as the
state of Florida; and the location of infrastructure such as canals, levees,
and transportation corridors. These factors are covered implicitly or explicitly in the rest of this chapter.

Approximately half of the South Florida region—the entire central
core—is under public ownership (see Figure 10-7). Thus the amount of
land available for development has been limited, affecting the overall
pattern of development. For example, westward agricultural and urban
expansion in the Atlantic coastal zone has been limited to approximately
20-35 kilometers. Moreover, because the region is a low-lying wetland,

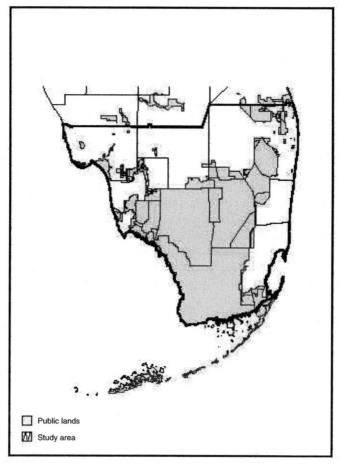

FIGURE 10-7 Public lands, South Florida, 1988. SOURCE: South Florida Water
Management District, 1988.

any development has required a significant capital investment in draining the land, protecting against floods, and building railroads and roads through the swamps.

Any historical description of the South Florida region would not be complete without mentioning another important driver of change in the region—natural hazards such as droughts, floods, hurricanes, and winter freezes. South Florida is highly vulnerable to the violent meteorological events characteristic of the Caribbean subtropical climate. The history of South Florida has been punctuated, for example, by the freezes of 1895 and 1989; especially violent hurricanes in 1926, 1928, and 1992 (Andrew); and the 1960–1961 drought.

While not the direct cause of extensive changes in land use, natural hazards have often spurred local and state officials to undertake hazard mitigation planning, which itself requires the relocation of people or industry, or the construction of infrastructure to prevent exposure to future events. Throughout the twentieth century, for example, citrus growers moved their operations ever southward into the Everglades region to escape the threat of freezes (Winsberg, 1991). On the coast, the massive eastern perimeter levee was constructed in the late 1940s and early 1950s in part to protect coastal communities from future floods. These and other examples are described more fully in the sections that follow.

Pre-1900: Frontier Settlement

South Florida was one of the last frontiers in the eastern United States. When Florida became a U.S. state in 1845, few nonnative inhabitants lived south of Lake Okeechobee and the entire population of Florida was less than 80,000. Through the late nineteenth century, most of the native and nonnative inhabitants (people of African or European descent) lived off of subsistence agriculture and resource extraction (hunting, fishing, logging). In the 1880s, however, small-scale, export-oriented agricultural activities began to take shape (USDA, 1884). Producers began to ship pineapples, sugar, and oranges to northern U.S. markets.

During this period, agriculture began to encroach on the region's wetland. In the agriculture sector, early state boosters envisioned reproducing the vital Caribbean sugar industry in Florida and creating a lucrative tropical fruit agriculture (Smith, 1884), but actual investments and changes in the landscape did not begin until the late 1800s. The impetus to development throughout the state, and particularly in the south, was favorable climatic conditions and optimistic appraisals of soil fertility. Development was made possible by the release of federal lands through the Swamp Lands Act of 1850. Ultimately, Florida received over 95,000 square kilometers of federal land, about 65 percent of its entire territory (Carter, 1974). These lands were used by politicians to entice capitalists to invest in drainage and land reclamation; a state bureaucracy, the Internal

Improvement Fund, was established to oversee this process. In the early years, the state ceded vast amounts of land to railroad companies for laying track in the Florida wilderness, much of it inaccessible at that time (Blake, 1980). Indeed, as recently as 1893 mail was delivered to Miami by means of a three-day hike from Boca Raton, 96 kilometers to the north (Derr, 1989).

In the wake of the Civil War, the state's development strategy, based on promoting railroad construction through land grants and railroad bond guarantees, collapsed with the bankruptcy of the railroads (Blake, 1980; Tebeau, 1971). The extensive swamp and overflowed lands ceded by the federal government were placed at risk as creditors demanded payment on their now worthless bonds. The legal process, an arduous one, was finally resolved when what was in essence a mammoth land sale—about 1.6 million hectares (16,000 square kilometers) at 62 cents a hectare, or 25 cents an acre—was held in the early 1880s. The purchaser, Henry Disston, restored the solvency of the Internal Improvement Fund, provided the railroads' creditors with a modicum of satisfaction, and allowed the state to resume using land as a lure to development. Unfortunately, though, Disston's efforts fell far short of expectations. His firm, the Atlantic and Gulf Coast Canal and Okeechobee Land Company, only managed to permanently drain about 202 square kilometers, calling into question early assumptions about drainage costs (Tebeau, 1971). In response to the demonstrated difficulties, private investors held back, although the dream of establishing a rich agriculture in the region lingered.

Even with these early activities, much of the land in South Florida remained little altered as the nineteenth century came to an end. In most respects, the integrity of the natural Everglades and adjoining watershed areas was still largely intact; only very small areas had been converted to agricultural and other human-dominated land uses. By 1900, probably fewer than a thousand people lived in the Everglades watershed area south of Lake Okeechobee.

1900–1930: Drainage and Land Conversion

With the construction in the early 1900s of a coastal railroad and the initiation of major drainage activities south of Lake Okeechobee, human manipulation of the South Florida ecosystem increased rapidly. Wealthy investors from Florida and northern cities took advantage of cheap land prices and government incentives to establish an extensive agricultural area south of Lake Okeechobee and coastal resort communities and port cities from Palm Beach through the Florida Keys. South Florida's population increased tenfold between 1900 and 1930 and marked the beginning of what would be exponential growth over the next six decades (Marth and Marth, 1993).

Because the state of Florida wanted to encourage settlement in South Florida but still lacked the money to provide the infrastructure, particularly the water control, needed for that settlement, it granted or cheaply sold land to various developers so they could drain it and then resell it to would-be settlers (Hanna and Hanna, 1948). In 1905 Gov. Napoleon Bonaparte Broward, a Progressive era politician and champion of small farmers and small business, was elected on a platform advocating further drainage of the Everglades (Proctor, 1996). The Everglades Drainage District (EDD), the institutional mechanism put in place to accomplish further drainage, was authorized to levy ad valorem taxes to finance the construction of drainage works. It was headed by the governor and his cabinet.

These initial phases of economic development were driven in part by tourism. The arrival of Henry Flagler's railroad in Miami in 1896 and the growth of tourism provided further impetus to agricultural expansion. Indeed, Flagler's vision centered on a two-way flow of traffic—tourists to the south and produce to the north, particularly pineapples and citrus (Derr, 1989). By 1909 Miami, whose population stood at 12,500, was enjoying 125,000 tourist visits a year (Derr, 1989).

With the creation of the Board of Drainage Commissioners in 1905 (it had created the Everglades Drainage District), drainage of the Everglades began in earnest (Finkl, 1995; Tebeau, 1971: 348). By 1913, 360 kilometers of canals had been dug in the district (Derr, 1989), and produce (tomatoes, beans, and other crops) was being shipped by steamboat to Fort Lauderdale and Fort Myers for both local consumption and shipment north (Blake, 1980). By 1917 the EDD had completed the construction of four major canals—Miami, North New River, Hillsboro, and West Palm Beach—from Lake Okeechobee through the Everglades to the tidewater. By 1925 the St. Lucie Canal extended from Lake Okeechobee eastward to the tidewater. Unlike the other canals, which were constructed at least partially along the alignment of natural creeks or rivers through transverse glades, the St. Lucie Canal wound through uplands with no natural drainage patterns. It served the single purpose of draining Lake Okeechobee. A little over 700 kilometers of canals were in place by 1931, connecting the southwest coast to the southeast coast and thereby opening the entire region to agricultural encroachment, human settlement, and environmental change.

In 1920, 23,000 persons were living on farms and in rural settlements in South Florida, cultivating 138 square kilometers; by 1927, 92,000 inhabitants were cultivating 186 square kilometers (Blake, 1980). Along the south shore of Lake Okeechobee, the soil was fertile, a mixture of mineral lake sediments and organic matter from submerged vegetation (Snyder and Davidson, 1994). But only a few kilometers from the lake and extending a hundred or more kilometers southward, the soils were very infertile because of their low mineral content stemming from the digotrophic conditions under which they were formed.

The land reclamation process went hand in hand with the demands of private investors for land and the state's willingness to manage the actual reclamation activity. Soon after the state demonstrated its intent to go forward with drainage, well-funded real estate speculators bought large tracts of land and resold them to smallholders, many of whom lived in other parts of the country. (The speculators collected fees from smallholders and paid the state to carry out the drainage.) This system functioned until the smallholders became aware that the reclamation process was much slower than had been advertised. In addition, deadly hurricanes struck in 1926 and 1928, exposing the riskiness of agriculture in the region. The willingness of the smallholders to continue funding this system dissipated, and dredging stopped. The momentum of growth was further slowed by the 1926 crash of the Florida real estate boom in the coastal, more tourist-oriented parts of the region.

Overall, the period 1900–1930 laid the foundation for the extensive growth and development of South Florida. Despite the impediments to growth, development produced a marked increase in the regional population—to 229,000 by 1930. Most population growth was concentrated along the southeastern Atlantic coast. Some areas in the newly drained portions of the Everglades also grew because they offered attractive agricultural opportunities.

1930–1950: Flood Control and Consolidation

The period 1930–1950 saw a fundamental restructuring of the South Florida region that changed the internal dynamics of the two emerging, yet increasingly separate, urban and agricultural systems. As a result, natural resource utilization and land conversion steadily increased throughout the period and accelerated in the 1950s. Between 1900 and 1953, approximately 2,625 square kilometers of natural lands were converted to agricultural or urban uses.

The Great Depression of the 1930s and World War II deflected attention from the early booster dreams for South Florida, but at the end of the war there was renewed investor interest in the region. In the meantime, however, a fundamental shift had occurred in the public's perception of the region's natural systems (Light and Dineen, 1994; Solecki et al., 2000). Many people had become aware of the side effects of unplanned drainage, as once-abundant wading birds began to vanish, as saltwater intruded into municipal well fields, and as the region's scenic splendor dissipated in clouds of smoke from muck fires.

Floridians' sense of unease was only exacerbated by the record floods of 1947 and 1948. The extensive flooding forced government officials and local residents to reconsider drainage and flood control in the region. In response to local economic and political pressure, Congress authorized the U.S. Army Corps of Engineers to establish an extensive public works undertaking known as the Central and Southern Florida (C&SF) Flood Control Project. Although several drainage projects had been tried in the Everglades area since the late 1800s, the C&SF project was a major turning point for water management in the region, because it served objectives beyond flood control and water conservation such as prevention of salt-water intrusion, improved navigation, preservation of fish and wildlife habitat, and maintenance of a water supply for Everglades National Park (ENP). Although there was no congressional prioritization of project purposes, flood control and water conservation were generally the guiding principles in project design (Light and Dineen, 1994).

The project authorization required the state to establish an agency to represent local interests in the design and financing of the project. The new agency, known as the C&SF Flood Control District, was later combined with the Okeechobee Flood Control District and reorganized as part of the 1972 Water Resources Act to become the South Florida Water Management District (SFWMD). The project sought to encourage agriculture to further expand south of Lake Okeechobee and in some areas to the east, and it sought to oversee the formal creation of the Everglades Agricultural Area (EAA). It envisioned that urban development, assured of flood protection and water supply, would expand rapidly along the Atlantic coast ridge and in the eastern Everglades.

Between 1952 and 1954, the U.S. Army Corps of Engineers built a 100-mile-long eastern perimeter levee that secured the Atlantic coast urban settlements from flood hazards (Light and Dineen, 1994). The Corps then followed with the Everglades Agricultural Area (1954–1959) and the Water Conservation Areas (1960–1963), producing a reconfiguration of the central and northern Everglades defined by levees, spillways, and pumping stations. Another 2,250 kilometers of levees and canals were added to what the state of Florida had already built (DeWitt, 1994).

In some respects, the demands for federal government intervention signaled not only a technological shift in the water management regime but also a shift in the attitudes of local residents. Although concern over natural disasters had long been an issue in South Florida, events of 1930–1950 offered graphic evidence of the region's vulnerability to major disruptions. Alarmed, residents and decisionmakers restructured the legal and institutional framework for water management in South Florida and agreed that government agencies should act to prevent damage from future flooding as well as initiate drainage projects (Blake, 1980). The government's response, which became known as multipurpose water management, produced at least two significant results. On a tangible level, the promise of flood protection meant heightened prospects for increased development of the upper Everglades and west of the coastal ridge. On a more symbolic level, the public recognized that radical alterations to the natural system were necessary to accommodate growing human demands.

Technological innovation during the period also facilitated the expansion of the agricultural sector. The problem was how to farm in a semitropical environment, something largely unfamiliar to U.S. farmers and other U.S. agricultural interests (Derr, 1989). Through the efforts of the federally sponsored Everglades Experiment Station in Belle Glade, however, much was being learned about how to overcome the fertility limitations of the saw grass muck soils. Vegetable production, in particular, increased as a result of such research—from approximately 6,900 hectares in 1929 to 30,000 hectares in 1943, or nearly three-quarters of the total cultivated area in the northern Everglades region (Elvove, 1943).

Livestock production also had been limited by the infertility of the saw grass soils. Yet even after some of the pasture fertility problems were overcome, cattle production was still limited by many other problems such as frozen winter pastures, foot rot, anaplasmosis, and severe insect and tick infestations (Kidder, 1979). Many of these problems, however, were resolved by the late 1940s with the development of new agricultural fertilizers and pesticides.

A primary agricultural sector that failed to change significantly during the 1930–1950 period was sugar, because government-imposed quotas constrained sugarcane production (Sitterson, 1953). Production increased from 2,800 hectares in 1930 to 15,300 hectares in 1950, but even that large percentage increase was still small when compared in absolute terms to the future expansion. Florida sugar producers consistently petitioned the federal government to increase their quotas, but the only suspension of the Sugar Act occurred during World War II (Salley, 1986).

Another major development of the 1930–1950 period was the full integration of South Florida into the nation's transportation network when all-weather federal and state highways and airline companies and airports joined the railroads in expanding access to the region. The earliest major highways into the region were U.S. Route 1, which paralleled Flagler's Atlantic Coast Line railway; U.S. Route 27, which ran across the southern end of the peninsula in a northwest–southeast direction; and the Tamiami (Tampa–Miami) Trail, which cut east–west at the southern end of the peninsula. These three highways became the main arteries of a denser highway network that took shape during the 1950s and 1960s. Earlier, South Florida had become one of the birthplaces of the airline industry. By the late 1920s, Pan-American Airlines had begun to make Miami the "Gateway to the Americas." It was joined shortly by another Miami-based carrier, Eastern Airlines (Chapman, 1991). The airline industry expanded during the early 1940s, as preparations for World War II affected the South Florida region.

From 1930 to 1950 population growth in South Florida slowed from the boom years of 1900–1930, but remained substantial. Reflecting the continued rapid growth in the Miami and Miami Beach areas and elsewhere, the population of South Florida climbed to more than 400,000 by 1940 and to just over 720,000 by 1950. The new in-migrants included retirees, workers drawn by the growing South Florida economy, and even a large number of World War II veterans, many of whom had trained in the region (Strong, 1991).

Middle-class tourists also flocked to the region, lured by effective marketing and aided by the increasingly efficient transportation networks. The transient population also included migrant farm workers who spent the winter months harvesting produce on the interior farms (Carlebach and Provenzo, 1993).

In the 1930s the vast majority of the population remained tightly clustered along the Atlantic coast. Only near Miami had the population moved more than several kilometers inland. The proportion of land converted to urban land uses remained small—no more than a few percent of the entire area. By 1940, only about 20 percent of the coastal population lived more than 8 kilometers from the coast (Schultz, 1991). During the 1940s, however, this growth began to spread across the Atlantic coastal ridge, with almost 30 percent west of this line (Schultz, 1991).

By the early 1950s some evidence of the shifts in land cover caused by these developments were already apparent (see Figure 10-4). Although most changes in land use until the early 1950s originated in agricultural production, the amount of land devoted to urban uses had begun to increase significantly, especially in Dade and Broward Counties.

Rapid urban growth also occurred in noncoastal (inland) communities. This growth was particularly significant, because for the first time the demand to shift land to urban uses outweighed the demand to shift land to agricultural uses over a large area. As a result, farmland was being converted to residential, commercial, and industrial land uses. Possibly in response, farmers seeking new agricultural land went even further inland, moving from the upland pine forests along the coastal ridge into the interior wet prairie and saw grass marsh areas. Among other things, the agricultural area south of Lake Okeechobee grew rapidly. Conversion was particularly evident along the major canals (for example, the Okeechobee, Hillsboro, and North New River).

1950–1970: Postwar Boom and Flood Control

The period 1950–1970 was one of tremendous growth for the South Florida region. During the 1950s and 1960s, it began to develop much of its contemporary socioeconomic conditions and land use patterns. Although earlier decades had witnessed greater percentage increases in population, the 1950–1970 period saw the greatest absolute increase in population to date, an increase from 0.75 million to almost 2.5 million. The greatest sources of in-migrants were the northeastern and midwestern United States. Many also came from Caribbean and Latin American countries, particularly Cuba. The anti-Castro policies of the U.S. Congress, which encouraged a large influx of Cubans, accelerated the growth in the population and the economy of South Florida. The population growth meant dramatic increases in the local demand for land, much of it in the noncoastal areas. By 1970 almost half of the population was located west of Interstate 95 (Schultz, 1991). Much of the housing development to accommodate the region's newest residents took the form of land-intensive, low-rise, single-family dwellings.

The southeastern section of the region grew especially quickly, and by the late 1960s the Miami area had gained many of the characteristics of a large, diverse metropolitan area. In 1968, after decades of simmering racial tensions and discrimination against African Americans, the city was the scene of the first in a series of race riots. The racial tension, coupled with the growing income disparities and a poverty-stricken underclass, rendered many of the older settled areas less desirable to middle- and upper-income residents and in-migrants (see Portes and Stepick, 1993). This trend helped to fuel the rapid residential development of inland sites and smaller urban areas on the Gulf of Mexico coast.

As the population of South Florida grew, so did its local economies, which were more service-based than those in many other parts of the United States. Indeed, the percentage of South Florida's workforce employed in service-related industries in 1970 was significantly higher than the national average. The service-based economy had an important influence on the demand for local natural resources. Because the economy had developed so recently and so quickly and because the region had become so completely integrated into the national economy, South Florida had moved rapidly through the stages of development during which populations typically place heavy direct demands on the local natural resource base. For example, by the 1950s most of the foodstuffs needed to feed the resident population could be brought in, and heavy industry and environmental pollution were not widely found. Other than the basic demands for water for consumption and land for housing, South Florida's population appeared to be creating economic growth and employment without overexploiting the environment. Furthermore, the rapid in-migration and the emergence of an economy based mostly on federal money transfers, ocean-based tourism, and other services were concentrating development mainly in coastal and urban centers.

The agricultural sector also grew dramatically during 1950–1970. The value of agricultural product sales in South Florida as a percentage of all farm sales in the United States more than doubled from 1949 to 1968

(Winsberg, 1991). Agricultural growth during the 1950s and 1960s was particularly vigorous because of the increased national demand for fresh winter produce, especially in the Northeast and Midwest (Winsberg, 1991). In the United States this produce could be grown only in Florida, California, and a few other Deep South states. During the period 1950–1970, the region's two primary agricultural areas—the area south of Lake Okeechobee and the Atlantic coast ridge area—continued to grow. The Everglades Agricultural Area primarily produced sugarcane and a variety of vegetables. By this time, most of the farms in the EAA had become large-scale agribusiness operations.

The 1959 Cuban revolution was largely the reason the Everglades became the greatest cane sugar-producing area in the United States. In 1959 sugarcane occupied 19,000 hectares in the Everglades and was processed in three mills. The United States had depended on Cuba to supply a large portion of the nation's sugar demand, but the embargo of Cuban produce after the revolution and the higher tariffs imposed on imported sugar ended that dependence.

During the embargo, many Cubans fled to Florida, including experts in all phases of cane sugar production. A few also possessed the wealth and expertise to invest in Florida's cane industry to help meet the domestic demand. As a result of these developments, sugarcane production increased spectacularly. By 1963 there were 55,800 hectares of sugarcane in the Everglades, which increased to 92,000 hectares by 1965, 121,000 hectares by 1979, and 162,000 hectares by 1987 (Salley, 1986; Snyder and Davidson, 1994). The new opportunities for sugarcane production came at the expense, however, of other EAA agricultural activities, especially the cattle industry, which declined significantly during the 1960s.

And what were the impacts of all these developments on the region's land use patterns? Tremendous changes took place from the early 1950s to the early 1970s. Two of the more obvious were the rapid increase of agricultural land in the EAA, and the increase in urban land, particularly around the cities of Miami and Fort Lauderdale, and along the entire coastline heading northward to West Palm Beach.

The rapid urbanization along the Atlantic coast led to other important shifts in land use patterns. From 1953 to 1973 most of the remaining upland pine forests and nearshore agricultural areas were converted to urban land uses. In 1973 just a few remnants of the coastal pine forest remained, and farms were found only in isolated pockets situated between the urban fringe and the public conservation lands to the west. In short, agricultural lands were largely reduced to the role of transition zone between the urbanized coast and the interior Everglades area. Meanwhile, other lands, typically in even more inland locations, were being shifted to agricultural production. These shifts were particularly evident

in the southern portion of Dade County and in a stretch of land running
northward from the Broward-Palm Beach county line.

1970–Present: Dynamic Growth and Constraints

Like the periods described earlier, the last 30 years have seen tremendous changes in South Florida. Absolute population growth has continued at a rapid rate, huge tracts of land have been converted to urban and
agricultural uses, and the demand for water resources has continued to
grow. As before, the two forces driving land use modification and conversion have been the growing national demand for Florida's agricultural
produce and increased in-migration. The population of the region, almost
2.5 million by the year 1970, was 3.6 million in 1980, and 4.6 million in
1990. Huge numbers of in-migrants have continued to stream into the
region from the Northeast and Midwest and from other countries, particularly Latin America and the Caribbean basin. Inland, significant
amounts of land have been cleared to make room for the construction of
large planned communities, mostly designed for retirees. Many of the
residents of these new inland communities have come from outside the
region and have raised the median household incomes (Walker et al.,
1997).

Tourism has continued to grow as a major industry in the region. By
the mid-1980s the region was the destination for approximately 15 million
visitors a year, and, together, Broward and Dade Counties maintained
over 75,000 hotel and motel rooms (Florida Department of Business and
Professional Regulation, 1994).

In the late 1980s, the basic pattern of land use remained the same, but
the shifts seen in the earlier 1950–1970 period had intensified (see Figure
10-5). The continuous strip of urbanized land along the Atlantic coast
became more clearly defined and dominated the roughly 160-kilometer
stretch from northern Palm Beach County to southern Dade County. Much
of the conversion of land to urban uses from the 1970s to the late 1980s
occurred within or adjacent to settled areas. The agricultural zone sepa-
rating the coastal settlements from the interior Everglades had become
significantly smaller. Far inland, shifts in land use were associated with
the conversion of land to agriculture, and in the EAA the amount of
agricultural land increased. Other, much smaller conversions to agriculture took place in the eastern coastal region in a broken string of parcels
often just alongside the publicly held lands.

Present-day agriculture in the region is mainly export-oriented (Snyder and Davidson, 1994). South Florida produces 21 percent of the nation's
sugar (Stone, 1992), and, as of the 1990 growing season, sugarcane, the
region's most important crop, occupied 178,200 hectares of Everglades
land, over 10 times the expanse in 1950. It is mostly grown just south of

Lake Okeechobee (Coale, 1994). Sales of sugarcane approached $500 million in 1990 (Alvarez et al., 1994).

But sugarcane production in Florida would not exist without the advantages given it by the U.S. government. Since 1934, the federal government has maintained a sugar quota, apportioning purchases among foreign and domestic producers and guaranteeing a price usually double that of the world market. As noted, up through 1960 the amount of sugarcane that could be produced in Florida was severely restricted and therefore relatively little land was devoted to it—19,000 hectares in 1959. After the Cuban revolution, the federal government placed an embargo on trade with Cuba, reapportioned its sugar quota, and suspended the domestic acreage restriction. (Up until this time, Cuba had maintained the largest sugar quota.) These events began the process that saw sugarcane production expand rapidly over the next several decades in Florida.

Since 1970, the other large agricultural production sectors also have experienced tremendous change stemming from a variety of causes. For example, winter freezes in more northerly locations in the state have accelerated the development of citrus production in South Florida, particularly Hendry County.

The continued rapid population growth and land conversion in South Florida have meant dramatic shifts in the agricultural economy of many areas within the region (Solecki et al., 2000). Particularly in the urban–rural fringe of Dade, Broward, and Palm Beach counties, the increased demand for land for urban uses and rising land values have led to the conversion of a significant amount of agricultural land either to urban land uses or to higher-value crops (for example, land used to raise vegetables was shifted to higher-value nursery products). In general, the agricultural sector has become increasingly open to land speculation and tenant farming, where farmland is purchased by land development companies and then leased back to the farmers. Such an arrangement keeps property taxes low while not limiting prospects for future development.

Although agriculture and tourism remain important components of the regional economy, a new component has emerged related to Miami's proximity to markets in Latin America and North America (Solecki, 1999). These market advantages have operated for both conventional and unconventional economic products. For example, with the narcotics boom in the mid-1970s Miami became the drug capital for much of the world; an estimated 70 percent or more of the U.S. supply of heroin, cocaine, and other illegal substances flowed through the region. This traffic brought drug-related wealth and crime to Miami. Indeed, throughout the 1980s, money laundering and cash surpluses were conservatively estimated to have added $1 billion to 2 billion a year to Miami's economy (Cartano, 1991).

Another major source of revenue was the more than 2 million Latin Americans who visited Miami each year from 1976 to 1983. Although the economic growth rate of Miami slowed significantly after the collapse of many Latin American economies in the early 1980s, by 1990 Miami had become a major international trade center. The Miami customs district handled only 2.1 percent of U.S. trade in 1990 ($19.1 billion), but it processed approximately 40 percent of the trade to Central and South America and the Caribbean (Nijman, 1996). Today, Miami continues its drive to gain prominence in global trade, particularly with Latin America (New York Times, 1996).

Thus as it enters the twenty-first century South Florida is a highly dynamic and increasingly diverse region. The regional economy has grown tremendously in recent decades (see Table 10-3), and the employment structure has changed to reflect the growth of the service sector (see Table 10-4). Income levels also have risen steadily, but then so has the degree of income disparity, thereby fueling crime and the formation of an underclass (Portes and Stepick, 1993). While the agricultural economy is still important, it has declined significantly relative to services. Throughout the region farmland is under intense conversion pressure, and in some counties agricultural activities are becoming scarcer.

Even though the South Florida economy has become more diverse and robust, profound questions have emerged recently about the general quality of life and social cohesion of the region (Croucher, 1997; Portes and Stepick, 1993). The critical issues behind these developments are the increasing diversification of the regional population as large numbers of Caribbean and Central and South American migrants have continued to pour into the region, and the increasing concern about the Everglades ecosystem and the growing sense of "paradise lost." These issues have had some direct and indirect impacts on the patterns of land use in the region.

Hundreds of thousands of permanent international migrants came into the region during the 1980s and 1990s. Joining the Cubans, most of

TABLE 10-3 Gross Domestic Product (GDP), Florida, Per Capita, Regional Estimate, 1960–1990

	1960	1970	1980	1990
Florida (millions of dollars)	14,443	$38,478	$118,301	$226,964
Per capita[a] (dollars)	2,917	5,667	12,138	17,543
Regional estimate[b] (millions of dollars)	4,735 (19.2)	13,852 (21.5)	43,622 (8.7)	81,522

[a]The years that data were acquired were: 1963, 1972, 1982, and 1989.
[b]Estimates based on regional population as a percentage of total Florida population. In parentheses are the average yearly growth rate by decades. Value for 1990s not yet available.

SOURCE: Calculated by authors from State of Florida Statistical Abstract data.

TABLE 10-4 Employment by Sector, South Florida, 1930–1990 (percent)

	1930	1940	1950	1960	1970	1980	1990
Primary sector employment							
Region	13.6	10.8	7.5	5.0	3.2	2.5	2.4
United States	24.4		14.1		4.5		3.3
Secondary sector employment							
Region	10.7	5.7	7.3	10.5	13.5	12.6	9.8
United States	29.3		25.9		25.9		17.7
Tertiary sector employment							
Region	75.7	83.5	85.2	84.5	83.3	84.9	87.8
United States	46.3		60.0		69.6		79.0

SOURCE: Census of Population, U.S. Census Bureau.

whom arrived from the 1960s to early 1980s, have been new streams of migrants from Colombia, the Dominican Republic, Ecuador, Haiti, Honduras, Jamaica, Nicaragua, Panama, Peru, and Puerto Rico. This immigration has given rise to tension between these groups and other groups in the region, primarily the African American and white Anglo populations. Conflicts have centered around employment shifts, political representation, cultural values, and community structure.

These ethnic population shifts have helped to cause land use shifts in the region beyond the obvious changes that come with increased population. The heightened Caribbean and Latin American presence in Dade County has been associated with the flight of whites northward to Broward and Palm Beach Counties (Boswell and Curtis, 1991). Hurricane Andrew, which hit southern Dade County in 1992, helped to accelerate the rate of relocation. In the early 1990s, areas like southwest Broward County were already growing quickly because of improved highway access, low interest rates, and the appeal of a less-urban location, but the hurricane helped to push land development "years ahead of schedule" (Solecki, 1999).

Also in the 1990s, concerns about the fate of the Everglades ecosystem and the region as a whole increased dramatically. It had been clear decades earlier that the hydrologic and landscape alterations were having negative impacts on the Everglades, but the size and potential impact of the problem finally brought the issue to the fore. In the mid-1990s the situation became so obvious that the governor of Florida convened a blue-ribbon panel to examine the current threats and create a framework for a more sustainable future.

As a result, restoration of the Everglades became a major national policy initiative. Scientists such as those working within the U.S. Man and the Biosphere, Human-Dominated Systems Directorate (Davis and Ogden, 1994; Harwell et al., 1996; U.S. MAB, 1994), nongovernmental organizations such as the Audubon Society and Everglades Partnership, and state and federal agencies such as the South Florida Water Management District and Federal Interagency Taskforce on Restoration, worked together and separately on developing a strategy for reversing ecological decline and promoting ecological sustainability in the Everglades.

No single project better exemplifies this effort than the massive one currently aimed at reviewing all of the water management policies in the region and modifying the Central and Southern Florida Flood Control Project of the U.S. Army Corps of Engineers first begun in the late 1940s. The $7.8 billion effort, known as the Restudy, calls for changes in the quantity, quality, timing, and distribution of water in the Everglades in order to restore the regional ecosystem and improve the general quality of life in Florida (see www.restudy.org for more information). The comprehensive plan recommended by the Restudy has more than 60 major infrastructural components. It was developed with the help of dozens of local, state, and national public and private groups and agencies. The fundamental goal of the plan is to capture most of the freshwater that now flows unused to the Atlantic Ocean and Gulf of Mexico and divert it to areas of greatest need. The bulk of the water will be reintroduced into the natural Everglades flow way to foster ecological restoration; the rest will be used to benefit local farming and urban demands. Implementation of the Restudy plan began in July 1999 and already has involved the purchase of approximately 50,000 hectares of new conservation lands. Although the full impact of the project on land use in the region will not materialize for another 20 years, the effort may well be as important as the Central and Southern Florida Flood Control Project first authorized in the late 1940s.

EMPIRICAL EVIDENCE OF THE PROCESS OF
LAND USE CHANGE

Thus far this chapter has described in very broad terms the process of land use change in South Florida and its links with population growth. It revealed that the tremendous decadal growth in population and incomes led to changes in land use in the Everglades throughout the twentieth century (see Figure 10-8). The rest of this chapter uses quantitative data to further illustrate the links between these various elements at both the regional and subregional levels.

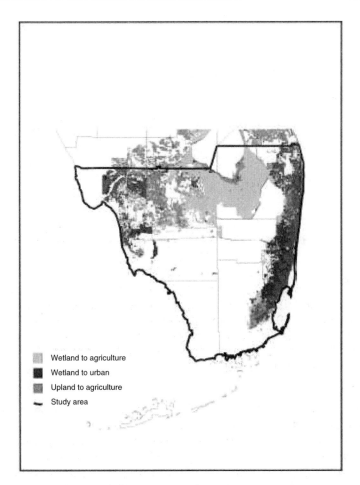

FIGURE 10-8 Land cover change, from natural to human-dominated systems, South Florida, 1900–1988. SOURCE: South Florida Water Management District, 1988.

The Impact of the Changing Regional Economy on Land Use

During the early period (pre-1930), the agricultural economy and urban settlement regions in South Florida were tightly linked. Although agricultural exports to areas outside the region grew during this period, much of the agricultural production went to feed the local residents and tourists. With the rapid drainage of land and construction of improved rail and road links, the development of export-oriented agriculture took off. Then, after World War II, the demand for agricultural and residential

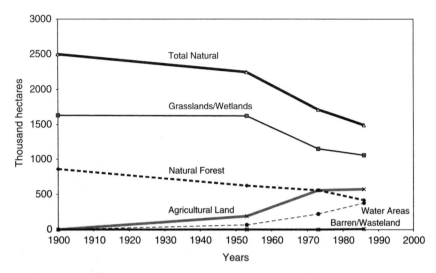

FIGURE 10-9 Land cover in South Florida, 1900–1988. SOURCE: Calculated by authors from data provided by the Center for Wetlands, University of Florida (1900, 1953, 1973) and South Florida Water Management District (1986). NOTE: Water areas are defined as open water, including lakes and bays. The high-resolution 1986 data allowed for increased identification of such features, which explains much of the increase in area.

land increased substantially as the regional economy increasingly responded to national and international markets.

The change in the rate of land use conversion throughout the century depicts the shifting demand (Figure 10-9). Based on the data available, the rate of conversion was much less during the early period (1900–1953) than during the periods 1953–1973 and 1973–1986. Between 1900 and 1953 about 2,625 square kilometers of natural lands were converted to agricultural or urban uses, or an average of 4,953 hectares a year. Between 1953 and 1973, nearly 5,800 square kilometers (28,997 hectares a year) of natural areas were lost to human uses, and from 1973 to 1986 another 2,650 square kilometers (20,387 hectares a year).

One partial explanation is the clear link between increased agricultural production for a national and international market and land use conversion. In 1939 the region accounted for 0.3 percent of all farm sales in the United States; in 1986, it accounted for 1.3 percent. Particular sectors were especially important. For example, South Florida's share of national sugarcane sales increased from 13.1 percent in 1939 to 46.1 percent in 1986; its share of national vegetable sales increased from 5.5 percent to 15.0 percent during the same period (Winsberg, 1991). Prices were set not by local supply and demand equilibrium but were the results of national and international markets and competition, with government support in the case of sugar.

The expansion of agricultural land was especially rapid during the middle part of the century, and the demands for urban land use also increased dramatically after World War II, particularly when automobile-oriented, land-intensive suburban development gained popularity. During the first and second periods, (1900–1953, 1953–1973), however, the conversion of natural areas to agricultural uses predominated and was greater than 70 percent for both periods. In fact, even with the rapid expansion of the urban population and the demand for land for urban uses during 1953–1973, the agricultural conversion of natural areas still climbed to 75 percent of the total amount of natural areas conversion, up from 72 percent in the preceding period. Much of this conversion took place inland from the Gulf of Mexico coast away from the urban populations. Later, though, the urban component increased appreciably. Between 1973 and 1986, urban expansion accounted for 124,169 hectares (or 47 percent) of the total 265,035 hectares of natural land converted. The agricultural component fell to 53 percent for the same period, down from 75 percent for the period 1953–1973.

The area of encroachment per new resident provides further evidence of the changing nature of the link between population growth and land use change. Over the periods 1900–1953 and 1953–1973, total encroachment per new resident grew from 0.26 hectares to 0.33 hectares. It slowed, however, for the third period (1973–1986) to a value of 0.18 hectares per new resident.[1] The decline during the third period of record is illustrative of the continued agricultural expansion in inland areas, particularly in Collier, Hendry, and Lee counties, and the suburban and exurban sprawl, particularly in western Broward and Palm Beach counties.

A land use shift of growing importance in the region was the conversion of farmland to urban land uses and the further conversion of inland natural sites to agricultural development. Over time, natural area sites for new residential areas declined, so developers turned to farmland. As farmers lost agricultural land, other more interior land was converted from natural land cover to agricultural production. The conversion of agricultural land to urban land more than doubled over the periods 1953–1973 and 1973–1986, growing from 32,733 to 75,160 hectares. In relative terms, the increase was more dramatic. As a percentage of the total conversion of natural areas, loss of agricultural lands to urban use climbed from 5.6 percent to 28.3 percent of total land conversion.

---

[1]The 1900 population was taken as 6,000. The 1953 population was interpolated between 1950 and 1960, the 1973 population between 1970 and 1980, and the 1986 population between 1980 and 1990.

The Impact of Infrastructure on Land Use

These regional phenomena indicate little about exactly how the process of land use change took place. In order to determine at the subregional scale how these changes occurred and what their relative impacts on the environment were, this section examines the role of infrastructure in steering development to specific sites. Although one might assume that land conversion is associated with infrastructure development, sites near some kinds of infrastructure, specifically canals and levees, were in fact the setting for the most extensive conversion from natural land use to other land uses.

Table 10-5 presents the fraction of land converted (natural areas to agriculture and natural areas to urban) for land that lies within 5 kilometers and 10 kilometers of specific canals and levees in South Florida. The data in Table 10-5, given for the periods 1900–1953 and 1973–1986, reveal the impact that public investments in infrastructure have had on the region's landscape evolution. In the first period, fully 73 percent of all agricultural and 79 percent of all urban conversion occurred within 10 kilometers of the 1930 canal system, showing that natural areas encroachment was clearly infrastructure-driven, even for the large expanses of uplands on both the east and west coasts of South Florida. By the second period, the importance of the canals had somewhat attenuated, although fully 56 percent of urban conversion still occurred within 10 kilometers of the 1930 canals. Note that the land within 10 kilometers of the canals constitutes approximately 10–20 percent of the land area of each county through which the canals pass.

Unfortunately, infrastructure projects also were associated with environmental problems. Even at canal sites remaining in natural ground cover (that is, nonagricultural and nonurban land), significant environmental degradation occurred, such as extreme changes in the natural pe-

TABLE 10-5 Canals and Natural Lands Encroachment, South Florida (percent)

	1900–1953	1900–1953	1973–1986	1973–1986
	Agricultural	Urban	Agricultural	Urban
5 kilometers	63	57	23	36
10 kilometers	73	79	43	56

NOTE: The canals considered were constructed by 1930. Percentages represent proportion of total natural areas converted. For example, 63 percent of all natural areas converted to agricultural use occurred within 5 kilometers of the canal system.

SOURCE: Calculated by authors from Center for Wetlands and South Florida Water Management District data.

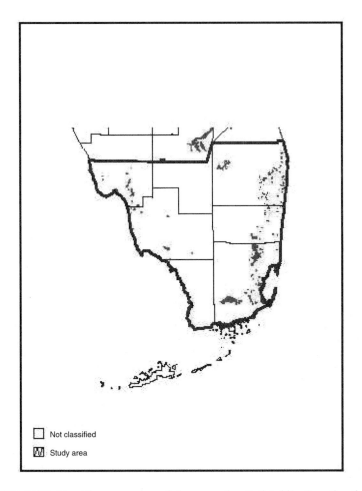

FIGURE 10-10 Brazilian pepper, melaleuca, and cattail infiltration, South Florida, 1988. SOURCE: South Florida Water Management District, 1988.

riodicity of the water table, the introduction and spread of nonnative,
alien species, and the inflow of water pollutants.

   We examined the spatial distribution of three well-recognized alien
species in the region: Brazilian pepper (*Schinus terebinthifolius*), melaleuca
(*Melaleuca quinquenervia*), and cattails (*Typha* spp.)—see Figure 10-10. These
species invade native species, eventually excluding and changing the local
ecosystem (for example, through increased transpiration of water). Then,
based on grid assignments to the South Florida region, we produced
frequency counts for the observance of these exotic species in relation to
three components of infrastructure—roads, canals, and levees. These data

TABLE 10-6 Exotic Species and Development Infrastructure, South
Florida

	Brazilian Pepper	Melaleuca	Cattails
Proximate[a]			
Roads	33	37	15
	(9)	(13)	(4)
Canals	18	23	6
	(5)	(7)	(2)
Levees	8	18	14
	(3)	(4)	(1)
Nonproximate[b]			
Roads	6	18	4
	(30)	(42)	(15)
Canals	21	32	13
	(34)	(48)	(17)
Levees	31	37	5
	(36)	(51)	(18)

[a]Entries for proximate categories show observed frequencies of GIS-generated grid cells (one square kilometer) containing both exotic species and an infrastructure component. Expected frequencies under null hypothesis of no spatial association appear in parentheses below the observed frequency. For example, in 33 (of 900) grid cells Brazilian pepper and roads are observed simultaneously. If the presence of roads did not affect the likely occurrence of Brazilian pepper, one would expect to observe 9 cells with both roads and the exotic species. Thus the observed value exceeds the value that would be expected in the absence of a spatial relation.

[b]Entries for nonproximate categories show the occurrence of exotic species in grid cells without the designated infrastructure component. Thus Brazilian pepper is found in 6 grid cells where no roads are observed. In the absence of a spatial relation the expected number of observations would be 30.

NOTE: The chi-square statistic was significant for all combinations of exotic species and infrastructure. The null hypothesis of spatial independence was uniformly rejected.

show strong spatial relationships between the presence of one of these elements of the built environment and the presence of one of three exotic species (Table 10-6). The upper panel of the table shows observed and expected frequencies of grid cells containing both an infrastructure component and some exotic species. Thus, in 33 grids can be found both a road and some Brazilian pepper. Under a null hypothesis of no spatial relation between the location of a road and the presence of Brazilian pepper, the expected frequency would be 9. Thus, there were many more instances of this combination than would be likely if no relationship existed.

Alternatively, in the cells where infrastructure components are absent, the frequency of some exotic species is lower. For example, in the case of Brazilian pepper, six cells contained roads but no Brazilian pepper. If no spatial relationship existed, the expected number of cells containing roads without Brazilian pepper would be 30. This same pattern is repeated for all combinations of exotic species and infrastructure components. There is always a more-than-expected frequency of observed exotic species in the presence of infrastructure and a less-than-expected frequency of nonoccurrence under the presumption of no spatial relationship at the 95-percent statistical confidence level.

THE KEY ROLE OF INSTITUTIONS AND MARKETS: A DISCUSSION

This historical perspective reveals the key role played by governments and markets in setting the stage for regional economic development and population growth and for subsequent changes in land use. Drainage of some areas of the region began in the late nineteenth century through the cooperative efforts of the state of Florida and investors from inside and outside the region. Several early efforts, such as Disston's project, ended with only partial success. Then, as part of Progressive era reformist policy at the turn of the twentieth century, the state of Florida became more directly involved in drainage efforts and sponsored some activities that lasted nearly 50 years, far beyond any individual's planning horizon. When drainage was finished, the federal government intervened for another period of sustained investments. By the late 1960s the ecology and hydrology of all South Florida had been fundamentally altered through dredging and filling operations.

Private interests profited tremendously from the common effort, realized through state intervention, to develop a viable economy in South Florida. But this economic development, while generating income and wealth, has fostered rapid population growth, which in turn has caused significant encroachment on surrounding natural areas. The most rapid population growth first took place along the Atlantic coast, particularly in and around some of the early towns, including Palm Beach, Fort Lauderdale, and Miami. Later, in mid-century, population growth accelerated on the Gulf of Mexico coast. The agriculture-based population in the interior remained relatively much lower throughout the century.

The region's early development phases expanded agricultural lands, but with ongoing regional development came a switch to urban encroachments. From 1900 to 1973 more than a half-million hectares of land were converted to agricultural uses. During the same period, 220,234 hectares of land were converted to urban uses. Later, from 1973 to 1986, urban-based populations demanded increasing amounts of residential space, particularly in the coastal zones. Since then, the expansion of human settlements has been deterred by physical constraints (such as extreme wetland locations) and institutional constraints (such as publicly protected lands) imposed by the system. Agricultural to urban conversions have become the primary land cover dynamic.

Over the years, several factors were involved in land use change. For one thing, there was a positive spatial association between the location of large capital infrastructure features—canals, levees, and roads—and heightened rates of land use conversion and the frequency of occurrence of alien plant species. These results present further evidence of how policy decisions at the local, state, and national levels guided the changes in the region's landscape.

One of the most interesting observations is the impact of the global economy on the South Florida region. As the South Florida economy expanded, it became increasingly integrated into the national and international economies, and in turn was increasingly influenced by events beyond the borders of Florida. The impact of the Cuban revolution and shift in the sugarcane market are the most obvious example. Currently, the economy of the region is being restructured through development of the Miami area into a major international finance and shipping center, which has brought increased flows of capital and in-migration to the region and will surely result in further changes to the landscape.

CONCLUSION

The analysis presented in this chapter suggests that changes in land use may be understood, at least in the South Florida case, through the study of institutional and market forces. Governmental intervention was key throughout the history of South Florida, especially when the study region was a frontier. The economic environment was simply too risky to sustain private interests alone, and state investment in infrastructure was critical. In more recent decades, federal action such as the U.S. embargo of Cuban sugar and the development and implementation of the federal environmental protection legislation had dramatic impacts on South Florida and the region's natural environment.

We must conclude that the common argument that population growth in South Florida led directly to changes in land use is overly simplistic. Government-supported infrastructure developments produced the economic opportunities that played a large role in land use changes in the region. In the early decades of the twentieth century, government-sponsored drainage operations fostered the expansion of agricultural development and settlement, and the canals attracted settlements and land use conversions. Government subsidies of population growth in the form of tax laws favoring large dwellings and utility pricing practices also added to the overall growth.

At mid-century, the expanded drainage operations and flood control activities carried out by the U.S. Army of Corps of Engineers led to further land use change. By the early 1960s much of the infrastructure needed to enable the conversion of land to agricultural and urban uses was in place. It was during this period that the amount of land converted per new resident in region was the highest—0.33 hectares per person from 1953 to 1973. From 1973 to 1986, as land became scarcer, the rate of natural land conversion per new resident began to slow.

Given these results, the connection between population growth and land conversion is best described as indirect. The relationship has been heavily influenced by shifts and turns in public policy at all levels of governance—local, state, national, and international. In South Florida these policies influenced land use change through two dimensions. First, the policies encouraged in-migration to the region, which led to increased exploitation of the land. During the past several decades, the U.S. embargo of Cuban sugar and the relaxation of controls on international immigration have had dramatic environmental impacts on South Florida.

Second, the policies channeled land development to particular types of sites or areas within the larger region. Federal responses to demands for increased flood control and now for increased environmental protection of the Everglades system have moderated the pace and distribution of land conversion. The most extreme examples of this are lands that are now under public ownership. There, all development has been excluded.

REFERENCES

Alvarez, J., G. C. Lynne, T. H. Spreen, and R. A. Solove. 1994. The economic importance of the EAA and water quality management. Pp. 194–223 in Everglades Agricultural Area: Water, Soil, Crop, and Environmental Management, A. B. Bottcher and F. T. Izuno, eds. Gainesville: University Press of Florida.

Blake, N. M. 1980. Land into Water—Water into Land: A History of Water Management in Florida. Tallahassee: University Press of Florida.

Boswell, T., and J. R. Curtis. 1991. The Hispanization of metropolitan Miami. Pp. 140–162 in South Florida: The Winds of Change, T. D. Boswell, ed. Miami: Department of Geography, University of Miami.

Carlebach, M., and E. F. Provenzo. 1993. Farm Security Administration Photographs of Florida. Tallahassee: University Press of Florida.

Cartano, D. G. 1991. The drug industry in South Florida. Pp. 105–111 in South Florida: The Winds of Change, T. D. Boswell, ed. Miami: Department of Geography, University of Miami.

Carter, L. J. 1974. The Florida Experience: Land and Water Policy in a Growth State. Baltimore: Johns Hopkins University Press.

Chapman, A. E. 1991. History of South Florida. Pp. 31–42 in South Florida: The Winds of Change. T. D. Boswell, ed. Miami: Department of Geography, University of Miami.

Coale, F. J. 1994. Sugarcane production in the EAA. Pp. 224–237 in Everglades Agricultural Area: Water, Soil, Crop, and Environmental Management, A. B. Bottcher and F. T. Izuno, eds. Gainesville: University Press of Florida.

Craig, A. K. 1991. The physical environment of South Florida. Pp. 1–16 in South Florida: The Winds of Change, T. D. Boswell, ed. Miami: Department of Geography, University of Miami.

Croucher, S. L. 1997. Imaging Miami: Ethnic Politics in a Postmodern World. Charlottesville: University Press of Virginia.

Davis, S. M. 1994. Phosphorus inputs and vegetation sensitivity in the Everglades. Pp. 357–378 in Everglades: The Ecosystem and Its Restoration, S. M. Davis and J. C. Ogden, eds. Delray Beach, Fla.: St. Lucie Press.

Davis, S. M., L. H. Gunderson, W. A. Park, J. R. Richardson, and J. E. Mattson. 1994. Landscape dimension, composition, and function in a changing Everglades ecosystem. Pp. 419–444 in Everglades: The Ecosystem and Its Restoration. S. M. Davis and J. C. Ogden, eds. Delray Beach, Fla.: St. Lucie Press.

Davis, S. M., and J. C. Ogden, eds. 1994. Everglades: The Ecosystem and Its Restoration. Delray Beach, Fla.: St. Lucie Press.

Derr, M. 1989. Some Kind of Paradise: A Chronicle of Man and the Land in Florida. New York: Morrow.

DeWitt, J. 1994. Civic Environmentalism: Alternatives to Regulation in States and Communities. Washington, D.C.: CQ Press.

Duever, M. J., J. F. Meeder, L. C. Meeder, and J. M. McCollom. 1994. The climate of South Florida and its role in shaping the Everglades ecosystem. Pp. 225–248 in Everglades: The Ecosystem and Its Restoration, S. M. Davis and J. C. Ogden, eds. Delray Beach, Fla.: St. Lucie Press.

Elvove, J. T. 1943. The Florida Everglades: A region of new settlement. Journal of Land Public Utilities Economics 19:464–469.

Finkl, C. W. 1995. Water resource management in the Florida Everglades: Are "lessons from experience" a prognosis in the future? Journal of Soil and Water Conservation 50(6):592–600.

Florida Department of Business and Professional Regulation. 1994. Master File Statistics: Public Lodging and Food Service Establishments, Fiscal Year 1994–1995. Division of Hotels and Restaurants. Tallahassee: Florida Department of Business and Professional Regulation.

Gleason, P. J., and P. Stone. 1994. Age, origin, and landscape evolution of the Everglades Peatland. Pp. 149–198 in Everglades: The Ecosystem and Its Restoration, S. M. Davis and J. C. Ogden, eds. Delray Beach, Fla.: St. Lucie Press.

Hanna, A. J., and K. A. Hanna. 1948. Lake Okeechobee, Wellspring of the Everglades. Indianapolis: Bobbs-Merrill.

Harwell, M. A., J. F. Long, V. Myers, A. M. Bartuska, J. H. Gentile, C. C. Harwell, V. Myers, and J. C. Ogden. 1996. Ecosystem management to achieve ecological sustainability: The case of South Florida. Environmental Management 20(4):497–521.

Kidder, R. W. 1979. From Cattle to Cane. Belle Glade, Fla.: Belle Glade Historical Society.

Light, S. S., and J. W. Dineen. 1994. Water control in the Everglades: A historical perspective. Pp. 47–84 in Everglades: The Ecosystem and Its Restoration, S. M. Davis and J. C. Ogden, eds. Delray Beach, Fla.: St. Lucie Press.

Lodge, T. E. 1994. The Everglades Handbook, Understanding the Ecosystem. Delray Beach, Fla.: St. Lucie Press.

Marth, D., and M. J. Marth. 1993. The Florida Almanac. Gretna, Fla.: Pelican Publishing Co.

Merchant, C. 1990. The realm of social relations: Production, reproduction, and gender in environmental transformations. Pp. 673–685 in The Earth as Transformed by Human Action: Global and Regional Changes in the Biosphere over the Past 300 Years, B. L. Turner, W. C. Clark, R. W. Kates, J. F. Richards, J. T. Mathews, and W. B. Meyer, eds. New York: Cambridge University Press.

Myers, R. L., and J. J. Ewel, eds. 1991. Ecosystems of Florida. Orlando: Central Florida University Press.

New York Times. July 25, 1996. Cuban-born commissioner is elected mayor of Miami. A7.

Nijman, J. 1996. Breaking the rules: Miami in the urban hierarchy. Urban Geography 17(1):5–22.

Ogden, J. C. 1994. A comparison of wading bird nesting colony dynamics (1931–1946 and

1974–1989) as an indication of ecosystem conditions in the Southern Everglades. Pp.533–570 in Everglades: The Ecosystem and Its Restoration, S. M. Davis and J. C. Ogden, eds. Delray Beach, Fla.: St. Lucie Press.

Portes, A., and A. Stepick. 1993. City on the Edge: The Transformation of Miami. Berkeley: University of California Press.

Proctor, S. 1996. Prelude to the New Florida, 1877–1919. Pp. 266–286 in The New History of Florida, M. Gannon, ed. Gainesville: University Press of Florida.

Robertson, W. B., and P. C. Frederick. 1994. The faunal chapters: Contexts, synthesis, and departures. Pp. 709–737 in Everglades: The Ecosystem and Its Restoration, S. M. Davis and J. C. Ogden, eds. Delray Beach, Fla.: St. Lucie Press.

Salley, G. H. 1986. A History of the Florida Sugar Industry. Miami: G. H. Salley (available from the Florida Sugarcane League).

Schultz, R. 1991. Population growth and migration: Southeast Florida in regional context. Pp. 43–62 in South Florida: Winds of Change, T. D. Boswell, ed. Miami: Department of Geography, University of Miami.

Sitterson, J. C. 1953. Sugar Country. Lexington: University of Kentucky Press.

Smith, B. 1884. Report on the Everglades. Sen. Doc. 242, 30th Cong., State of Florida, Tallahassee.

Snyder, G. H., and J. M. Davidson. 1994. Everglades agriculture: Past, present, and future. Pp. 85–115 in Everglades: The Ecosystem and Its Restoration, S. M. Davis and J. C. Ogden, eds. Delray Beach, Fla.: St. Lucie Press.

Solecki, W. D. 1997. The role of coalitions and interest groups in regional environmental change. Paper presented at a meeting of the Association of American Geographers, Fort Worth, Texas.

Solecki, W. D. 1999. Environmental hazards and interest group coalitions in contemporary megacities: A case study of changing metropolitan Miami after Hurricane Andrew. In: Megacities and Vulnerability, J. K. Mitchell, ed. Tokyo: United Nations University.

Solecki, W. D., J. Long, C. Harwell, V. Myers, E. Zubrow, T. Ankerson, C. Deren, R. Hamann, R. L. Hornung, and G. Snyder. 2000. Human-environment interactions in South Florida's Everglades region: Systems of ecological degradation and restoration. Urban Ecosystems. In press.

Stone, J. A. 1992. Agriculture and the Everglades. Journal of Soil and Water Conservation 47:207–215.

Strong, W. 1991. The southeast Florida economy. Pp. 70–86 in South Florida: Winds of Change, T. D. Boswell, ed. Miami: Department of Geography, University of Miami.

Tebeau, C. W. 1971. A History of Florida. Coral Gables, Fla.: University of Miami Press.

U. S. Department of Agriculture (USDA). 1884. Yearly Report on Agricultural Production in the United States. Washington, D.C.: U.S. Department of Agriculture.

U.S. Man and the Biosphere (MAB) Program, Human-Dominated Systems Directorate. 1994. Isle au Haut Principles: Ecosystem Management and the Case of South Florida. Publication 10192. Washington, D.C.: U.S. Department of State.

Walker, R. T. 1998. An Integrated Agricultural, Urban, Land Use Model. Washington, D.C.: Resources for the Future.

Walker, R. T., and W. D. Solecki. 2000. Development and land cover change: The case of South Florida. Annals of Association of American Geographers. Under review.

Walker, R. T., W. D. Solecki, and C. Harwell. 1997. Land use dynamics and ecological transition: The case of South Florida. Urban Ecosystems 1:43–57.

Winsberg, M. 1991. South Florida Agriculture. Pp.17–30 in South Florida: Winds of Change, T. D. Boswell, ed. Miami: Department of Geography, University of Miami.

11

Evolution of the Chicago Landscape: Population Dynamics, Economic Development, and Land Use Change

Edwin S. Mills
Kellogg School of Management,
Northwestern University
Cynthia S. Simmons
Department of Geography,
Michigan State University

Over the years the natural landscape of the Chicago region in the American Midwest has changed dramatically, from near-pristine prairie and forests in the pre-settlement period of the early 1800s, to an agriculture-dominated landscape by 1880, to the major metropolis of the twenty-first century. Chicago has become one of the world's great industrial, financial services, and transportation centers because of the interaction between its urban core, with its vast array of services, and some of the world's most productive farmland, which stretches several hundred kilometers from the southwestern corner of Lake Michigan where Chicago is situated. Indeed, Chicago has been aptly characterized by Cronon (1991) as "Nature's Metropolis."[1]

This chapter examines the changes in land use associated with the historical evolution of economic development, population growth, and environmental interactions in the city of Chicago and its surrounding area. The Chicago region, as defined here, lies in the northeastern corner of the state of Illinois, and is made up of Cook, DuPage, Kane, Lake, McHenry, and Will counties (see Figure 11-1). The significant industrial development to the east in Indiana is not included. The upcoming sections describe the salient geographic features and land use patterns of this region, as well as its demographic characteristics and economic structure.

---

[1]In addition to Cronon's remarkable geographic and environmental history of Chicago, Chicago has been the laboratory for pioneering studies of urban spatial structure, location theory, planning and design, and urban ecology by scholars at the University of Chicago and by Chicago planners.

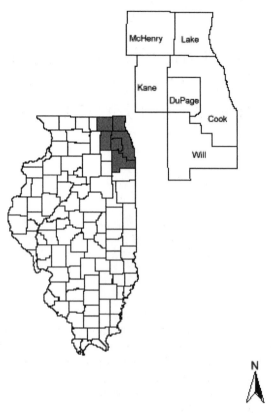

FIGURE 11-1 Illinois and the Chicago study region. SOURCE: U.S. Geological
Survey.

An examination of the two main environmental impacts that development has had on the Chicago region—resource exhaustion and pollution—follows. The chapter concludes with a discussion linking the major
drivers of land use change with the Chicago region's evolving landscape.

DESCRIPTION OF THE STUDY REGION

The six Illinois counties making up the Chicago study region (Figure
11-1) have a total land area of approximately 9,700 square kilometers.
Overall, the region can be characterized as a flat plain. In the early nineteenth century the land was covered primarily with natural prairie grass
(bluestem, side oats grama, Indian grass, and others). Some forested areas, consisting of old oak and hickory hammocks, were found in the
northeastern reaches of the region (Sullivan, 1998). As the agricultural

frontier moved west, however, the landscape was quickly transformed. The natural grasses were burned, plowed, and eventually replaced with domestic crops such as wheat, corn, and oats. The soils in the region are predominantly mollisols, dark, nutrient-rich soils created by the degradation and regrowth of prairie grass. The alfisols found in northern Lake County are light in color and provide a mixture of rich and poor-quality nutrients. The region's average annual temperatures range from 24°C to 26°C in the summer months and from –4°C to 0°C in the winter months. The average annual precipitation is somewhat less than 1 meter.

Overall, then, the region has an ideal combination of soils, precipitation, and temperature for high agricultural productivity. Historically, the resource base of fertile soil and abundant timber provided the impetus for the local economy. Today, Chicago depends on its rural hinterland much less than in earlier years, but its business service sector still provides sales and financing of agricultural property and legal, financial, processing, and transportation services for agricultural products.

Land use in the Chicago region has changed dramatically since the early 1800s when it was still primarily unsettled, except for scattered indigenous encampments. This natural environment quickly gave way to agricultural production, and by 1900 more than 90 percent of the region was under cultivation (see Table 11-1 and Figure 11-2).[2] Although agriculture has dominated land use in the region even up to the present day,

---

[2]Because detailed land use data for early time periods were not available for the Chicago region, a geographic information system (GIS) was created that compiled existing data on built-up areas (urban) and approximated agricultural and natural land use data. The results of the land use change analysis for urban, agricultural, and natural areas are presented in Tables 11-1 and 11-2, and Figures 11-2 and 11-3.

The pre-settlement landscape of around 1821 was presumed to be a near natural setting based on a re-creation of the landscape by Philip Hanson in 1969 and reproduced by Chicago's Field Museum in 1998. Data on built-up areas were provided by the U.S. Geological Survey (USGS) for 1876, 1900, and 1955. The data for natural areas were derived from data provided by the Illinois Department of Natural Resources for the 1990s, and these data also were used for the earlier time periods. It was assumed that natural areas in the 1990s would most likely correspond to natural areas in the earlier time periods because natural lands today were probably areas not suitable for agriculture. All other land not built-up or classified natural was designated as agricultural, which accounted for about 90 percent of the land area in 1900. This designation is supported by the agricultural census for 1900, which reported that 89 percent of the region was farmland. The land use data for 1972 and 1992 provided by USGS were classified using the Anderson classification system: (1) urban, (2) agriculture, (3) grass/rangeland, (4) forest, (5) water, (6) wetland, (7) barren. For the aggregate analysis of the three main land uses (agriculture, urban, and natural), categories 3–7 were combined into one category—natural. The land use change analysis presented in Table 11-3 and Figure 11-4 for 1972 and 1992 used the USGS land use data and classification system. This analysis is intended to indicate general land use trends and not produce precise estimates of changes in land use.

278

GROWING POPULATIONS, CHANGING LANDSCAPES

TABLE 11-1 Land Use in the Chicago Region, Pre-settlement–1992 (percent)

	Pre-settlement	1900	1955	1992
Built-up	0	6	12	34
Agriculture	0	90	84	48
Natural	100	4	4	19

SOURCES: Calculated by authors from data provided by the U.S. Geological Survey (1900, 1955, 1992) and Illinois Department of Natural Resources (1990).

the landscape patterns in Figure 11-2 reveal the expanding urban influence. By 1900 urban areas made up 6 percent of the region. This trend intensified as agricultural areas dwindled by about 43 percent between 1955 and 1992 and urban areas nearly tripled, from 12 percent in 1955 to 34 percent in 1992. Overall, from 1900 to 1992 urban areas increased six-fold and agricultural land decreased by nearly half.

Table 11-2 provides estimates of land use change for three conversion episodes: (1) pre-settlement-1900; (2) 1900–1955; and (3) 1955–1992. The data reveal the increasing urban encroachment into agricultural land. The most substantial loss of agricultural land occurred between 1955 and 1992, when more than a quarter of the land classified as agricultural in 1955 was shifted to urban use. The greatest land cover conversion, however, occurred during the pre-settlement period to 1900; the conversion from natural areas to agriculture left less than 5 percent of the natural areas

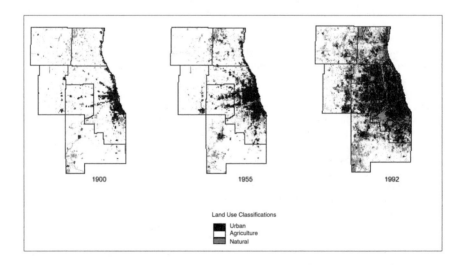

FIGURE 11-2 Evolution of land use, Chicago region, 1900, 1955, 1992.

TABLE 11-2 Land Use Change Matrix, Chicago Region, Pre-settlement–1992

	Land Use Change (as a percent of initial land cover)		
	Pre-settlement–1900	1900–1955	1955–1992
Agriculture to agriculture		91	56
Agriculture to natural		0.8	17
Agriculture to built-up		8	26
Natural to agriculture	92	17	11
Natural to natural	4	82	84
Natural to built-up	4	0.9	4
Built-up to agriculture		11	1
Built-up to natural		0.4	6
Built-up to built-up		88	93

SOURCE: Calculated by authors from data provided by the U.S. Geological Survey (1900, 1955, 1992) and Illinois Department of Natural Resources (1990).

remaining. The decades that followed saw the substantial loss of natural areas to both agriculture and urban expansion (see Table 11-2).

Early foresight by private and public interests resulted in some preservation of natural areas, albeit relatively small. For example, in 1909 the Burnham Plan outlined a system of protected parklands along the shore of Lake Michigan and throughout the study region. And in 1915 the Illinois General Assembly enacted legislation creating public preserves (Chicago Region Biodiversity Council, 1999). The actual quantity and spatial distribution of these areas are difficult to ascertain for early time periods because of a lack of accurate maps. However, U.S. Geological Survey land use data for 1972 and 1992 indicate that land classified as natural has expanded (see Table 11-3). Taken as a whole, natural areas, which include the categories grass/rangeland, forest, water, wetland, and barren land, increased from 11 percent in 1972 to 19 percent in 1992. A disaggregation of the category natural areas into its respective categories (Table 11-3) shows that the greatest degree of recovery (an increase of nearly 6 percent) occurred on forestland. About 8 percent of land classified as agricultural in 1972 and 9 percent of land classified as urban were classified as forest in 1992, representing 36 percent and 27 percent of total forestland, respectively. Wetland and grassland areas also have experienced recovery; they have more than doubled.[3]

---

[3]Much of this apparent recovery, however, may stem from classification differences from one period to the next and from the fact that the actual land area represented by these land classifications is relatively small.

TABLE 11-3 Land Use Classification and Change Matrix, 1972 and 1992 (square kilometers)

Land Use Classification, 1972	Land Use Classification, 1992							1972^a Total Area	1972^b Percent of Total Area
	1	2	3	4	5	6	7		
1 – Built-up	2,587	175	35	300	50	30	9	3,186	33
	(81)	(5)	(1)	(9)	(2)	(1)	(0)		
2 – Agriculture	457	4,269	110	408	50	73	13	5,380	56
	(8)	(79)	(2)	(8)	(1)	(1)	(0)		
3 – Grass/rangeland	0	0	0	0	0	0	0	0	0
	(0)	(0)	(0)	(0)	(0)	(0)	(0)		
4 – Forest	65	74	19	349	21	78	0	606	6
	(11)	(12)	(3)	(58)	(3)	(13)	(0)		
5 – Water	9	7	2	13	93	10	0	134	1
	(7)	(5)	(1)	(10)	(69)	(7)	(0)		
6 – Wetland	6	22	3	17	11	27	0	86	1
	(7)	(26)	(3)	(20)	(13)	(31)	(0)		
7 – Barren	107	66	8	37	24	10	9	261	3
	(41)	(25)	(3)	(14)	(9)	(4)	(3)		
1992 Total area^c	3,231	4,613	177	1,124	249	228	31	9,653	100
1992 Percent of total area^d	33	48	2	12	3	2	0	100	

NOTE: Land use data across rows represent the distribution of 1972 land cover as of 1992. In parentheses is the percentage of the 1972 total area by classification. For example, 2,587 square kilometers or 81 percent of the built-up area in 1972 remained built-up in 1992. The land use data in the columns sum to the total land area by classification for 1992.

^{a} Total 1972 land area in each classification, which is the sum of the data across the rows.
^{b} Percent of total land area represented by each classification. For example, 33 percent of land area in 1972 was classified built-up.
^{c} Total 1992 land area in each classification, which is the sum of the data in the columns.
^{d} Percent of total land area represented by each classification. For example, 33 percent of land area in 1992 was classified built-up.

SOURCE: Calculated by authors from data provided by the U.S. Geological Survey (1972 and 1992).

Both governmental and nongovernmental groups—such as the Open-lands Project and Chicago Wilderness—have pursued efforts to protect and expand natural areas. Overall, more than 80,000 kilometers of land in the Chicago region are currently held in protective reserves by federal, state, county, and municipal governments, as well as private organizations (Chicago Region Biodiversity Council, 1999).

MAJOR DRIVERS AND CONSEQUENCES OF LAND COVER CHANGE

The major factors driving land use change in the Chicago region are population dynamics, economic development, and environmental changes.

Settlement and Population Dynamics

For centuries, Native Americans lived at low population densities near the point where the small Chicago River empties into Lake Michigan, within a kilometer of what is now the center of Chicago's business district. The first European fur traders arrived about 1770, and in 1803 the U.S. Army built Fort Dearborn where the river emptied into the lake. Mixed European and Native American settlements expanded slowly during the early decades of the nineteenth century, but rapid growth began with the westward movement of the frontier.

Starting from a base of fewer than 5,000 people in 1840, the population of the city of Chicago grew at the extraordinary rate of 20 percent per year until 1850 (Table 11-4). During the half-century after 1840, the city's

TABLE 11-4 Population of the City of Chicago, Chicago Region, and United States, 1840–1990 (thousands)

Census Year	City	Region[a]	United States
1840	5	35	17,062
1850	30	115	23,191
1860	112	259	31,443
1870	299	493	38,558
1880	503	771	50,155
1890	1,100	1,391	62,947
1900	1,699	2,084	75,994
1910	2,185	2,702	91,972
1920	2,702	3,394	105,710
1930	3,376	4,449	122,775
1940	3,397	4,569	131,669
1950	3,621	5,177	150,697
1960	3,550	6,220	179,323
1970	3,367	6,978	203,211
1980	3,005	7,103	226,545
1990	2,784	7,261	248,709

[a] In this table the Chicago region consists of the six counties that comprise the Northeastern Planning Commission Region.

SOURCES: City population: 1840–1980, Local Community Fact Book, Chicago Metropolitan Area. n.d. Chicago: Chicago Review Press; 1980 and 1990, U.S. Census as reported in Woods and Poole. 1997. MSA Profile. Washington, D.C.: Woods and Poole Economics. Region population: 1840–1990, U.S. Census Reports. U.S. population: U.S. Census of the Population.

population grew at a rate of more than 11 percent per year. The city's growth reflected in part the rapid urbanization under way nationally and in part the massive influx of people into the Midwest attracted by its economic prospects. The Chicago region grew more slowly than the city itself. Nevertheless, the region's annual population growth was about 7.3 percent during the same period.

From 1900 to 1950 the city's growth rate declined dramatically, to 1.5 percent per year, and from 1950 to 1990 the population actually decreased about 0.5 percent per year. Although between 1840 and 1920 the population of the city grew much more rapidly than the population of the region and the United States, after the mid-twentieth century the population of the city declined, while both the region and the United States experienced slow but steady population growth.

As noted, the initial population growth of the Chicago region can clearly be attributed to the massive influx of migrants. Later, however, natural population growth was at work. The unusually low natural population growth in 1930 was an anomaly reflecting the low national birth rates attributable to the dire conditions brought on by the Great Depression. Natural growth accelerated, however, with the return of prosperity during the 1940s and especially during the "baby boom" decade of the 1950s. After this peak period, natural population growth in Illinois and elsewhere steadily declined with significant reductions in both birth and death rates. As some baby boomers reached their childbearing years during the 1980s, the natural growth rate increased slightly.

In the early time periods, population was concentrated in the core of the city, and the hinterlands were sparsely populated (see Figure 11-3). In 1950 population growth began to intensify beyond Cook County. And from 1970 to 1990 the massive suburbanization pattern was unmistakable. In fact, from 1970 to 1990 the region's population grew by more than 4 percent, whereas Cook County's population fell 7 percent.

Cook County has been almost entirely urban since urban data became available in 1900, when Chicago reached its present land area which is about half of Cook County (see Table 11-5, which provides state data for 1900–1990, but they are dominated by the Chicago region). The non-Chicago half of Cook County contained only 8 percent of the county's population, most of whom lived in relatively small suburban centers. According to Table 11-5, urban trends for the region are greatly influenced by the sheer number of urban residents in Cook County. Consequently, aggregate urban measures for the region indicate that the population has been more than 90 percent urban since the turn of the century. This figure is misleading, however; outside of Cook County the population was only 45 percent urban in 1900, and that percentage increased markedly during the century, to 91 percent by 1990.

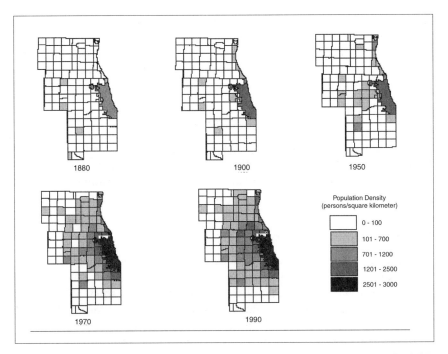

FIGURE 11-3 Population density trends, Chicago region, 1880–1990. SOURCE: U.S. Census of Population.

Today Chicago is the third-most-populous metropolitan area in the United States, after New York and Los Angeles. In 1997 the official Chicago metropolitan area was home to 7.8 million residents, making it almost as large as the two or three largest metropolitan areas of China and India. By contrast with China and India, however, U.S. metropolitan areas have low population densities. In 1997 the density of the Chicago

TABLE 11-5 Percent of Urban Population, Chicago Region, Illinois, and United States, 1900–1990

	1900	1910	1920	1930	1940	1950	1960	1970	1980	1990
Cook County	96	97	97	98	97	99	99	100	100	100
Chicago region (excluding Cook County)	45	50	56	64	62	67	77	83	88	91
Region total	90	91	93	94	93	95	95	96	97	97
Illinois	54	62	68	74	74	78	81	83	83	85
United States	40	46	51	56	57	64	70	74	83	75

SOURCE: U.S. Census Report of Population.

region was 594 persons per square kilometer. In 1994 the city of Chicago contained 2.7 million residents, or 4,704 per square kilometer. The densities of U.S. metropolitan areas and their central cities have declined substantially during recent decades as population and employment have dispersed from centers to peripheries, or suburbs.

Economic Structure

The second driver of land use change is economic development. The Chicago region began the twentieth century as the major agroindustrial region in the nation and ended it as a center of international trade and financial services.

Resource-Related Activities

The half-circle centered on Chicago and extending from the southern shores of the Great Lakes upward across the southern parts of Wisconsin and Minnesota—all in all, an area of about 1 million square kilometers with a radius of about 800 kilometers—contains some of the world's best grain-producing farmland. Until recently, most of the region's grain was shipped to Chicago. Some was processed in the region, but most was shipped unrefined to the East Coast and Europe for processing. Chicago's primary contributions were storage, marketing, grading, financing, and transportation. Many of the technical advances in grain production originated in the "breadbasket" surrounding Chicago—plows designed for the rock-hard virgin midwestern soils and other farm equipment, fertilizers, grain genetics, and harvesting techniques. Sophisticated financing, futures, and options markets were invented in Chicago, which to this day is the site of the world's most important grain and livestock financial and speculative markets. Even in the early nineteenth century, farmers could mitigate the risk of crop price fluctuations by contracting sales of their crops on futures markets prior to or early in the crop season. These were complex speculative markets in which prices for future delivery fluctuated with plantings, weather conditions, and forecasts in crop-growing regions and with economic conditions and forecasts of supply and demand on the East Coast and in Europe. Great fortunes were made, and sometimes lost, in Chicago's speculative grain, timber, and livestock markets.

Before it became farmland, much of the land west of Chicago was well-watered natural grassland. To the east was extensive timberland, cleared for farms by early in the nineteenth century. Some of the timber was used for structures, but much was burned. Extensive forests also were found north of Chicago, in Wisconsin and Michigan, where by 1830 commercial timber cutting and sawing had become established businesses. These operations began just north of Chicago in primeval forest, but gradually moved, as land was denuded, to about 500 kilometers north of Chicago at the northern end of Lake Michigan. Timber was cut and moved to sawmills scattered up and down the lake. Much of the cutting took place in winter, when logs could be dragged across the snow by mules. The work was wretched, poor paying, and dangerous. Many of the cutters were farmers, who were free of farmwork during winter months. The lumber was used to build houses in Chicago and houses and barns on surrounding farms, but some was shipped east. The best markets, however, were west, where there were almost no trees; the eastern part of the country had its own timber.

By 1900 most of the usable timber in the Chicago region had been cut, over a forested area of perhaps 50,000 square kilometers, and the lumber business shrank. Much of the timberland was converted to grazing and farming, and those activities are still under way in parts of Wisconsin and Michigan. Nevertheless, in northern Wisconsin and Michigan large tracts of land have reverted to beautiful second-growth forest.

Because of the costs of transportation, most sawmills were located close to the forests and not in Chicago. Chicago's contribution was processing (mostly drying), fabrication (some prefabricated houses were shipped from Chicago), wholesaling, storage, financing, and transportation of lumber. Lumber storage occupied large tracts of land in Chicago (on the east bank of the south branch of the Chicago River, about 3 kilometers south of the present central business district). Apparently, the lumber business has not caused significant environmental problems in Chicago. Sawdust and wood chips have long had a variety of uses.

Partly because of the availability of grain and partly because of cheap land, the Midwest also has been the major beef- and pork-producing region of the country since even before the Civil War (1861–1865). Cattle and hogs replaced the bison that numbered 20–40 million on the fertile grassland in the early part of the nineteenth century. Bison herds dwindled as railroads crisscrossed the plains, making the land valuable for grain and domestic animal production. At first, most of the livestock was shipped live to Chicago, where it was also shipped live eastward. By mid-century, however, livestock were being slaughtered, graded, and processed in Chicago and the carcasses then shipped on to the East Coast. Indeed, in 1870 about half of all hogs and more than a quarter of all cattle received in Chicago were slaughtered there. By 1900, more than 83 percent of the hogs and 65 percent of the cattle received were being slaughtered in Chicago. Thus between 1870 and 1900 the number of livestock slaughtered in Chicago increased more than eight times (U.S. Census Bureau, 1902).

Shipment was restricted initially to cold months to provide natural refrigeration, but by the end of the nineteenth century electrically refrigerated rail freight cars were in use. Early in the twentieth century, as freight transportation switched from rail and water to trucks and then to refrigerated trucks, it became cheaper to slaughter animals closer to the agricultural areas where they were raised and to ship carcasses instead of live animals to Chicago. By the late 1940s, then, most slaughtering had left Chicago for Des Moines, Omaha, and other smaller cities near where animals were grown.

At their peak in the late nineteenth and early twentieth centuries, slaughterhouses posed massive environmental problems for the Chicago region. They were first located on the south side of the stem of the Chicago River, near its mouth. Massive amounts of animal waste were simply dumped in the river, and the stench, especially in hot weather, was sickening. Later, the stockyards were moved to the southwestern part of the city, near what is now Midway Airport. Because prevailing winds blow across the city from there, this site also was unsatisfactory. The stockyards, however, were major employers of poorly educated workers, and the city was loath to press the employers hard. Technology, in the form of refrigerated trucks, ultimately solved the problem by dispersing the source of pollution.

The agricultural sector, especially grain production, has been another important economic activity in the study region. The percentage of land area devoted to farms increased steadily from 53 percent in 1850 to 84 percent in 1900 (Figure 11-4). Excluding Cook County, the proportion of farmland at the turn of the century was even greater, 90 percent. Since then, that percentage has fallen, but 50 percent of this region was still farmland in 1990. Similarly, employment data reveal that by 1840, 83 percent of the region's workforce (excluding Cook County) and as much as 53 percent of

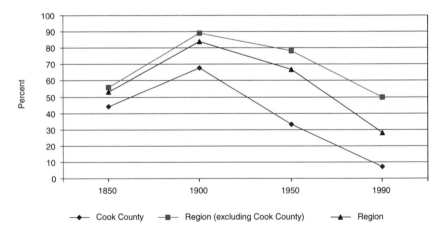

FIGURE 11-4 Percent of land in farms, Cook County and Chicago region (excluding Cook County), 1850–1990. SOURCE: U.S. Agricultural Census.

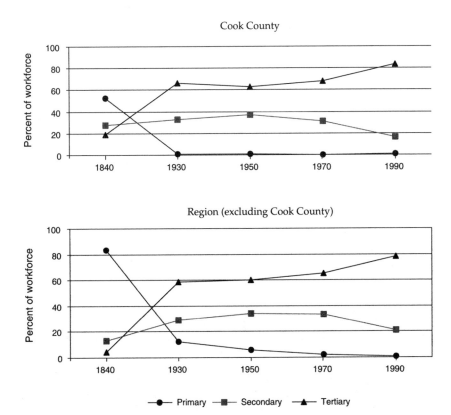

FIGURE 11-5 Distribution of workforce: primary, secondary, and tertiary sectors, Cook County and Chicago region (excluding Cook County), 1840 and 1930–1990. SOURCE: U.S. Census Report of Population.

Cook County's workforce were in the resource-based primary sector (see Figure 11-5). By 1930, however, the percentage of the region's workforce in the primary sector had dropped to little more than 12 percent and has continued to decline in tandem with state trends. In Cook County the share of employment in the primary sector had dropped sharply to 0.8 percent by 1930 and has not exceeded 0.5 percent since then.

Despite the reduction in workforce and land dedicated to agriculture, crop yields have risen over time (see Figure 11-6). Many factors influence grain productivity: soil type, weather, demand, transportation, technology and machinery, and government policies. Production and productivity have especially complex influences in the Chicago region. On the demand side, urban population rose rapidly until about 1950, then slowly. That growth added to local demand for grain products. But the urban population occupied increasing amounts of the region's space, which cur-

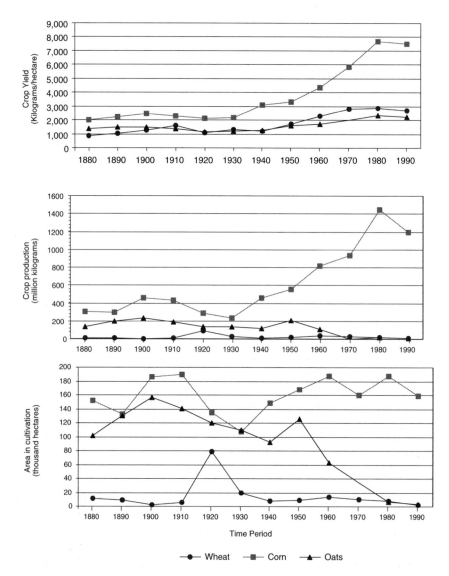

FIGURE 11-6 Grain production, Chicago region, 1880–1990. SOURCE: U.S. Agricultural Census.

tailed production, especially in the region's inner counties. Demand also was influenced by the transportation capability from the farms to Chicago and from Chicago to the East Coast and European cities. Economic conditions on the East Coast and in Europe influenced demand as well.

Agricultural productivity increased markedly in the past half-century because of the mechanization that enhanced productivity per unit of labor and because of the increased application of chemicals and the introduction of new plant varieties. Farm electrification, which started early in the twentieth century but was strongly stimulated by the federal government in the 1930s, led to rapid productivity growth, and various technologies also have had massive influences on productivity. In the nineteenth century, special plows were designed to cope with the rock-hard prairie soils, and crop planting and rotation became more scientific. In the twentieth century, planting, fertilization, rotation, and harvesting benefited from scientific advances, stimulated by research and advisory assistance sponsored by the federal government. Since World War II, hybrid corn and other genetic improvements, computerized technology, and much better-educated farmers have been extremely important.

From 1880 to 1900 the region's corn and oats production increased by 52 and 66 percent, respectively (see Figure 11-6). Wheat production, which grew erratically, was by 1920, its peak year, more than 10 times its 1880 volume. The dramatic increase in wheat production in the 1920s, often referred to as the "Golden Age" of agriculture, can be attributed to new technologies such as mechanization and fertilizers that allowed more land to be cultivated. In addition, wartime concerns led the U.S. government to encourage farmers to increase domestic production in order to reduce dependence on imports (Mumford, 1930). Unfortunately, by the end of the decade the surplus production resulting from the reduced demand for exported grain had led to low prices for the major food crops, with the result that wheat production and area under cultivation declined sharply over the next decade. Wheat and oats production also decreased after 1960 and 1950, respectively, because these crops were being pushed out by the growth and suburbanization of Chicago. Nevertheless, yield per hectare has increased for all three crops since the early post–World War II years. The region's extraordinary growth in corn production through 1980 represents rapid growth in output per hectare, which permitted continuing increases in total production despite a shrinking land area.

The quality of the Chicago region's soils and its farms is demonstrable; for all three crops, the region's yield per hectare exceeded the national average despite dwindling farmland and labor. The proximity of the region's farms to the Chicago market, and the resulting high agricultural land values, evidently stimulated farmers to use land intensively. Today the Chicago metropolitan area is no longer a major processing site for the region's grain production. Only small amounts of wheat and oats are presently grown in the region, and much of the region's corn production is now used for animal feed and shipped directly to feedlots.

Many observers have suggested that the growth of metropolitan regions has resulted in the loss of the prime farmland, thereby threatening the nation's agricultural production (Greene and Harlin, 1995; Vining et al., 1977). Such a loss of prime farmland has, in fact, occurred in the Chicago region, where low-density residential land uses are transforming the landscape at a rapid rate (Greene, 1997). Nevertheless, the implications for national-level agricultural production are debatable (Vesterby et al., 1994). For 40 years the United States has produced excess grain, and livestock also were produced in excess during the 1990s. Indeed, the domestic demand for grain products is saturated, and dietary changes (to reduce fat consumption) have weakened demand for animal products. In addition, the limitations of foreign demand (by Russia, Japan, and much of East Asia) caused reductions in exports during much of the 1990s. Nevertheless, the United States is a major exporter of agricultural products. In the 1990s such products accounted for 10 percent of all U.S. exports, and the positive agricultural balance of trade during that period was between $16 billion and $26 billion.

Urban Activities

The economic hallmark of the city of Chicago in the nineteenth century was extremely rapid growth with almost no regulation or taxation by governments. Although Chicago was probably a higher-wage city than Boston or New York (both native-born and immigrant workers tended to move west, partly because of higher wages), much of the work was dull, ugly, and dangerous. Nevertheless, living standards were probably somewhat higher than those on farms in the region. Entrepreneurship and practical innovation characterized the city, and some of the great American fortunes were accumulated in Chicago in railroads, steel, meatpacking, grain, real estate development, and speculation.

One of the most impressive characteristics of nineteenth-century Chicago was its ability to bring together imaginative entrepreneurs, financial capital, large numbers of productive workers, innovative financial and production techniques, and transport innovation. Massive investments were made in what is now called infrastructure capital: docks, dredging, landfill, streets, water supply, transportation, and, near the end of the century, electrified commuter subway and elevated rail lines. Private companies, with almost no government intervention or support, built most.

Another important characteristic of Chicago's early development was the deep and intimate interaction between the urban and resource-related sectors. In 1900 Chicago had little complex industry, and its industrial base did not compare with the textile, garment, and leather industries of southern New England. Although entrepreneurship, worker productivity, and capital (large amounts of it sent from Europe) all played important roles, Chicago owed its early growth and prosperity to its surrounding land and to the workers, many of them immigrants from northern Europe, who extracted its bountiful products.

For the post–World War II period, detailed sectoral employment data are available at the county level. For the longer period, the only data available are classified by sector—primary (described earlier), secondary, and tertiary. The secondary sector includes manufacturing, construction, and public utilities. The tertiary sector includes the business and consumer services provided by both government and the private sector. Some private services are provided by profit-seeking firms and some by non-profit organizations. In the United States the maintenance and repair of produced goods are included in the tertiary sector, unlike in some other countries that include them in manufacturing.

The vast majority of secondary and tertiary jobs are located in urban areas. In the United States, about 20 percent of workers live in rural areas and have nonfarm jobs, but in recent decades most of those jobs have been located in nearby urban areas.[4] Even in 1840, 56 percent of Chicago's workforce held secondary sector jobs. For Cook County's entire workforce, the percentage was about half of that, and for the rest of the Chicago region (excluding Cook County), the percentage was about half that of Cook County (see Figure 11-5). By World War II, the city's secondary sector workforce was about 35 percent, a figure now typical of a developing country. Across the geographic scales, the percentage of the workforce in the secondary sector has declined steadily since the early postwar period (Figure 11-5).

By 1990 the secondary sector constituted less than 18 percent of the total national workforce, and 17 percent of the Chicago region's workforce. Most of the decline in secondary employment in both the nation and in the Chicago region has been in the manufacturing sector. By the late 1990s the Chicago region workforce had become even less concentrated in manufacturing and the secondary sector than in the country as a whole. Manufacturing remains an extremely important sector nationally and regionally, but because of rapid productivity growth it has not been a source of significant job growth for at least 30 years.

Figure 11-5 reveals the massive shift in the region's workforce to the tertiary sector. From 7 percent in 1840, the tertiary sector's workforce share grew to almost 80 percent in 1990. What is not widely appreciated is that the tertiary sector's share for the region had already grown to nearly 60 percent in 1930 and hardly changed until the decade of the 1970s. In the 1970s and 1980s there was a further explosion in service sector jobs. And by 1990 the Chicago region had a somewhat greater concentration of employment in the tertiary sector than the country as a whole.

---

[4]Data are by place of residence, not by place of employment. Even in the nineteenth century, some workers commuted to Cook County urban jobs from rural residences in outer counties. By the 1920s inward commuting by both public and private vehicles was substantial.

In the Chicago region, as in most metropolitan areas, tertiary jobs are much more centralized than secondary sector jobs. In 1990 the percentage of Cook County employment in the secondary sector was smaller than that of the region as a whole, whereas the percentage in the tertiary sector was larger than that for the entire region (see Figure 11-5). Retailing and elementary and secondary education are large tertiary subsectors, and they are about as dispersed as population. Almost all other tertiary subsectors are more centralized than population, including wholesaling, finance, consulting, law, professional services, and hotels. The region's movement from secondary to tertiary sector jobs has been remarkably smooth over recent decades. The proportion of the region's workforce employed in the tertiary sector rose from 67 to 80 percent between 1970 and 1990. The region's income per capita remained more than 20 percent above the national average, and during that period manufacturing employment fell by about one-third and tertiary employment rose by almost two-thirds.

In summary, in Chicago's earliest days it was a center for processing, transporting, and financing the bounty produced by the agricultural land in the region and hundreds of kilometers beyond. By the end of the nineteenth century, most of the region's industry was engaged in processing the output of the surrounding rural and resource-based agricultural, livestock, and forestry products. Early in the twentieth century, much of the region's secondary sector began to veer toward "heavy industry" in which resource inputs came from farther away and in which Chicago's most important attraction was as a shipping and rail (then road, then air) transportation center. The city became the financial capital of the Midwest, which it remains today. Although the region is a center for industry, for a half-century most employment growth has been in the tertiary sector, making the metropolitan area much more similar to large metropolitan areas elsewhere in the country than it was a century ago.

Environmental Issues and Resource Exhaustion

All large metropolitan areas inevitably pose serious threats to the environment. Protection against morbidity, mortality, and aesthetic degradation requires a massive investment in infrastructure and regulation of the behavior of people and businesses. Yet in most countries morbidity and mortality rates are lower in large metropolitan areas than elsewhere, because highly populated regions are better able to mobilize both the resources and the expertise needed to protect the environment. Morbidity and mortality are also lower in high-income countries than in low-income countries. Although high-income countries produce large amounts of pollutants, they have the resources needed to keep the environment relatively clean. Consequently, most national measures of U.S. air and water quality have improved steadily during recent decades (U.S. Census Bureau, 1999). The elimination of steam railway engines and a ban on burning coal to heat buildings may have contributed to improvement in air quality. Pollution-sensitive game fish have reappeared in many lakes and streams, and specific ambient measures, such as dissolved oxygen, have improved pervasively. Indeed, over the last decade national ambient measures have improved for all six pollutants for which data are available (carbon monoxide, ozone, sulfur dioxide, particulates, nitrogen dioxide, and lead). Although air and water quality is inevitably worse in large metropolitan areas than elsewhere, the Chicago region's air and water quality is good by both U.S. and world standards. Some credit goes to natural conditions. Chicago has moderate summer temperatures, and its winters are cold enough to keep tropical and many warm weather diseases at bay. It also has good natural air movements that dissipate airborne wastes.

Lake Michigan is by far the metropolitan area's most important water resource. The city and its suburbs near the lake obtain their water from intakes located a kilometer or so from the shore. Historically, that arrangement, which dates from the late nineteenth century for the city and twentieth century for the suburbs, has been ideal. The lake's northbound flow is many times the current withdrawal volume, and withdrawals are limited by the needs of other metropolitan areas along its shores and by a treaty between the United States and Canada that limits U.S. withdrawals. Chicago has not had a water shortage since it began its withdrawals from the lake, and none appear to be on the horizon. The quality of lake water is high along the metropolitan area's 75 kilometers of shoreline, in part because much of the shoreline is government property and in part because private and local government discharges are strictly regulated. As a result, public swimming beaches dot the shoreline, and the public water supply is provided with only minimal treatment of lake withdrawals. Occasionally, however, one or more city beaches are closed for a day or two, mainly because during heavy rains wastewater exceeds the capacity of the treatment system and some is pumped directly into the lake. Completion of an expensive massive storage facility under the city will permit wastewater storage during periods of high flow.

The Chicago River, the largest of several small rivers that empty into the lake within the metropolitan area, flows into the lake less than a kilometer north of the center of the central business district. Animal slaughtering and other polluting activities along its banks made the river a cesspool even in the nineteenth century. Carrying out an ingenious scheme completed in 1900, workers dammed the mouth of the river, reversed its flow, and dug a sanitary canal from the south branch of the river to connect it with the Mississippi River system. The scheme protected the water intakes in the lake, but left the Chicago River a cesspool and drained wastewater into the Mississippi system. Once the animal slaughter and other polluting activities moved away from the river, however, the quality of the river's water improved gradually. Over the last quarter-century, the increasingly stringent controls on discharges to the river have further enhanced water quality.

Within the metropolitan area, Lake Michigan's watershed extends only a kilometer or two west of the western shore of the lake. Other substantial rivers in the metropolitan area—notably the Fox and Des Plaines—flow south and southwest and drain into the Mississippi system.

The Illinois Environmental Protection Agency has an extraordinary collection of data on some 30 water quality indices that have been measured several times a year since the late 1980s at about 40 stations located on streams within the metropolitan area. These data are objectively summarized in the agency's annual (in recent years) water quality report. The measurements reveal that, first, water quality is lower the closer one is to the high-density eastern edge of the metropolitan area (Dreher, 1997). Second, most dimensions of water quality have shown improvements at most locations over the decade covered by the data. And, third, flooding is a problem in areas near the Fox and Des Plaines Rivers, partly because suburban development has increased the runoff during spring thaws.

Land is by far the Chicago region's most valuable natural resource, demonstrated by the expansion of waterfront land into Lake Michigan. On a broader scale, the land area encompassed in this study is flat and well connected to both rural and urban markets by natural and manmade transportation systems. Moreover, there is no evidence that increasingly intensive agriculture has reduced the productivity of the region's soils during the last 150 years. Urban growth has greatly reduced the region's agricultural land, but a shortage of agricultural land is not considered a national problem or prospect (Vesterby et al., 1994). The United States, a large net exporter of agricultural products, has had agricultural surpluses for most of the last 40 years, and there is no prospect of agricultural shortages for the foreseeable future.

LINKS BETWEEN DRIVERS AND PROCESSES
OF LAND USE CHANGE IN CHICAGO

This section examines more closely the connection between demographic and economic factors—the drivers of land use change—and the major land use patterns experienced in the study area. In particular, this analysis looks at the events leading to the dramatic conversion of the natural environment to a predominantly agricultural landscape at the turn of the twentieth century, the encroachment of urban and built-up areas into the agricultural frontier, and, finally, the expansion of built-up areas through the process of suburbanization.

Incorporated in this analysis is the concept of land use coupling, which pertains to the functional relationship between an agricultural hinterland and its urban settlements (Walker et al., 1997). A regional land use system is considered "coupled" when interdependence exists between activities in the agricultural hinterland and those in the urban center. Conversely, "decoupling" occurs when this interdependence is disrupted and economic activities within the region are disassociated. This section describes how land use demands and thus land use patterns in the Chicago region changed in response to the evolution of the regional economy and the shift from a coupled to a decoupled system. The discussion is divided into three periods: pre-settlement–1900, 1900–1955, and 1955–1992.

Pre-settlement–1900

Chicago became the metropolis of the Midwest because of its ready access to the Great Lakes and, after the opening of the Erie Canal in 1825, to New York and Europe. In 1848 a short canal connecting Lake Michigan with the Mississippi River system was opened after long turmoil about financing and construction. The canal, which was financed through a complex web of government and private initiatives, was relatively short and technically easy to build, but controversy surrounded attempts to make the waterway profitable. Even so, the canal served as a major stimulus to the region's economic development during the second half of the nineteenth century.

By the mid-nineteenth century, Chicago had rail connections with New York, Philadelphia, and Boston, and by 1869 rail lines through Chicago reached the Pacific Ocean. The opening of the twentieth century found Chicago the world's greatest rail center. Not only could products be shipped from Chicago to all eastern cities, and thus on to Europe from East Coast ports, but raw materials within a 2,000-kilometer radius could be transported to Chicago.

During this period of development, the agricultural economy and urban settlements in the Chicago region were tightly connected, or coupled—that is, the agricultural hinterland produced the raw goods that were processed in the urban center. Most of those products were then shipped to external markets. The conversion of this region from a near natural setting around 1820 to an agriculture-dominated landscape at the turn of the twentieth century resulted from external demand, the abundance of fertile land, and the ability of Chicago's urban center to serve the processing and transporting function. By 1900, about 9,255 square kilometers of natural land had been converted to human-dominated systems, with agriculture accounting for 92 percent of the land use change (see Table 11-2).

Chicago was indeed the center of the nation's breadbasket, and throughout this period the agricultural productivity of grains exceeded the national averages by more than a third. In 1840 about 83 percent of the population was employed in agriculture, and 13 percent was employed in food-related manufacturing such as meatpacking and milling (U.S. Census Bureau, 1840). By 1862 Chicago had become the nation's meatpacking center (U.S. Census Bureau, 1902).

1900–1955

From 1900 to 1955, urban areas in the Chicago region doubled in size, and agriculture began to decline (see Table 11-1). Indeed, 8 percent of agricultural land, or about 700 square kilometers, shifted to urban use (Table 11-2), reflecting the apparent structural transformations that were occurring in the regional economy. As noted earlier, throughout the nineteenth and early twentieth centuries Chicago industry was engaged mainly in processing resources derived from the hinterland. In 1900 meatpacking was the principal economic activity and employer in the region. Its importance began to erode, however, and by the mid-twentieth century most slaughterhouses had left Chicago. Subsequently, a transformation, or decoupling, of the regional economy began with the shift to heavy industry and the importation of raw goods. By 1930 the regional economy had little more than 2 percent of its workforce in the primary sector, a third in the secondary sector, and nearly two-thirds in the tertiary sector (Figure 11-5). Although northern Indiana is not included in the study area, it is important to note that from 1900 to 1945 expansion into that region resulted in the Chicago area becoming one of the world's greatest centers of heavy industry. By 1950 primary sector employment was inconsequential, and manufacturing was by then centered on metal fabrication and machinery (U.S. Census Bureau, 1950). The principal employers in the tertiary sector were wholesale trade, finance and real estate, and railroad services.

Despite the decline of employment in the primary sector and an approximate 14 percent reduction in land devoted to crops (wheat, corn, and oats), aggregate yields show that the crop productivity of the Chicago region increased by nearly 27 percent (see Figure 11-6). The increase in productivity resulted from technological innovations that enabled both intensive and labor-saving production.

Finally, the urban population of the Chicago region (excluding Cook County) increased from 45 percent in 1900 to 67 percent in 1950 (see Table 11-5). Overall, population in the region tripled, at an average annual growth rate of 3.4 percent (see Table 11-4).

1955–1992

During the third period, the predominant land cover conversion patterns in the study region were loss of agricultural land and an increase in urban and natural areas. From 1955 to 1992, about 2,100 square kilometers, 26 percent, of agricultural land was converted to urban use, and nearly half that amount reverted to areas classified as natural (see Table 11-2). Overall, agricultural land declined 50 percent, urban areas nearly tripled, and natural cover increased almost fivefold (see Table 11-1). As with the other conversion episodes, changes in land use can be linked to demographic and economic patterns.

In this last period the economic activities in the agricultural areas were decoupled from urban activities. Less than 1 percent of the workforce was employed in the primary sector; nevertheless, grain productivity based on crop yield rose 70 percent, despite an almost 50 percent reduction in land devoted to crops (see Figures 11-4, 11-5, and 11-6). Most of the value-added processing of crops during this period occurred on-site or in regions outside of Chicago. The secondary sector accounted for less than a quarter of the workforce, and most industry was light manufacturing with little or no connection to the agricultural hinterland or to regional consumption (see Figure 11-5). Overwhelmingly, the greatest increase in employment was in the tertiary sector.

The land use pressures created by the growth of the tertiary sector differ from those generated by agricultural and manufacturing activities. In particular, recent population growth and economic development have increased the demand for residential land. Figure 11-3 graphically depicts this process of suburbanization from 1880 to 1990 based on population density. Although apparent by 1950, the population shifts were most intense from 1970 to 1990. Finally, a comparison of the population trends for Cook County with those for the remainder of the region for this time period shows that, while growth rates slowed for the entire region, population growth rates in Cook County actually declined (see Table 11-4). Corroborating this conclusion is a detailed land use change analysis, which indicates that between the mid-1970s and 1990s approximately 194 square kilometers of agricultural land were converted to residential use (Greene, 1997). The growing demand for residential land resulted from the movement of secondary and tertiary production from the urban core to the suburban fringes, a phenomenon recently referred to as edge city development. This development of suburbia was promoted in Chicago as elsewhere by a variety of public policies involving road construction, housing finance, and taxes, as middle- and upper-income households moved outward and as businesses followed purchasing power and households. As noted earlier, Chicago became the major transportation center for the central United States. This expansion included not only the major interstate railway system, along with metropolitan transit, but also an extensive network of interstate highways. In addition, O'Hare Field, located about 40 kilometers west of downtown Chicago, is the nation's busiest airport. The westward urban expansion of the built-up area includes land even further to the west of O'Hare field, itself a center of regional economic activity.

Meanwhile, from 1955 to 1992 there was an apparent recovery of natural areas, which by 1992 had increased to nearly four times the 1955 measure (see Table 11-1). As noted earlier, most of this regrowth was in forested areas and land converted from agriculture. Forest recovery is not a process unique to the Chicago region. In fact, an historical analysis of land use data in both the developed and developing world suggests the existence of a landscape turnaround point, at which the factors causing deforestation dissipate and forest recovery occurs (Walker, 1994). The Chicago region fits well within a two-stage model of landscape change, in which deforestation gives way to reforestation as labor- and land-saving agricultural technologies, and rural–urban migration, alleviate pressure on the landscape, thereby allowing forest recovery (Walker, 1994). An additional phenomenon that has contributed to the increase in natural areas has been the conversion of urban areas to forest through the creation of urban parks, an important effort pursued by most local governments.

CONCLUSION

In the Chicago study area, the regional land use system is largely governed by the degree of interdependence between the agricultural hinterland and urban center. During the period of early development, from about 1820 to 1900, the regional land use system was coupled with the agricultural hinterland producing the raw goods that were processed in the urban center. Land use during this period shifted from a predominantly natural landscape to an agricultural one.

The second period of development, 1900–1955, saw the rise of an increasingly decoupled system as manufacturing in the urban center shifted from its reliance for feedstock on nearby agricultural products to heavy industry based on imported materials. Likewise during this period, many agricultural goods once processed on-site were exported outside the Chicago region for value-added processing. The major land use change during this period was the encroachment of urban land use into agricultural land.

The final period of development, 1955–1992, saw the nearly complete decoupling between economic activities in the rural areas and urban centers. Land use changes during this period included the loss of agricultural land to residential use and the recovery of natural areas. Although the region's population grew slowly during the third period, the rapid suburbanization of both population and employment dramatically increased the land devoted to urban purposes.

REFERENCES

Chicago Region Biodiversity Council. 1999. Biodiversity Recovery Plan. Chicago: Chicago Region Biodiversity Council.

Cronon, W. 1991. Nature's Metropolis. New York: Norton.

Dreher, D. 1997. Watershed urbanization impacts in stream quality indicators in northwestern Illinois. Northeastern Illinois Planning Commission, Chicago.

Greene, R. P. 1997. The farmland conversion process in a polynucleated metropolis. Landscape and Urban Planning 36:291–300.

Greene, R. P., and J. M. Harlin. 1995. Threat to high market value agricultural lands from urban encroachment: A national and regional perspective. Social Science Journal 32:137–155.

Illinois Environmental Protection Agency. Illinois Water Quality Report. Springfield. Annual.

Mumford, H. W. 1930. Introduction. Proceedings from the Illinois Agricultural Adjustment Conferences of 1930. Urbana: University of Illinois.

Sullivan, J. 1998. Chicago Wilderness: An Atlas of Biodiversity. Chicago: Chicago Region Biodiversity Council.

U.S. Census Bureau. 1840. Recapitulation of the aggregate value, and produce, and number of persons employed in mines, agriculture, commerce, manufactures, by counties. Pp. 298–309 in Compendium of the 6th Census. Washington, D.C.: U.S. Department of Commerce.

U.S. Census Bureau. 1902. Manufactures: Special Report on Select Industries. P. 414 in 12th Census of the U.S., Vol. 9, Part 13. Washington, D.C.: U.S. Department of Commerce.

U.S. Census Bureau. 1950. Economic characteristics of the population, by sex, for counties: 1950. Pp. 168–179 in Census of the Population: Characteristics of the Population, Vol. 2, Part 13. Washington, D.C.: U.S. Department of Commerce.

U.S. Census Bureau. 1999. Statistical Abstract of the United States. Washington, D.C.: U.S. Department of Commerce.

Vesterby, M., R. Heinlich, and K. Krupa. 1994. Urbanization of Rural Land in the United States. Agricultural Economic Report 673. Washington, D.C.: U.S. Department of Agriculture.

Vining, D. R., T. Plaut, and K. Bieri. 1977. Urban encroachment on prime agricultural land in the United States. International Regional Science Review 2:43–156.

Walker, R. T. 1994. Deforestation and economic development. Canadian Journal of Regional Science 16(3):481–497.

Walker, R. T., W. D. Solecki, and C. Harwell. 1997. Land use dynamics and ecological transition: the case of South Florida. Urban Ecosystems 1:37–47.